The enlargement of Europe

MANCHESTER
UNIVERSITY PRESS

Political Analyses

Series editors: Bill Jones and Michael Moran

Roland Axtmann
*Liberal democracy into the twenty-first century: globalization, integration
and the nation-state*

Lynn Bennie, Jack Brand and James Mitchell
How Scotland votes: Scottish parties and elections

John Burton
Violence explained: the sources of conflict, violence and crime and their prevention

Stuart Croft
Strategies of arms control: a history and typology

E. Franklin Dukes
Resolving public conflict: transforming community and governance

Brendan Evans and Andrew Taylor
From Salisbury to Major: continuity and change in Conservative politics

Michael Foley
The politics of the British Constitution

Michael Foley and John E. Owens
Congress and the Presidency: institutional politics in a separated system

Nick Moon
Opinion polls: history, theory and practice

The enlargement of Europe

Stuart Croft, John Redmond,
G. Wyn Rees and Mark Webber

Manchester University Press

Manchester and New York

distributed exclusively in the USA by St. Martin's Press

Published by Manchester University Press
Oxford Road, Manchester M13 9NR, UK
and Room 400, 175 Fifth Avenue, New York, NY 10010, USA
http://www.man.ac.uk/mup

Distributed exclusively in the USA by
St. Martin's Press, Inc., 175 Fifth Avenue, New York,
NY 10010, USA

Distributed exclusively in Canada by
UBC Press, University of British Columbia, 6344 Memorial Road,
Vancouver, BC, Canada V6T 1Z2

British Library Cataloguing-in-Publication Data
A catalogue record for this book is available from the British Library

Library of Congress Cataloging-in-Publication Data applied for

ISBN   0 7190 4970 9   *hardback*
       0 7190 4971 7   *paperback*

First published 1999

06 05 04 03 02 01 00 99   10 9 8 7 6 5 4 3 2 1

Typeset by Ralph J. Footring, Derby
Printed in Great Britain by Biddles Ltd, Guildford and King's Lynn

This book is dedicated to Sam and Theo.

Contents

Tables

Series editors' foreword

The *Politics Today* series has been running successfully since the late 1970s, aimed mainly at an undergraduate audience. After over a decade in which a dozen or more titles have been produced, some of which have run to multiple copies, MUP thought it time to launch a new politics series, aimed at a different audience and a different need.

The *Political Analyses* series is prompted by the relative dearth of research-based political science series which persists despite the fecund source of publication ideas provided by current political developments. In the UK we observe, for example: the rapid evolution of Labour politics as the party seeks to find a reliable electoral base; the continuing development of the post-Thatcher Conservative Party; the growth of pressure group activity and lobbying in modern British politics; and the irresistible moves towards constitutional reform of an arguably outdated state.

Abroad, there are even more themes upon which to draw, for example: the ending of the Thatcher–Reagan axis; the parallel collapse of communism in Europe and Russia; and the gradual retreat of socialism from the former heartlands in Western Europe.

This series seeks to explore some of these new ideas to a depth beyond the scope of the *Politics Today* series – whilst maintaining a similar direct and accessible style – and to serve an audience of academics, practitioners and the well-informed reader as well as undergraduates.

Foreword

The political upheavals in central and eastern Europe that began in 1989 have inspired the greatest change in the political and economic landscape of Europe since the end of World War Two. Across the region, democracy and the market economy have displaced totalitarianism and central planning. The European Union has been quick to respond to these opportunities, offering the possibility of EU membership to countries in central and eastern Europe, negotiating agreements that aim at free trade, and providing a billion ECU a year to help them modernise.

In July 1997, the European Commission published a report – entitled 'Agenda 2000' – on the challenges facing the EU in the next century. In this report, the Commission recommended that accession negotiations be opened early in 1998 with Cyprus, the Czech Republic, Estonia, Hungary, Poland and Slovenia. The Commission has backed up its commitment to keep the other applicants squarely part of the enlargement process with a promise to double financial assistance to all applicants and to review their progress in 1998. The Commission will recommend that accession negotiations be opened with Bulgaria, Latvia, Lithuania, Romania and Slovakia once they have made sufficient progress in their membership preparations. By the early years of the next century, the first applicants from central and eastern Europe will have joined the Union.

The EU for its part faces a considerable challenge in preparing itself for the next enlargement. Decision-making procedures that were designed in the 1950s for six member states have remained largely unaltered. In the coming years fundamental changes will have to be made if decision-making in the Union is to remain transparent, flexible and fair.

This book will make a valuable contribution to the evolving debate within the Union on these key issues and I welcome the initiative of the authors in this regard.

Hans Van Den Broek
European Union Commissioner

Acknowledgements

This book is the product of a collaborative effort between the four authors that has included a series of meetings at the Universities of Birmingham, Leicester and Loughborough. During the project we have developed many debts of gratitude, but would only mention a few here. David Allen is to be thanked for his intellectual contribution regarding the issues examined in the book. Thanks are due to Richard Purslow for supporting the idea at the outset and to Nicola Viinikka for her patience in seeing it through to completion. Stuart Croft and Wyn Rees would like to acknowledge NATO for their Research Fellowships, which enabled them to undertake research for the project. In addition, appreciation is extended to Walter Kemp of the Public Information Department at the OSCE for his having read and commented on chapter 5.

Notes on the authors

Stuart Croft is Professor of International Relations at the University of Birmingham, where his teaching focuses on the security politics of Europe. He is co-editor of the journal *Contemporary Security Policy* and his most recent publication is *Strategies of Arms Control: A History and Typology* (Manchester University Press, 1996).

John Redmond is Professor of European Studies at the University of Birmingham. His teaching lies principally in the political economy of the European Union. His recent publications include *The 1995 Enlargement of the European Union*, which he edited (Ashgate, 1997), and *From Versailles to Maastricht: International Organization in the Twentieth Century* (Macmillan, 1996).

G. Wyn Rees is Lecturer in International Relations at the University of Leicester. His teaching concentrates on European politics and security. His recent publications include *The Western European Union at the Crossroads: Between Trans-Atlantic Solidarity and European Integration* (Westview, 1998) and *Rethinking Security in Post-Cold War Europe*, which he edited with W. Park (Longman, 1998).

Mark Webber is Lecturer in the Department of European Studies, Loughborough University, where he specialises in the teaching of Russian government and foreign policy. His recent publications include *CIS Integration Trends: Russia and the Former Soviet South* (Royal Institute of International Affairs, 1997) and *The International Politics of Russia and the Successor States* (Manchester University Press, 1996).

Abbreviations

CAP	common agricultural policy
CEECs	central and east European countries
CFE	Conventional Forces in Europe (Treaty)
CFSP	common foreign and security policy
CIS	Commonwealth of Independent States
CJTF	Combined Joint Task Force
COE	Council of Europe
CSBMs	confidence and security-building measures
CSCE	Conference on Security and Cooperation in Europe
ECHR	European Convention on Human Rights
EDC	European Defence Community
EEA	European Economic Area
EFTA	European Free Trade Association
EU	European Union
FSU	former Soviet Union
GNP	gross national product
IFOR	Implementation Force
IGC	intergovernmental conference
MEP	Member of the European Parliament
NACC	North Atlantic Cooperation Council
NATO	North Atlantic Treaty Organisation
PACE	Parliamentary Assembly of the Council of Europe
PFP	Partnership for Peace
ODIHR	Office for Democratic Institutions and Human Rights
OMRI	Open Media Research Institute
OSCE	Organisation for Security and Cooperation in Europe
SFOR	Stabilisation Force

TEU	Treaty on European Union
UN	United Nations
WEU	Western European Union
WTO	Warsaw Treaty Organisation

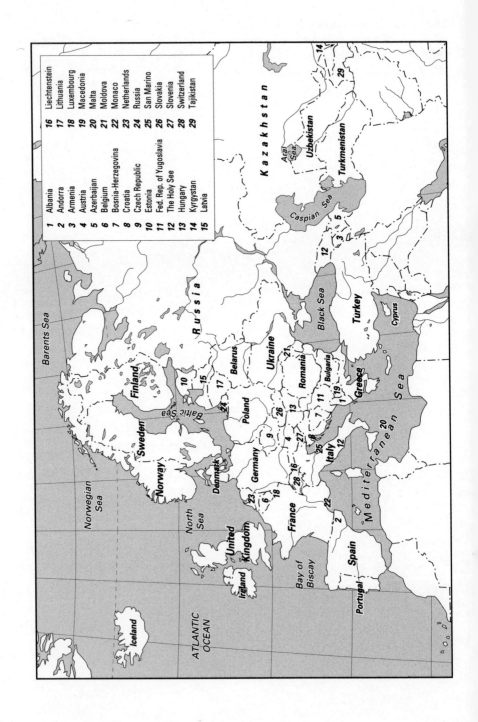

1	Albania	**16** Liechtenstein
2	Andorra	**17** Lithuania
3	Armenia	**18** Luxembourg
4	Austria	**19** Macedonia
5	Azerbaijan	**20** Malta
6	Belgium	**21** Moldova
7	Bosnia-Herzegovina	**22** Monaco
8	Croatia	**23** Netherlands
9	Czech Republic	**24** Russia
10	Estonia	**25** San Marino
11	Fed. Rep. of Yugoslavia	**26** Slovakia
12	The Holy See	**27** Slovenia
13	Hungary	**28** Switzerland
14	Kyrgystan	**29** Tajikistan
15	Latvia	

1

Organisations, Europe and enlargement

Introduction

European politics have been dominated since the end of the Cold War by questions of inclusion and exclusion. Who should be included in the institutional clubs that have been developed, largely in western Europe, and on what grounds? And as a consequence, who should be excluded, and how should that exclusion be justified? Different approaches have been apparent on the part of the major institutions: a diplomatic 'big bang' from the Organisation for Security and Cooperation in Europe (OSCE), the swift but as yet uncomprehensive enlargement of the Council of Europe (COE), the planned but slow and unfulfilled movement east of the European Union (EU) and the Western European Union (WEU), and the timid and limited expansion of the North Atlantic Treaty Organisation (NATO).

These five organisations form the core of the study for this book, and significantly all existed during the Cold War. Their survival reflects the fact that despite the radical change in European life brought about by the abandonment of communism and the dissolution of the Soviet Union, western Europe's political, economic and military leaders have looked to entrench that which they know, rather than to create new bodies. And those new bodies that have emerged – such as the Commonwealth of Independent States (CIS) and the Visegrad Group[1] – have been notable for their lack of development. Does this imply that, in trying to understand enlargement of institutions in Europe, we need look no further than bureaucratic inertia as our primary explanation?

That would surely be too simplistic an approach. Certainly officials in major organisations have a vested interest in the survival and political health of their employers. But beyond that, states have seen a utility in those organisations. How 'utility' is defined is rather controversial, as will be examined later in this chapter, but that there is some utility is not at question. However, as the institutions have enlarged, one of the most notable features has been the lack of coordination in those enlargements. There may be a meta-value of enlargement in Europe, but it has not been pursued in a coordinated fashion. What is clear is that there has been no macro concept of enlargement that can be deconstructed. This is very important, for not only does it mean that there has been no blueprint for change, but it means that there is no common standard for comparison. As will be seen, it is not possible to compare the enlargement of, say, NATO and the EU either favourably or otherwise because there is no independent standard for judgement. All that can be done is, first, to evaluate the institution's enlargement practice in the light of its policy statements and, second, to identify contradictions in the pattern of so-called interlocking institutions created by those enlargement practices.

Before proceeding with the examination of the enlargement debates, policies and practices of the EU, COE, OSCE, WEU and NATO, three important conceptual foundations will be laid. The next section will ask how 'Europe' may be understood. What is meant by 'European'? Does it imply those states of the EU? Does it stretch to those countries that have Association Agreements with the EU? Or a geographically wider group, such as those that are in NATO's Partnership for Peace? Such questions are complex, for they take us from the relatively straightforward arena of geopolitics into the much more murky area of identity. For example, how do we distinguish between 'western' and 'European' in the context of the Council of Europe? Are European values the same as western values? Such an idea would be anathema to many in France and elsewhere in continental western Europe, but much less so to many in the United Kingdom. But the question is sharper elsewhere: is Turkey 'western' but not 'European'? Or what of Malta? Is it European or North African, or does the answer depend on the nature of its government?[2] And there is yet another complex level to this question: who decides the answer to the question 'Who is European?' This is difficult enough when viewed at the state level, but even more divisive at the individual level: when is a person born in France not French, or a worker employed in Germany for thirty years not German, or a British passport holder not British?

Having clarified the complexity inherent in the term 'European', this chapter will then ask the question 'Do institutions matter?' The reader will expect the answer in this book to be in the affirmative, for if the authors were predisposed to be hostile to the notion that institutions play an important role, this book would not have been written. There are many different theoretical positions in international relations that would support this perspective – neo-liberal institutionalist, social constructivist, the English school of international relations – and support for different theoretical positions has been apparent among the authors. Major projects have been undertaken examining whether institutions matter, but as this is not the primary focus of this book we cannot expect to make a major contribution to that debate. Rather, we will portray the contours of the neo-realist/neo-liberal debate, which has been the dominant feature of this question in the European studies literature, and will briefly touch on the variant of constructivism.

The final section of this chapter will examine concepts of enlargement. The idea of enlarging Europe's institutions is, of course, not a new one, but in the 1990s it has been largely unidirectional: it has been the western European organisations that have attracted the central and eastern Europeans, not those organisations developed or proposed in that part of the continent during the Cold War (such as the Council for Mutual Economic Assistance – the CMEA, or Comecon) and in the post-Cold War period (such as the Central European Initiative). But, echoing a point made earlier, there has been no overarching concept of enlargement in Europe; so how, then, should we understand what is meant by enlargement?

This first chapter lays the foundation for subsequent chapters on individual organisations. By outlining the concepts of Europe, institutions and enlargement utilised in this book, this chapter will provide the framework for the later analyses.

What is Europe?

The question 'What is Europe?' has long been a difficult one. On a simple geographical level, Europe stands as a peninsula on the Eurasian land mass, dwarfed by territories to its east. Yet the term 'Europe' has tended to be used as a shorthand to denote a sense of identity. This identity has varied in its definition but has been built upon a sense of common history, values and culture, as well as shared living space. To quote from Lewis, 'Europe is as much a concept and cultural construct as a territorial entity'.[3]

Identity is itself a notoriously complex issue, as it depends upon both self-perception and the views of others to secure legitimacy. Identity has traditionally been defined in terms of communities with particular characteristics, such as a common language, or in terms of nation states. Yet a sense of 'European-ness' necessitates transcending these other identities and asserting an identity at a higher level. At the same time it raises the question of whether there is a tension for an individual or a community in possessing multiple identities. This is a pertinent issue for western Europe at the present time as there are fears within many countries that national identity could be lost amid the process of political and economic integration.[4]

During the Cold War, security was the issue that defined the various perspectives on what constituted Europe. Geographical and other considerations were regarded as secondary to the security alignment of a state – whether it was a part of the western or eastern bloc. In the eyes of many, much of the hostility was ritualistic and the product of posturing. It served to divide the continent to suit the political interests of states outside Europe and enabled them to maximise their influence and control. The demise of the Cold War has resulted in a reassessment by states of where the interests of Europe truly lie.

Nevertheless, the Cold War was extremely important in asserting rival conceptions of Europe. Two conceptions were especially influential.[5] The first included either the United States or the Soviet Union, or both. Over issues such as arms control, it was recognised that the two powers played a central role and it was unrealistic to analyse the security of the continent without them. This thinking was evident in the creation of the Conference on Security and Cooperation in Europe (CSCE – the predecessor of the OSCE), which encapsulated territory from Vancouver to Vladivostock. The Soviet Union was always careful to emphasise its European credentials during the Cold War and this was built upon by Gorbachev with his rhetoric of a 'Common European Home'.[6] This was cleverly advanced because it implicitly excluded the United States from a role in Europe. Charles de Gaulle had attempted a similar manoeuvre when he defined Europe as existing from Portugal to the Ural Mountains, thus including the western half of the Soviet Union but excluding the United States.

The other and more common usage of the term 'Europe' was in relation to the states of the western half of the continent. These were the states that were party to the Treaty of Rome and comprised one of the two pillars of the Atlantic Alliance. As for a broader conception of Europe, the west was often accused of losing sight of eastern Europe owing to its pre-occupation with the Soviet Union. Eastern Europe was viewed as part of the Soviet empire, without any meaningful differentiation between the various states.[7] This broader definition of Europe covered all the territory from the Atlantic Ocean to the borders of the Soviet Union. This contained an implicit emancipatory message that countries on the continent should be free to decide upon matters of concern without the overlay of super-power interests.

Thus, the way in which Europe was defined during the Cold War reflected the ideological alignments of states. For some countries there was little choice in the matter, as it was apparent that notions of self-identity were subordinated to superpower interests. The results were sometimes peculiar – for example, Turkey was treated as part of the west because of its membership in the Atlantic Alliance, while Czechoslovakia was seen as part of the east because of its position in the Warsaw Treaty Organisation (WTO). Furthermore, the attempt to view the continent through a super-power lens left some regions blurred around the edges. The neutral countries of the north and some of the southern states, such as Yugoslavia, failed to fit into these simplistic typologies.

The end of the Cold War

Geopolitically, it has been possible to discuss a more diverse concept of Europe since the end of east–west confrontation. Rather than conceiving of the continent as a whole, it can be helpful to classify it in terms of four regions, or sub-systems, which share certain characteristics. Although not entirely comprehensive, this approach has the benefit of drawing on common features from before as well as during the Cold War and blending them with geography.[8]

The first region is western Europe, determined by the states that make up the EU. This is often regarded as the kernel of Europe, comprised of states that have grown accustomed to an economically integrated and inter-dependent relationship over the last fifty years. Even this region is not without its oddities, however, as some states, such as Switzerland and Norway, are considered as part of western Europe yet they have stood apart from much of the process of integration. The United States has also been considered as an integral actor in this part of the continent, particularly in security matters, yet in geographical terms it remains an extra-European power.

A second tranche of states exists in central Europe, what is sometimes referred to as 'Mitteleuropa'. This includes countries such as Poland, Hungary, the Czech Republic and Slovakia, which few would dispute possess a strong claim to be in the European family. Yet beyond these states it becomes difficult to determine where the boundaries of this region should be drawn. In essence, the question arises as to how far east one should proceed. Should, for instance, the Baltic states of Latvia, Lithuania and Estonia be incorporated into this grouping in the light of the fact that they were occupied by the Soviet Union during the Cold War?

A third group of countries includes the successor states of the former Soviet Union. The Russian Federation has emerged as the dominant actor, yet it symbolises the contradictions among them as its own claim to be a European state is deeply contentious. Throughout its history there has been a tension within Russia between those who look east and those who look west. The elite have tended to look to the west and have emphasised Russia's influence on Europe in terms of culture, music and literature. Nevertheless, even they cannot deny that Russia has borders extending well beyond Europe. This problem is shared among the states that broke away from the Soviet Union in 1991. Countries such as Ukraine and Georgia have a claim to be geographically linked to Europe. However, the same cannot be said for countries such as Uzbekistan or Kazakhstan, which are geographically part of central Asia and whose paths of political development blend the rhetoric of liberal democracy with authoritarian practices divorced from the mainstream of European political organisation. Such states as these are more likely to look to their Muslim neighbours to the south for their models of development than to the west.

The last group of states with a claim on European status are those situated in the Balkans, regarded as the southern flank of the continent. This has traditionally been an area of instability, serving as the spark for World War One and, more recently, the conflict in the former Yugoslavia. Countries in the region include Bulgaria, Romania and Albania; their common characteristics have tended to be a reliance on agriculture, a relatively low level of technological development and a high degree of political centralisation.

Creating a Europe whole and free?

For the countries of central Europe, the end of the Cold War heralded a time of great optimism. The Berlin Wall, which had represented the political division of Europe, was dismantled and Soviet occupation forces began to be pulled back to their home territory. The revolutions in states such as Czechoslovakia were remarkably peaceful and the example of the rapid integration of the German Democratic Republic into the Federal Republic gave the central and east European countries (CEECs) hope for the future. Now that the blocs had been dissolved without resort to violence, it became possible for them to conceive of a 'return to Europe'.

The argument of some countries, such as the Visegrad members, was that the Cold War witnessed a skewing of their normal pattern of development and that only with its disappearance could they return to a common set of European values. They could justifiably claim to have shared a European heritage in terms of their history, culture and religion. Indeed, even during their experience of Soviet hegemony, the existence of strong civil societies had ensured that their value systems retained a pro-western orientation. The fact that it had been necessary to impose socialist unity on them by force lent credence to this argument. They now embraced western political and economic values in the form of multi-party systems, market economies and the rule of law. In their eyes, western Europe represented economic modernisation, stability and a sense of a happier destiny.

However, there were undeniably problems to be overcome. There was considerable diversity between states in the region and uneven levels of political and social development. It was far from clear that western political models would be appropriate for all states. Moreover, while there were historical linkages with states in western Europe, it was impossible to ignore forty-five years of communist rule. Linked to this was the issue of where to draw the line between states that could be assimilated quickly into western organisations and those that would have to be left outside. A country such as Romania was eager to be brought into the western family yet it lacked the traditions of democratic government that were discernible in a state such as the Czech Republic. But to exclude Romania, while accepting other countries in central Europe, would threaten to leave that state in a political vacuum.

There was also an enormous range of inherent practical problems among the CEECs. For example, their economies exhibited varying levels of stagnation and their physical environments were almost universally polluted and suffering from neglect. Furthermore, few states could claim to be ethnically homogenous. Tensions over minority rights were bubbling up as authoritarian control was relaxed and these were contributing to a resurgence of nationalism. The most extreme example was in Yugoslavia, where rivalries and antagonisms between the various communities propelled the country into disintegration and war. West European states were alarmed that such a destructive and bloody conflict could occur so close to their own territories.

Is there still an enemy?

Security was one of the dominant issues that divided Europe into its constituent parts during the Cold War, but with its end the WTO, which had maintained the cohesion of the eastern bloc, was rapidly dissolved. In 1991, the Soviet Union itself broke up as various constituent republics asserted their independence.

As for the western half of Europe, its experience of security was very different. Western Europe had developed after World War Two into a 'security community', where war was not considered to be a viable instrument for resolving disputes. Although this community was not uniform across the whole of the west, it still was strong enough to outlive the end of the east–west antagonism.[9] Despite the fact that there were no immediate post-Cold War threats to western territorial integrity, there was a recognition that shared risks existed on their periphery. The war in the former Yugoslavia bore out the fact that western powers had a common interest in promoting stability within Europe and on its borders.

The west continued as an island of security stability while the east entered a period of uncertainty. Many states in the east hoped that a pan-European framework would replace the bloc structures and provide for a system of collective security. These hopes were dashed by the lack of commitment the leading western states demonstrated towards the CSCE Paris summit in November 1990, as well as by evidence that the Soviet Union was still willing to use its military strength to further its interests. This resulted in a growing demand to extend the western zone of security to include states in the former rival bloc. Once more, however, this raised the perennial problem of drawing new lines in Europe. Critics could argue that little had changed with the end of the Cold War, that the western paradigm of adversarial relationships was still in place, albeit in an altered form.

Russia, in a manner similar to its Soviet forebear, was the foremost obstacle to the idea of enlarging the western security zone. On the one hand, it was still an enormously powerful state militarily and was perceived as presenting a residual danger to its neighbours. Yet, on the other hand, there was a genuine fear in the west of alienating Russia and stimulating a return to mutual suspicion and hostility. Russian leaders made it clear that they expected a privileged relationship with the west in light of their continued power and influence and that this should extend to those territories on Russia's periphery, its so-called 'near abroad'. Western discussion of enlarging the security zone to draw in states along the borders of Russia has elicited a consistently negative response from the Kremlin and has prompted Russia to attempt to draw some successor states, notably Belarus, back into a closer relationship.

Building Europe through institutions

Western Europe had pursued successfully, throughout the post-war period, a policy of integration which had created a set of interlocking institutions in the areas of security, economics and human rights. It could claim to have 'won' the Cold War by outlasting its adversary: its economic system had proved to be superior and its values had proved to be durable. In this way western institutions offered an explanation of past success while at the same time articulating a vision of Europe's future. It was these very same institutions that eastern states were now clamouring to join as they lacked suitable alternative structures in their half of the continent.

Western states were eager to signal their approval of the revolutionary changes in the east but there was no universally accepted vision about admitting new members to established organisations. Both the process of enlargement and the timetable for undertaking it became topics of dispute in the west.

A contradictory pressure from within the western half of the continent has been to push ahead with a 'core Europe' concept. This has been demonstrated with the movement in the 1990s to political and monetary union within the EU. As the integrative process in the west has still considerable ground to cover, there has been a desire to avoid sacrificing its momentum in order to incorporate the CEECs. Institutions have sought to adapt their own structures before admitting new members, so as to prevent any impairment of their decision-making dynamism. This approach has been strengthened further by the differences of emphasis among west European states. While countries such as Germany have focused on the CEECs, others such as Italy and Spain have called for greater attention to be paid to the needs of southern states.

In seeking to determine which applicants should be admitted to western institutions, a host of complex problems have been generated. A set of agreed values underpinned each of the organisations, based on Roman law, Judaeo-Christian ethics, traditions of civil rights and market economic systems. In the light of these, it remained to be agreed how new adherents would qualify for admittance. In addition, it had to be assessed how the organisation itself would be affected by the influx of new and disparate states. Many were considered to be in a volatile condition and open to reverses of orientation. This was particularly the case among those countries, such as Poland, that had undertaken economic shock therapy. Rather than providing a quick fix, as some had expected, shock therapy resulted in economic dislocation, rising unemployment and soaring inflation. It was not inconceivable that states might abandon their radicalism and revert to less arduous policies.

Overall then, it seems clear only that the concept of 'Europe' means different things to different people; there is no identikit. Indeed, Jean Monnet, one of the founding fathers of west European integration, declared that 'Europe' had never existed but that it must be genuinely created.[10] In essence, the idea of 'Europe' is about a sense of shared fate and common problems. This has direct implications for institutional enlargement. For some in the west, the priority must be to deepen integration in case the process should grind to a halt or even go into reverse.[11] For others, the future lies in widening existing institutions, while accepting the attendant costs.

Some countries are unquestionably considered to be a part of 'Europe'; other states are deemed to be close to joining, while another group, by virtue of their geography and makeup, are viewed as outsiders. In such a way, a dominant vision of 'Europe' emerges by default, namely those countries that are, and those countries that are not, invited into western institutions.

Do institutions matter?

One of the central concerns of the discipline of international relations is to discover those conditions that make possible cooperation between states. Several explanations for such cooperation have been forwarded. In recent years much has been made of the role of political values and the effects of economic prosperity. Both of these would seem to be important in the west European context. It could be argued quite convincingly that since 1945 the consolidation of democracy and the common experience of economic growth (and, by the same token, the absence of periods of catastrophic economic depression) have been central in explaining the avoidance of war and the proliferation of collaborative efforts between states in the region. A third, and equally important, factor has been the development of international 'institutions', a term which refers to a range of cooperative practices, including those associated with formal international organisations.[12]

In the post-war period, western Europe has been subject to a dense process of institutionalisation. This, it is argued, has drawn the states of the region together in overlapping and mutually beneficial forms of military, economic and political activity. These forms of cooperation are not only important in their own right, but have also contributed to a broader process, fostering a climate of trust and moderating the competitive behaviour of states.[13] What is more, if this argument is correct, it has profound implications for the wider continent, for it suggests that an extension of the institutional process to central and eastern Europe is a realisable way of bringing some form of stability to the more troubled and turbulent half of the continent.

Yet is it really so self-evident that states have an interest in institutionalised forms of cooperation? To help us understand the reasons why institutions arise and survive it is worth considering three schools of thought, those of neo-realism, neo-liberal institutionalism and social constructivism.

Neo-realism: assuming the worst

As summarised by one of its most insistent advocates, neo-realism proceeds from five basic assumptions. First, the ordering principle of the international system is a condition of anarchy, taken to mean the absence of an overriding authority above states. Second, states possess military capacities, which have an offensive nature. Third, states are uncertain of and, therefore, suspicious of other states. Fourth, states are motivated above all by a desire for survival, or, in other words, the protection of their sovereignty. And finally, states are 'instrumentally rational' – they act strategically to ensure they survive.[14]

From these assumptions, certain kinds of behaviour are seen to arise. In a world in which a higher authority is absent and distrust is prevalent, self-help becomes the order of the day. Cooperation is inhibited by fears of cheating and considerations regarding 'relative gains' (the suspicion on the part of one state that collaboration benefits other states more than itself).[15] This is clearly not a propitious environment for the operation of international institutions. To make matters worse, because the doctrine of state sovereignty generally prohibits external agencies from interfering in the priorities of states, institutions lack the ability to impose some collective interest or enforce rules of conduct. In fact, to the extent that international institutions do carry out important roles, these have less to do with promoting mutually beneficial cooperation and more with advancing the particular interests of powerful states. To paraphrase John Mearsheimer, the leading states create and shape institutions so that they can preserve their share of world power, or even add to it.[16] Hence, institutional outcomes reflect the balance of power between states. In some instances this is clear cut – take American dominance of NATO or Soviet preponderance in the WTO. More ambiguous are situations where the balance does not clearly favour one state. Such has been the case in the United Nations (UN), where, during the Cold War, both the United States and the Soviet Union exerted comparable influences. It has also been the case within the EU and the OSCE, where several states have been influential. In such situations, the result is either institutional paralysis or at best a temporary and ephemeral meeting of minds.

Neo-realism also holds a less than sanguine outlook on the post-Cold War order in Europe. The passing of the Soviet threat and the transition from a bipolar to a multi-polar world has been seen as marking the arrival of a period of instability and danger. The assumptions upon which this assertion rests are largely structural in nature. With a power configuration of three or more, rather than two, major powers,[17] instability increases owing to a proliferation of 'conflict dyads', deterrence strategies become more complex and the chances of misperception and miscalculation proliferate.[18] While neo-realists are shy about taking the next step in this argument by asserting that a war involving the major powers is likely, this is certainly a scenario consistent with their line of thinking. The emergence of a string of weak states in central and eastern Europe, the Balkans and the former Soviet Union has increased the opportunities for intervention in order to carve out zones of influence. This has already had potentially catastrophic consequences. As Jack Snyder has suggested, 'the balance-of-power policies of small east European states released from the grip of Soviet hegemony, may help catalyse war among the great powers'.[19] And even in the absence as yet of such a war, neo-realists can still point to the eruption of civil wars, such as in the Soviet successor states of Transcaucasia, as confirmation of their generally pessimistic position.

For the neo-realist, the post-Cold War order has implications for international institutions on two principal grounds. First, insofar as the states of western Europe had, during the Cold War, been able to bury their differences in the face of a common external threat, the disappearance of that threat, with the passing of the Soviet Union, could lead to the re-emergence of old antagonisms, rendering cooperative efforts between them that much more difficult.[20] Second, the new threats posed by the eruption of civil wars on Europe's periphery have presented challenges which international institutions have been hard pressed to meet. There is no better proof of this than the war in the former Yugoslavia, which has severely tested the credibility of the OSCE, the UN, the WEU and the EU.[21] Even NATO's belated success following the Dayton agreement of 1995 was achieved only after what was, in effect, a unilateral diplomatic intervention by its most powerful member state, the United States.

Neo-liberal institutionalism: emphasising the possible

Neo-liberal institutionalism seeks to demonstrate that cooperation is easier to achieve than is recognised by the neo-realists. This view is willing to accept certain core neo-realist tenets, such as the position of states in a condition of anarchy and the subsequent pursuit of self-interest, but asserts that even the self-interested state will recognise the benefits of cooperation. Following arguments derived from models such as the prisoners' dilemma, it is argued that cooperation avoids outcomes which are sub-optimal, that is, situations in which states will be worse off owing to their neglect of mutual agreement. Institutions offer the means to formalise and facilitate such cooperation in world politics.[22]

Institutions also address the structural obstacles to cooperation perceived by the neo-realists. Cheating, for instance, can be deterred by, first, establishing punishment regimes for transgressors and rewards for cooperative states and, second, by creating expectations that the benefits of future cooperation will be jeopardised if a state seeks unilateral advantage. As for the relative gains dilemma, this institutions help overcome by facilitating an environment of security among states which, according to Robert Keohane, 'allow[s] government to emphasise absolute ... gains'.[23] In such an environment, states measure success in terms of their own returns, rather than whether their gains are greater or less than those of other states. This allows them to cooperate even in the knowledge that they will not be the only or the greatest beneficiary.[24] Moreover, while states will still be concerned with the pursuit of self-interest and will utilise institutions as instruments for furthering this, it is also possible that institutions can affect how states define those interests and therefore 'play roles that go beyond instrumentalism'.[25] Insofar as states are increasingly thrown together in institutional arrangements by the imperatives of interdependence, habits of contact will be formed that lead states to recognise that their interests are not necessarily at odds. International institutions thus become the vehicles for the pursuit of common concerns and states learn to take the interests of others into account when framing their own policies: they become 'joint-maximisers rather than self-maximisers'.[26] Furthermore, an institution can obtain an identity that is autonomous from the states that inhabit it. The institution becomes an international actor in its own right, pursuing the aggregated interests of its member states. This, to an extent, has occurred with the office of the UN Secretary-General and is even more evident in the case of the Commission of the EU.[27]

Turning to the mechanics of cooperation more specifically, here we might consider the roles played by intergovernmental organisations, perhaps the most familiar embodiment of institutionalised behaviour among states. Oran Young has identified three important roles performed by these bodies. They help create and administer international regimes, that is, standards of behaviour within a range of issue areas;[28] they provide a framework for the pooling of resources in the service of a common interest (the classic example being military alliances); and third, they provide a setting for multilateral diplomacy and negotiation. The last is especially important and in this regard international organisations have considerable merit. In political terms, according to Young, they facilitate 'the linking of issues for the purposes of devising mutually acceptable agreements'. In efficiency terms, meanwhile, they are able to handle with relative ease discussions on issues that involve 'large-scale multilateral interactions' (migration, the environment, the law of the sea), thereby eliminating the transaction costs of overlapping and repeated interactions associated with bilateralism.[29] Success in these areas, in turn, generates further action; a virtuous circle is created whereby success leads to positive expectations of future relations and states 'get caught up on a continuing process through which the areas of cooperation are widened'.[30]

By the institutionalist view, international organisations are accorded a pivotal role in post-Cold War Europe. Liberated from the paralysis of the period of east–west stand-off, they are now free to play a more constructive role in international affairs. Moreover, for Robert Keohane and Joseph Nye, the dense institutionalisation of western Europe will help sustain continued cooperation there despite the disappearance of the binding circumstances provided by a common external threat. The habits of proven and beneficial cooperation will not simply evaporate under the new circumstances. But what of those regions where institutionalisation is less developed? The task in this connection is to extend the model to eastern Europe and the former Soviet Union. This will serve to stabilise the potentially disruptive international consequences attendant upon the end of the Cold War and to impress upon these states the worth of democratic values and norms, and the western system of managed capitalism.[31] New initiatives on the part of NATO (notably offshoots such as the North Atlantic Cooperation Council, Partnership for Peace and the Euro-Atlantic Partnership Council) and the EU, an extension of the role of the UN and the OSCE in conflict resolution, and the preservation and extension of arms control and disarmament regimes are all seen as germane in this regard.[32]

Neo-liberal institutionalism is not totally optimistic in its outlook. Institutions do not offer a shortcut to utopia. To paraphrase Dag Hammarskjold's view of the UN, they are created 'not in order to bring us to heaven but in order to save us from hell'.[33] In the drier and more cautious language of the political scientist, international institutions are 'sometimes, but not always, capable of exerting significant effects';[34] 'they have the *potential* to facilitate cooperation'.[35] The readiness of states to enter into such activity, even the institutionalists admit, is coloured by calculations of self-interest. While international institutions may mitigate the competitive drives of states, they can neither transform interests that are fundamentally in conflict nor foster altruism. The trick of international institutions rather is to create alluring material outcomes of cooperation when interests are congruent. Furthermore, the success of institutionalised cooperation is seen as dependent on the number of states involved – with fewer numbers likely to prove more successful than larger numbers.[36] This has a particular significance in terms of enlargement. The logic of the argument would seem to be that an enlarged institution is a less effective one. More members mean that the possibilities for a clash of interests are increased and the problems of coordination, administration and communication are multiplied. Merely posing the question of enlargement, meanwhile, courts the danger of opening up divisions among existing members of an institution. All of this is not to say that enlargement is treated suspiciously by institutionalists – in fact quite the reverse, as the process also entails rewards as well as losses. However, a basic dilemma is apparent: enlargement versus cohesion. How institutions have dealt with this dilemma will be a central concern of the case-study chapters.

The constructivist challenge

The debate between the neo-realists and the neo-liberals has been a dominant one in the international relations literature, and particularly so in the European studies literature, as the EU (and, to a lesser extent, NATO) has been seen as the key test case. National urges in the EU are seized upon by the neo-realists to illustrate their case; collaborative initiatives are developed by the neo-liberals to critique the neo-realists. Despite the heat generated by the neo–neo debate, a further paradigm has developed which has important insights to offer to the debate on institutions: social constructivism.

Constructivism, drawing implicitly upon earlier work and in particular that of the English school of international relations, suggests that the neo-realist–neo-liberal debate is too narrow.[37] Indeed, there are so many points of convergence that Ole Wæver has recently suggested that a 'neo–neo' synthesis has emerged.[38] Moreover, constructivism sees both the neo schools as part of a 'positivist' approach to international politics that they reject. Positivism suggests that there is an objective truth that can be discovered through reason, and that there is only one correct form of reasoning, which, through empiricism, enables the analyst to test propositions. Positivism therefore requires a distinction between observer and observed.

Constructivism suggests, by contrast, that there is no objective truth in international relations, no one uniform 'reason', that reliance on empiricism is therefore analytically dangerous, and that observer and observed cannot be separated. In place of this, constructivists argue that knowledge is socially constructed. As Neufeld has put it:

> ideas, words, and language are not mirrors that copy the 'real' or 'objective' world – as positivist conceptions of theory and knowledge would have it – but rather tools with which we cope with 'our' world. Consequently, there is a fundamental link between epistemology – the question of what counts as reliable knowledge – and politics – the problems, needs, and interests deemed important and legitimate by a given community.[39]

Hence, the 'real' world is constructed by the language and the values of the agents in that world. 'Thus,' as Spike Peterson argues, 'objectivity, understood as a "perspectiveless gaze" is impossible in a socially constructed world; rationality is not transcendental but historically specific, learned activity; and methods are necessarily contextual, and therefore shaped by culture and particular values.'[40]

This is important for consideration of the role of institutions and their enlargement in post-Cold War Europe. If the EU has been the focus of the engagement of neo-realism and neo-liberalism, it has been the future and nature of NATO which have provided an important theme in the constructivist challenge to neo-realism. The neo-realists argue that where there are objective threats to states, they will respond by forming an alliance. If that objective threat dissipates, the cohesion of that alliance will weaken. Thus, with the collapse of Soviet power, and the objective impossibility of an equal replacement, NATO must wither away.[41]

The constructivist approach to NATO is rather different. This has perhaps best been expressed by Thomas Risse-Kappen.[42] First, constructivists reject the notion of an objective threat. As Risse-Kappen argues, 'Threat perceptions do not emerge from a quasi-objective international power structure, but actors infer external behaviour from the values and norms governing the domestic political processes that shape the identities of their partners in the international system.' Second, once functioning, alliances are shaped by shared values: 'the Western Alliance represents an institutionalization of the transatlantic security community based on common values'. Third, this institutionalisation of common values is robust in the face of political change, for 'It is easier to adjust an already existing organisation, which encompasses an elaborate set of rules and decision-making procedures, to new conditions than it is to create new institutions of security cooperation.'[43]

Thus, international institutions are, for neo-realists, responses to real threats and to changes in the balance of power; to constructivists they can be fundamental representations of values and, as such, can be and often are constructed to play a central role in international affairs.

The debate between the constructivists and neo-realists has been about explaining NATO's survival rather than focusing upon its enlargement, but there are clear constructivist implications for understanding institutional enlargement. To the constructivists, enlargement represents an attempt to broaden the base of those who share the common values. This needs to be considered carefully, in the light of three points. First, it does not follow that members of an institution want to share their values with all applicants; it also does not follow that members of an institution believe that all applicants can share those values. Consider the case of Russia: who wants Russia to share the values (and benefits) of EU membership? Who believes that Russia can share the values of NATO? Second, it also does not follow that all institutions are equally important in representing the shared values of states. Institutions can collapse because they do not represent shared values, or states can withdraw if, owing to revolutionary domestic changes, their new value system leads them to radically reconstruct their international identity and loyalties.[44] On this point, perhaps it was easier for western countries to expand the COE before, and more widely, than the EU or NATO because the Council represents European/western views more weakly than they do. Third, the constructivist view does not imply that western organisations share the same values. For example, Paris seems to believe that there is a difference between European and western/trans-atlantic powers, and this was important in the early 1990s when France did not want to see NATO enlarge before the EU.[45]

Concepts of enlargement

It is important to bear in mind that there has not been one concept of enlargement applied to the institutions of Europe. There has been no master plan, no one architect, to bring a semblance of order to the complexity of widening the membership of so many organisations over a relatively short period of time. If there is not *a* concept of enlargement to be deconstructed, it makes the task of this volume rather more difficult. If one concept of enlargement could have been identified, it would have been possible to explain how the enlargement strategies of each institution related to the overarching whole, where problems had emerged, how they were resolved and how compromise was managed. But instead of this picture of *an* enlargement process, Europe's institutions have been subjected to *individual enlargement processes*.

In such circumstances, even the task of comparison becomes difficult. In what sense can the enlargement of the COE be compared to that of the WEU? Obviously, many of the agents involved – member states and appli-cants – have been the same in both cases, but the dynamics of the enlargement debates have varied because the context of each has differed.

Enlarging the COE has been in large part about giving a symbol of democratic respectability to post-communist states and also about encouraging others to 'improve' their behaviour. In contrast, debates about enlarging the WEU have been about the inter-relationship between the EU and NATO and their relative political positions in Europe as well as enlargement. Without a dominant narrative of enlargement, it is analytically difficult to relate the two processes in such a way that would allow judgement as to whether the enlargement of one organisation was in any sense more successful than that of the other.

Thus, the lack of a grand strategy for the enlargement of Europe's institutions provides an analytical difficulty for this volume. In addition to being unable to find clear grounds for comparison, the lack of a blueprint means that there is no clear empirical basis for the selection of the five institutions to be examined in this volume: NATO, the EU, the WEU, the OSCE and the COE. The authors judge these five to be more important than, say, Visegrad, but the agents of institutional enlargement have not stipulated this. These difficulties are compounded by the need to consider two forms of enlargement: of membership, and of function. All of the institutions under examination in this volume have been the subject of debates regarding both types of enlargement. The emphasis in the book is on enlargement of membership but, as will be seen in successive chapters, it is rarely possible to separate membership from function. Often, a debate about an increase in membership has led to a debate about enlargements of function and, similarly, debates about function have impacted upon debates regarding membership. This widening–deepening inter-relationship has been most apparent in the context of the EU, but it can be seen in each of the five institutions under examination.

A subsidiary point of importance is that although there has been no grand strategy of enlargement, the dominant theme has been the enlargement of western institutions, and the dominance of western institutions formed during the Cold War over new, post-Cold War creations. There is, in other words, a unidirectional nature to the enlargement processes: central and eastern Europe have looked west, while western Europe has not looked east for its institutional homes. This westward movement, characterised by the slogan 'back to Europe', has surely largely been about symbolism. It may be fair to suggest that actors such as Gorbachev won the Cold War as much as did the United States and western Europe, but that does not disguise the rhetorical dominance of the values of liberal democracy, the market economy and a broader notion of security in Europe. And yet, for many post-communist states, liberal democracy, the market economy and a broader notion of security for the state and its citizens are much easier to achieve by rhetorical declaration than they are by convincing their populations. Thus, the allure of the western community, for an association with those that have apparently achieved these three goals (something much less accepted in western Europe than in central and eastern Europe), is seen as helping to convince citizens in countries aspiring for membership of various organisations that things are improving. And, according to this perspective, the more badges of membership that are achieved, the better. It would be difficult to argue against this, in either psychological or material terms: would not Czech membership of the EU and NATO offer Prague the prospect of greater prosperity and security, at least in the medium term? And because it has been difficult to argue against this, organisations created since the end of the Cold War have simply been unable to compete with the western institutions in terms of attractiveness.

The one apparent exception to this unidirectional picture is the OSCE, for it was never a western organisation, rather representing a balance of interests among the states in the Vancouver to Vladivostok space. And it has certainly played an important role in the 1990s in terms of election monitoring and notably, but not exclusively, in the area of preventive diplomacy. Yet even here the unidirectional impulse is evident, in at least two senses: first, in terms of western values and interests; and second, in terms of the rejection of any alternative.

First, of the three 'baskets' of objectives underlying the establishment of the CSCE – security cooperation, economic cooperation and common human rights – it is only the last which has really emerged into the post-Cold War OSCE. Security cooperation has operated at some levels, for example in the Contact Group in the former Yugoslavia (although this was outside the OSCE), but the dominant norm has been of very different levels of security within the OSCE space. There may, eventually, have been large-scale military inter-vention in Bosnia, but not in Tajikistan, or Nagorno-Karabakh. In economic terms, certainly from the perspective of the CEECs, post-Cold War Europe has been about self-help rather than economic cooperation: certainly there has been no new Marshall Plan. But the third basket, that of human rights based on western notions (political and legal freedoms) rather than Cold War eastern notions (economic rights such as that to employment), has predominated.

Second, it has been within the OSCE that the powerful pull of western institutions has been most apparent. Russia has sought to redevelop the OSCE, to furnish it with, in effect, a security council, and to make other institutions in Europe, notably NATO and the CIS, answerable to it. By making the OSCE the paramount organisation in Europe, important symbolic and practical changes to European governance would have been made. Perhaps not surprisingly, members of the NATO Alliance have been hostile to such an idea. But much more importantly, Russia has been unable to generate any significant support for this idea in central and eastern Europe. In this way, the CEECs have ratified the unidirectional orientation of post-Cold War enlargement and rejected alternatives.

Conclusion

This chapter has sought to demonstrate that 'Europe', 'institutions' and 'enlargement' are all complex phenomena, capable of multiple and often conflicting interpretations. Although some actors, perhaps notably the United States, have come to play particularly important roles, there has been no grand strategy. However, policies cannot simply be ascribed to the nature of the post-Cold War European structure. The enlargement of Europe's organisations, therefore, cannot be explained in terms of a largely agent-centred approach, but neither can it be portrayed as a product of predominant structural pressures. Instead, as Anthony Giddens would suggest in his concept of 'structuration', agents' policies have influenced the structure, or architecture, of Europe but also the European structure has influenced the policies of agents.

This volume will illustrate this complex inter-relationship by examining each of the enlargement processes for the five main international organisations in Europe. Each chapter will first examine the history of the organisation in terms of prior enlargements, to see whether such enlargements relate to the contemporary debate; it will then examine the chronological development of enlargement debates and policies from the end of the Cold War; and finally it will examine tensions involved, arguments for and against enlargement of that particular organisation, the role of key actors and future implications. Finally, the concluding chapter will assess the key issues in the enlargement of Europe.

Notes

1   The Visegrad states are Poland, Hungary and, after their division, the Czech Republic and Slovakia.
2   Dom Mintoff's government had close relations with Libya; that of Eddie Fenech Adami with Italy. Malta's domestic political debate has to a certain extent revolved around the identity question.
3   P. Lewis, 'Europe and Russia', in B. Waites (ed.), *Europe and the Wider World*, London: Routledge in conjunction with the Open University, 1995, p. 74.
4   S. Garcia (ed.), *European Identity and the Search for Legitimacy*, London: Pinter for the Eleni Nakou Foundation and the Royal Institute for International Affairs, 1993.
5   These arguments draw upon some of the ideas advanced by Ole Wæver. See B. Buzan, O. Wæver, M. Kelstrup, E. Tromer and P. Lemaitre, *The European Security Order Recast*, London: Pinter, 1990, pp. 45–50.
6   M. Gorbachev, *Perestroika*, London: Fontana, 1988.
7   See T. Judt, 'The rediscovery of Central Europe', in S. Graubard (ed.), *Eastern Europe ... Central Europe ... Europe*, Boulder, CO: Westview, 1991.
8   This approach can be found in H. Miall (ed.), *Redefining Europe: New Patterns of Conflict and Cooperation*, London: Pinter for the Royal Institute for International Affairs, 1994.
9   Buzan *et al.*, *European Security Order*, p. 28.
10 D. Gowland (ed.), *The European Mosaic: Contemporary Politics, Economics and Culture*, London: Longman, 1995, p. 289.

11 B. Buzan, 'The changing security identity in Europe', in O. Wæver, B. Buzan, M. Kelstrup and P. Lemaitre, *Identity, Migration and the New Security Agenda in Europe*, London: Pinter, 1993.

12 J. J. Mearsheimer defines institutions 'as sets of rules that stipulate the ways in which states should cooperate and compete with each other.... These rules are typically formalized in international agreements, and are usually embodied in organisations with their own personnel and budgets.' See 'The false promise of international institutions', *International Security*, Vol. 19, No. 3, 1994/5, pp. 8–9.

13 See P. van Ham, 'Can institutions hold Europe together?', in Miall (ed.), *Redefining Europe*, pp. 186–7.

14 Mearsheimer, 'False promise', pp. 10–11; see also K. Waltz, *Theory of International Relations*, Reading, MA: Addison-Wesley, 1979, pp. 88–93.

15 J. M. Grieco, 'Anarchy and the limits of cooperation: a realist critique of the newest liberal institutionalism', *International Organisation*, Vol. 42, No. 3, 1988, especially p. 499.

16 Mearsheimer, 'False promise', p. 13.

17 K. Waltz has suggested that by the first decade of the twenty-first century the United States and Russia will remain great powers, and may have been joined by Germany (or a united Europe), Japan and China. See 'The emerging structure of international politics', *International Security*, Vol. 14, No. 4, 1990, p. 9.

18 J. J. Mearsheimer, 'Back to the future: instability in Europe after the cold war', *International Security*, Vol. 15, No. 1, 1990, pp. 14–15.

19 J. Snyder, 'Averting anarchy in the new Europe', *International Security*, Vol. 14, No. 4, 1990, p. 9.

20 Mearsheimer, 'False promise', p. 9.

21 van Ham, 'Can institutions hold Europe together?', pp. 193–5.

22 O. R. Young, 'International regimes: towards a new theory of institutions', *World Politics*, Vol. 39, No. 1, 1986, p. 109; R. O. Keohane, 'International institutions: two approaches', *International Studies Quarterly*, Vol. 32, No. 4, 1988, p. 386.

23 R. O. Keohane, 'The diplomacy of structural change: multilateral institutions and state strategies', in H. Haftendorn and C. Tuschhoff (eds), *America and Europe in an Era of Change*, Boulder, CO: Westview, 1993, p. 53.

24 A. A. Stein, *Why Nations Cooperate: Circumstance and Choice in International Relations*, Ithaca, NY: Cornell University Press, 1990, pp. 115–17. Robert Keohane and Lisa Martin have also argued that even when relative gains considerations apply, institutions play an important role by helping to settle these 'distributional conflicts', by 'assuring states that gains are evenly divided over time'. See their 'The promise of institutionalist theory', *International Security*, Vol. 20, No. 1, 1995, pp. 44–5.

25 R. O. Keohane and S. Hoffmann, 'Conclusion: structure, strategy and international roles', in R. O. Keohane, J. Nye and S. Hoffmann (eds), *After the Cold War: International Institutions and State Strategies in Europe, 1989–1991*, Cambridge, MA: Harvard University Press, 1993, p. 401.

26 Stein, *Why Nations Cooperate*, p. 53. See also G. M. Lyons, 'International organisations and national interests', and O. Young, 'System and society in world affairs: implications for international organisations', both in *International Social Science Journal*, No. 144, 1995.

27 C. Archer, *International Organisations*, London: George Allen and Unwin, 1983, pp. 141–9.

28 While the concept of an 'international regime' has been contested, S. Krasner's widely cited definition has been followed: that regimes are 'sets of implicit or explicit principles, norms, rules and decision-making procedures around which actors' expectations converge in a given area of international relations.' See his 'Structural causes and regime consequences: regimes as intervening variables', *International Organisation*, Vol. 36, No. 2, 1982, p. 2.

29 Young, 'System and society in world affairs', pp. 203–4.

30 Lyons, 'International organisations', p. 263.

31 Keohane and Hoffmann, 'Conclusion', p. 401.

32 C. Archer, *Organising Europe: The Institutions of Integration*, London: Edward Arnold, 2nd edn, 1994, pp. 281–2; van Ham, 'Can institutions hold Europe together?', pp. 197–203.

33 Cited in T. G. Weiss, 'The United Nations at fifty: recent lessons', *Current History*, Vol. 94, No. 592, 1995, p. 228.

34 R. O. Keohane, 'Redefining Europe: implications for international relations', in Miall (ed.), *Redefining Europe*, p. 233.

35 Keohane, 'International institutions: two approaches', p. 393, emphasis in the original.

36 R. Axelrod and R. O. Keohane, 'Achieving cooperation under anarchy: strategies and institutions', *World Politics*, Vol. 38, No. 1, 1985, pp. 234–46.

37 On the constructivist–English school linkage, see the excellent T. Dunne, 'The social construction of international society', *European Journal of International Relations*, Vol. 1, No. 3, 1995, pp. 367–89.

38 O. Wæver, 'The rise and fall of the inter-paradigm debate', in S. Smith, K. Booth and M. Zalewski (eds), *International Theory: Positivism and Beyond*, Cambridge: Cambridge University Press, 1996.

39 M. Neufeld, 'Reflexivity and international relations theory', in C. Turenne Sjolander and W. S. Cox (eds), *Beyond Positivism: Critical Reflections on International Relations*, Boulder, CO: Lynne Rienner, 1994, p. 15.

40 V. S. Peterson, 'Introduction', in V. S. Peterson (ed.), *Gendered States: Feminist (Re)Visions of International Relations Theory*, Boulder, CO: Lynne Rienner, 1992, p. 12.

41 This is the argument made most notably by Mearsheimer in 'Back to the future', pp. 5–56, and it is an important theme in his 'The false promise'.

42 T. Risse-Kappen, 'Identity in a democratic security community: the case of NATO', in P. Katzenstein (ed.), *The Culture of National Security*, New York: Columbia University Press, 1996, pp. 359–99.

43 *Ibid.*, pp. 367, 395 and 396.

44 The best examination of this is D. Armstrong, *Revolution and World Order: The Revolutionary State in International Society*, Oxford: Clarendon Press, 1993. Armstrong is a leading proponent of the English school rather than constructivism, but if one will allow the point made earlier, the linkages between the two theoretical perspectives are very strong.

45 Although, of course, the French position was complicated by their desire to deepen the Union before extending it.

2

The enlargement of the
North Atlantic Treaty Organisation

Introduction

During much of the forty years of east–west hostility, NATO – along with the Warsaw Pact – was seen as the quintessential Cold War institution. The guarantee of the security of the west Europeans by the United States, backed by the deployment of American conventional and nuclear forces on the European continent, and the integration of those forces with those of the west Europeans through NATO's integrated military command, provided a political and diplomatic framework for security relations in Europe. With the end of the Cold War, NATO clearly lost its *raison d'être*, and yet the political leaders of the Alliance were most unwilling to allow NATO to fold.

Following the revolutions in the CEECs in 1989, there was a great deal of argument that NATO should be replaced, like the Warsaw Pact, with a pan-European security system under the CSCE. However, the terms of the debate quickly changed from the interest of the CEECs in the abandonment of NATO into a desire to join the organisation.[1] Enlargement therefore quickly came to be seen as one means by which a new NATO could make a contribution to post-Cold War Europe. However, importantly, this was an argument coming not from inside NATO, but from central Europe. It was Warsaw, Prague and Budapest that saw the key future role for NATO in terms of enlarging the western security community, at a time when in London, Washington and Bonn the main argument in favour of maintaining NATO revolved around inertia: maintain NATO in case it became useful in the future.

Arguments in favour of the enlargement of western security institutions therefore focused on NATO expansion. The reasoning in favour of expansion was focused on three points. The first was that the Soviet Union, and later Russia, clearly provided a threat to the independence of central Europe, or at least could do so in the future. The second was that the central

Europeans had the right to join western institutions as part of their 'return to Europe', and that neither Moscow nor the western countries could properly deny the CEECs this right. The third was that access to security institutions had to go alongside the key goal of the CEECs – joining the EU.

These different arguments led to an emphasis on enlarging different institutions. For the first argument, that connected to a Soviet/Russian threat, only NATO membership would suffice. Only NATO had the organisation and capabilities (above all, the American link) to extend security guarantees beyond western Europe. The third argument, related to the enlargement of the EU, raised in profile the importance of membership of the WEU, which at Maastricht became the defence arm of the EU. This would have certain knock-on effects on the debate over NATO enlargement, as will be seen later. And the second argument – connected to the 'return to Europe' – seemed to imply that the expansion of both NATO and the WEU, perhaps in parallel, was important.

Underlying all of this debate was the deeply controversial nature of the question of NATO enlargement between NATO members and within NATO governments (above all, those of Germany and the United States). This was, to a large extent, probably inevitable, for any discussion about NATO enlargement would be, in fact, argument over the nature of European security, the future of the Alliance, alternative architectural designs for post-Cold War Europe and, fundamentally, debates over identity, over who 'deserves' to be included in the NATO security community. As Simon Lunn has argued, many fail 'to recognise the powerful symbolic appeal that NATO has for the CEECs, and that the drive for membership is powered as much by the need for the psychological reassurance of belonging to a democratic club, as it is by the immediate need for physical security.'[2]

However, this was not the first time that NATO faced a question of enlargement. There have been three previous instances when the organisation expanded its membership.[3] The first wave was in 1952, with the accession of Greece and Turkey. In one sense, this was not a controversial enlargement, for Greece and Turkey had been the object of the Truman Doctrine in 1947, at the origin of containment and of the Cold War. On the other hand, neither state could claim to be North Atlantic, each was involved in competition with the other and the accession of Turkey brought NATO directly against the Soviet border. Nevertheless, given American aid to both states since 1947 and British aid in the period up to 1947, it was clear that they were part of the western security environment, and they became members of the Alliance in February 1952. The second case came two years later, with the accession of the Federal Republic of Germany. In response to the militarisation of the East German police force, the perceived communist threat as epitomised by the Korean War and the failure of the European Defence Community, a conference in London in September 1954 agreed that West Germany should be armed and integrated into NATO, which formally occurred in May 1955. In response, the Soviet Union renounced treaties with Britain and France, and formed the Warsaw Pact. The third enlargement was the inclusion of Spain, which formally became a member in 1982. This accession was extremely controversial in Spain because many felt that NATO in general, and the United States in particular, had done much to keep Franco in power for many decades. Although the referendum was close, there was a majority in favour of membership.[4]

From these three cases, few clear models emerge for what could be seen as a fourth wave of enlargement, but one that has been termed the 'first' wave (i.e., first post-Cold War). NATO has had experience of incorporating more than one state at once (with Greece and Turkey); of carrying through an enlargement in the face of massive international hostility (with the accession of West Germany); and in managing enlargement in the context of major internal resistance (in Spain). Any future enlargement decisions may have one or all of these characteristics; however, the specificities of such future enlargements are likely to outweigh any superficial similarities to past enlargements.

This chapter will examine the nature of the disagreement and discussion within NATO over enlargement in the 1990s in two parts. The first part will proceed with a chronological account of the debate over NATO enlargement. This part will itself be divided into three sections: the first examines the period from 1989 to 1991, when NATO opposed enlargement; the second will examine how NATO deferred enlargement decisions from the end of 1991 to the end of 1993; and the third will analyse the moves towards actual enlargement, which began at the end of 1993, accelerated after September 1995 and which culminated in the decisions taken at Madrid in 1997. The second part will be thematic, and will assess the main conceptual arguments that have been raised against NATO enlargement from a variety of sources – both official and academic, and from both within the Alliance and outside – along with suggestions of how to meet these dilemmas. The conclusion will derive a model of NATO enlargement from the analysis which precedes it, and will offer some possible future paths.

The enlargement debate

NATO's opposition to its enlargement: 1989–91

The first clear move that NATO would adjust to the end of the Cold War came with the London summit in June 1990. At the end of that meeting, the NATO heads of state and government issued a document that was grandly entitled the 'London Declaration'. The document changed the nature of NATO language towards the Warsaw Pact and offered a series of meetings. The London Declaration stated that NATO would 'reach out to the countries of the East which were our adversaries in the Cold War, and extend to them the hand of friendship.'[5] In terms of meetings, Pact leaders were invited to Brussels to address the North Atlantic Council (NATO's governing body) and were invited to establish regular diplomatic liaison with NATO, while contacts between military staffs were to be intensified.

NATO made a great deal of the London Declaration, indicating that it signalled the end of Cold War competition. However, the motives for the statement suggest that the change was not as great as NATO's leaders indicated. All the governments of NATO agreed that the dramatic political change in Europe had to be managed and not allowed to spin out of control. To that end, to the NATO leaders it seemed logical and sensible to attempt to shore up the political position of Mikhail Gorbachev, as President of the Soviet Union. When communism came under great pressure in eastern Europe, it had fundamentally been Gorbachev who had restrained hard-liners in Moscow and who had brought about the replacement of the Brezhnev Doctrine with the so-called 'Sinatra Doctrine'.[6] One of the great Cold War fears had been a clash over an East German population rising against their communist rulers. Therefore, the fact that Soviet tanks had not intervened in East Germany in 1989, as pressure for exit visas led to the collapse of the Berlin Wall, was something for which all the western leaders had to be grateful. This was not only in terms of allowing the emergence of a democratic transition in central and eastern Europe, but also in terms of avoiding an east–west crisis of proportions not seen, arguably, since the Cuban missile crisis. The change in the NATO language at London was, then, based on two firm assumptions: first, that significant change was under way in the east and that that change had to be carefully managed; second, in order to bring about managed change, the political position of Gorbachev in Moscow had to be cemented as far as possible. To this, the post-communist CEECs were of secondary importance, and deep military relations between NATO and the CEECs were certainly not on the agenda, for this would have been seen to undermine Gorbachev's position in the political confrontation between reformers and hard-liners in Moscow.

During 1990, the CEECs were content not to press NATO for security commitments because they did not see the Soviet Union under Gorbachev as a particular threat, because they still had Soviet troops on their soil and because they felt that NATO as well as the Warsaw Pact should be folded in favour of enhancing the CSCE. However, all of this was to change in early 1991. On 8 January, Soviet troops were deployed around Vilnius in order to try to impose the conscription of Lithuanians into the Soviet army, which had been resisted since the Lithuanian parliament had voted on 11 March 1990 to re-establish Lithuanian sovereignty. On 11 January 1991, those Soviet forces were involved in violent struggles in the streets of Vilnius, in which there were several deaths. It is difficult to overstate the psychological impact that this event had on policy-makers in the CEECs and, indeed, upon nationalists in the Soviet Union outside Russia.[7] Whereas in 1990 the Soviet Union had been associated with the peaceful conclusion of the Cold War, in early 1991 pictures of the Soviet use of force alerted many in central Europe to the dangers of being so close to Russian power.

This use of force by Moscow was followed by a clear change in the foreign policy of the CEECs. On 25 February, a decision was taken in Budapest to wind up the Warsaw Pact on 1 July. The last Soviet units left Hungary and Czechoslovakia in June 1991, although the last Soviet/ Russian forces did not leave Poland until November 1992.[8] By the middle of 1991 it became clear that a key aim of Soviet diplomacy was to sign bilateral treaties with the CEECs that would restrain their rights to join alliances.[9] For example, Article 3 of the proposed Soviet treaty with Czecho-slovakia, Poland and Hungary would have prevented those countries from joining any anti-Soviet alliance, which was interpreted by all as meaning NATO.[10]

The combination of the events in Lithuania and the harder line in Soviet diplomacy led the central Europeans into a policy of seeking membership of NATO.[11] Thus, the key aims underlying NATO policy at the London summit were coming apart as the CEECs were increasingly unhappy about playing a secondary role in the post-Cold War period. In order to try to take account of these changing central European attitudes, NATO issued a document at its Copenhagen North Atlantic Council meeting in the spring of 1991 that committed the Alliance to a series of intensified military contacts at SHAPE (NATO's military headquarters) and at major NATO command centres.[12] At Copenhagen the NATO countries declared 'we reiterate that our own security is inseparably linked to that of all other states in Europe, particularly to that of the emerging democracies.'[13]

However, these NATO moves were not adequate for the central Europeans. From this point onwards, successive governments in Warsaw, Prague, Budapest and, later, Bratislava began to argue consistently for NATO membership.[14] Political leaders in central Europe began to calculate that only security guarantees from NATO would ensure the medium-term survival of their countries as independent and democratic. Czechoslovak Foreign Minister Jiri Dienstbier said, 'I have only one objection [to NATO]. We are not a member.'[15] Gyula Horn, Hungary's premier, commented, 'With regard to not being able to extend the western defence umbrella to central and eastern Europe in order not to irritate the Soviet Union: I apologize – but what do they offer instead?'[16]

NATO had committed itself at the London summit to a review of its relations with the post-communist states and of NATO strategy, and this review meeting was scheduled to be held in Rome at the end of 1991. The central Europeans began to argue that this was the point at which NATO should commit itself to enlargement. This demand became even stronger during the coup in Moscow in August 1991, despite the fact that the coup collapsed after only a few days and that it fundamentally undermined what little cohesion remained in the Soviet state. As the Rome summit became fixed in NATO diaries, a clear decision had to be taken on the central European demands for membership.[17] Should a commitment to enlarge be given, particularly at a time when the Soviet Union was collapsing? Or should emphasis be placed on Yeltsin and Russia as the partner leader and state to manage the continuing process of political change?

Deferring enlargement: 1992–3

It became clear to all at the Rome summit that NATO had decided to defer any decisions on enlargement. The summit produced not a statement about an intention to enlarge at some point in the future, but rather a new institution – the North Atlantic Cooperation Council (NACC) – that would include all post-communist states on the basis of non-discrimination. The NACC would be a forum for NATO states and the ex-Warsaw Pact countries to discuss how to further cooperation and dismantle the remnants of the Cold War.

Without doubt, NATO's decision to form the NACC rather than make moves towards enlarging membership was a disappointment to the CEECs. Some 'saw the Council as a "cheap consolation prize" for countries like Poland that had sued for NATO membership and had been rejected.'[18] As one parliamentarian of the Czech and Slovak Federal Republic, Jaroslav Suchanek, noted, 'We were slightly disappointed by the results of the Rome meeting.... We really need some guarantees from the west concerning our security.'[19] And the Hungarians argued that given NATO leaders had said that the Alliance might enlarge should the threat return – meaning Russia – NATO should have enlarged in 1991 because of the threat of Serbia to Hungary.

Yet not only were the central Europeans disappointed by the lack of progress on membership, they were also disturbed by NATO's decision to use non-discrimination as the operating principle for the NACC in the new relations with the former communist states. All the ex-Warsaw Pact countries (plus the Baltic republics) were invited to the first NACC meeting. The Hungarians, reflecting other views in central Europe, argued that 'the relations of NATO with Hungary, Czechoslovakia and Poland, those countries that will conclude association agreements with the EC should differ: they should reflect that these states have made progress on the way to European integration.'[20] The institutionalisation of non-differentiation in the NACC in effect lumped together in one category all the ex-Warsaw Pact states. This was graphically illustrated at the first NACC meeting, where the number of participants meant that each of the twenty-five political leaders who addressed the group had only five minutes in which to speak.[21] For Jan Zielonka, the commitment to non-differentiation in the NACC meant that 'Central European frustration at not being admitted to NATO increased rather than decreased after the creation of the Council.'[22] Even after the collapse of the Soviet Union, non-differentiation remained. In the meeting held in Brussels on 10 March 1992, representatives of Armenia, Azerbaijan, Belarus, Kazakhstan, Kyrgyzstan, Moldova, Tajikistan, Turkmenistan, Ukraine and Uzbekistan, as well as from Russia, joined the NACC proceedings. In Oslo in June, Albania and Georgia joined. Non-differentiation now implied that NATO would treat Poland and Turkmenistan in the same manner.

There was yet further criticism of the NACC, in terms of duplicating the membership and taking over the functions of the CSCE. In a powerful critique of the NACC published in the *Financial Times*, Edward Mortimer argued that the NACC was 'an unnecessary and possibly mischievous institution'.[23] Mortimer suggested that the 'CSCE could have been given a boost, had it been made the forum for the kinds of security cooperation now to be carried on in NACC'.[24] Were the NATO members seeking to enshrine the pre-eminence of the NACC in Europe, partly as a counter to the popularity of the CSCE in certain countries the previous year? Many functional responsibilities would inevitably be carried out less efficiently within the NACC than the CSCE, given that the former did not include Europe's neutral and non-aligned as members. 'It is as though NATO believed that Moldova and Tajikistan, which are members of the NACC had somehow become more deserving, more reliable, or more important to North Atlantic security than Ireland, Sweden, Finland and Austria: a manifestly absurd proposition.'[25] As John Chipman put it, 'On the surface, Morocco would have a higher claim for association to North Atlantic structures than Tajikistan.'[26] The creation of the NACC both strengthened NATO's position in relation to the CSCE and also ensured that in the emerging pan-European relationship it would always be NATO that would be in control of the agenda through the NACC, rather than the NATO countries having to share that control as would be the case in the CSCE.

The work of the NACC developed over the next couple of years and had successes in several areas: over the reorganisation of the Conventional Forces in Europe (CFE) Treaty after Soviet collapse;[27] through deepening military contacts;[28] and in conflict management, with discussions and debates over Nagorno-Karabakh, Moldova, Georgia and the former Yugoslavia, and in the withdrawal of Russian troops from the Baltic republics. A final area of important work in the NACC was in terms of developing peacekeeping concepts.[29] But the NACC did not receive significant support from the central Europeans, who preferred to see the institution as a holding measure. This view was well expressed by Christopher Conliffe: 'As for the NACC, the point must be made that whatever it may be doing at the moment, it is more or less a gesture on the part of the Alliance towards the states of the former USSR, and that is the best that can be said at the present.'[30] Thus, inevitably, the pressure that had developed for enlargement in 1991 was not dissipated by the invention of the NACC, and that pressure returned in 1992 and especially in 1993.

Even though the NACC had apparently made a contribution to European security on a number of levels, by the end of the summer of 1993 dissatisfaction remained, for three reasons. First, it was unclear how much progress was due to debate within the NACC and how much to bilateral pressures and multilateral negotiations in other fora. Second, it was not clear how much of a contribution many of the partner countries were actually making. Even a strong supporter of the NACC, such as William Yerex, noted that 'some delegates from the East show up for nearly every meeting sponsored by the NACC. They simply change [job] titles, ask for air fare and hotel accommodation at NATO expense and appear at meetings more as spectators than as sources of any real intellectual input.'[31] Third, the NACC did not seem to be moving the central Europeans towards membership, and the dilemma over non-differentiation deepened. While the CEECs continued to press for membership, pressure grew for the incorporation of yet more members into the NACC, especially the neutral and non-aligned members of the CSCE, such as Sweden and particularly Finland, which was already an observer in the NACC.[32] Far from enhancing the status of central Europe, the NACC seemed in danger of weakening it.[33] Thus, enlargement of the Alliance itself came back on to the agenda.

The NACC had, originally, been a German–American diplomatic innovation. However, there was no consensus in either the German or the American governments that the NACC was a long-term solution to the two conflicting goals of maintaining influence over a stable process of change through influence in Moscow, and providing reassurance to the CEECs that Russia would not be allowed to dominate.

German dissatisfaction with the NACC, and support for expanding NATO, had been expressed as early as December 1992 by Wolfgang Schaüble, a leading figure in the German Christian Democratic Union.[34] However, the main German proponent of enlargement was the Defence Minister, Volker Rühe. The quick expansion of NATO, he argued, was in Germany's interests in order to create further stability on its eastern borders. He went on to say that 'The Atlantic Alliance must not become a "closed shop". I cannot see one good reason for denying future members of the European Union membership in NATO.'[35] Rühe's arguments certainly did not have total support in the German government and an alternative model for enlargement was presented by Foreign Minister Klaus Kinkel, who emphasised taking longer and linking the process to the enlargement of the EU.[36] However, importantly, both agreed that enlargement of the Alliance *should* take place, setting the parameters of the German debate.

In the United States, there had also been evidence that officials supported NATO expansion. A high-level draft of the 1992 Defense Planning Guidance suggested that 'Should there be a threat from the Soviet Union's successor state, we should plan to defend against such a threat in eastern Europe, should there be an alliance decision to do so.'[37] After the 1992 Oslo NACC meeting, Lawrence Eagleburger, then American Deputy Secretary of State, had suggested that NATO could expand 'at the appropriate time', while the US permanent representative to NATO, William Taft IV, submitted that, for certain countries, membership could come well within a decade.[38] In December 1992, US Secretary of Defense Dick Cheney argued for 'Ultimate membership in NATO for at least some of those nations of central and eastern Europe that meet the basic fundamental test that we've required of others.'[39] Yet for many in the American government, nothing should have been done to alienate the reformists in Moscow. Admiral William D. Smith, the American military representative to NATO, argued on 18 June 1993 that 'what happens in Poland and Hungary, for example, is important to us, but what happens in Russia is crucial'.[40] This conventional wisdom, however, came under increasing attack from those within the United States who were becoming concerned that Russian policy was hardening.[41]

A key event was the circulation of a paper, written by Ronald Asmus, Richard Kugler and Stephen Larrabee of the RAND Corporation, among American, NATO and western European government and semi-official circles. The paper argued for the immediate expansion of NATO to Poland, Hungary and the Czech Republic, and also possibly to Slovakia. It also advocated a twelve-division rapid-reaction force, and a more fulsome re-integration of France into the military command.[42] A version of the paper was published later in *Foreign Affairs*, in which the authors argued that the 'NACC does not go far enough. It is essentially a holding operation that provides only meagre psychological reassurance.'[43]

This debate was focused by the joint Russian–Polish statement of 25 August 1993 in which Russia recognised Poland's right to join NATO, stating that such membership would not be against Russian security interests.[44] Subsequently, the Polish Prime Minister, Hanna Suchocka, said that 'Any further delay in this question does not seem possible,' a position to which the Hungarian Foreign Minister, Geza Jeszensky, immediately subscribed.[45] This led Senator Lugar, a member of the US Senate Foreign Relations Committee, to press for the inclusion of the Visegrad countries into NATO at the forthcoming NATO January 1994 summit, arguing that the Russians were less hostile and that NATO needed new members, as well as new missions, in order to survive.[46] Chancellor Kohl stated that 'At these talks in January I will raise the question of how we can give these countries not only the feeling but also a guarantee that they have a security umbrella.'[47] Thus, many in central Europe began to believe that the argument had been won and that membership would be a serious issue at the January summit. In the words of Andrzej Towpik, from the Polish Foreign Ministry, 'For too long we feel we have been standing knocking on a door without getting any response. Now as far as NATO membership goes, the question no longer seems to be whether, but when.'[48]

However, two key events were to slow the progress towards enlargement. First, in Poland, general elections in the autumn of 1993 removed the Solidarity-oriented Democratic Union government from power, and replaced it with the Democratic Left Alliance, the former communist party. The chair of the Democratic Left Alliance, Wlodzimierz Cimoszewicz, argued that 'There was never any debate on Poland's future security possibilities or about NATO membership and its implications.... We don't say no, but we believe it would be wise to explore other possibilities.'[49] The loss of momentum in the central European campaign was picked up by those who were not persuaded that the January summit should be dominated by NATO expansion. The British and French were, for different reasons, both uncomfortable with the expansion of NATO. For Britain, it was not clear that stability would be enhanced, while the cohesion of NATO could, it was feared, have been damaged.[50] The French were still concerned that the EU, and the WEU, should be allowed to play a significant role in the European security debate.[51]

The second key issue that slowed the expansion argument was the hostility in Moscow to Yeltsin's acceptance in August 1993 that the Poles could join NATO. Yeltsin's 'official statement, however, was soon counteracted by Foreign Minister Kozyrev and other Russian politicians.'[52] In the aftermath of the violent defeat of the conservatives in the Russian parliament that October, Yeltsin, perhaps to appease those in the military who had stood by him in the attack on parliament, wrote to several western governments to suggest that the time was not right for the extension of NATO.[53]

The 'window of opportunity' for expanding NATO without alienating the Russians – if it ever really existed – seemed to have closed. The Poles argued that the violence around the Russian parliament demonstrated once again that events in Russia were unpredictable and that Poland could be secure only within NATO.[54] However, those in the west sceptical about expanding NATO were again in the ascendancy. To move forwards to incorporate Poles, Czechs and Hungarians now would, surely, reduce the west's influence in Moscow and enhance the strength of the anti-reformists. From central Europe, this appeared very much like a Russian veto over their membership of NATO.

The solution to the dilemmas posed by disagreement within NATO was for the Alliance increasingly to steer a middle course from 1991 to 1994: to offer the prospect of NATO membership to some, but not to create a concrete means of access. As Rolf Clement put it, the NACC's role was 'to manoeuvre on the borderline between membership and rejection'.[55] Not only did this strategy allow NATO to manage relations between the CEECs on the one hand and Russia on the other, but it also enabled the Alliance to maintain a balance between different groups within NATO itself. That is, NATO's policies towards the east at this time were also determined by a need to maintain balance within the Alliance itself. In such a manner, the potential for open and bitter public argument, both within NATO and between NATO and the partner countries, was minimised. However, within this overall framework, it is clear that spokespersons, often interpreted as speaking for the Alliance, actually contributed to the weakening of NATO's relations with central and, increasingly, other eastern European countries, especially during 1993. Thus, by the end of that year, it had become clear that some new initiative would be required. But would that initiative be the acceptance of new members with a clear timetable, or the creation of a new holding mechanism?

On the precipice of enlargement: 1994–7

The third period began at the end of 1993 with the discussion over the nature of decisions to be taken at the January 1994 summit, in Brussels. The context had been set by a number of meetings and speeches in October to resolve the disagreement between those in the German government in favour of a quick enlargement (above all, Volker Rühe), and the dominant line in the US administration, which stressed that delay was still important. In early October, NATO Secretary-General Manfred Wörner had suggested that 'we should now open a concrete perspective for expanded NATO membership.'[56] However, the changed perceptions of the implications of NATO expansion turned the NATO debate away from a decision to expand the Alliance in the short term. On 20 October, NATO defence ministers met at Travemünde, where the concept later to be known as Partnership for Peace (PFP) was proposed by US Defense Secretary Les Aspin and accepted as the policy framework for formal adoption at the summit in January.[57]

The adoption of PFP at the January 1994 Brussels summit was central to the continued vitality of the Alliance. At this time, NATO faced two deep problems. First, it was deeply split over the issue of enlargement. Second, no one could decide what the purpose of the Alliance was. PFP resolved both problems, for it gave a purpose to NATO – projecting stability into central and eastern Europe – and it offered the prospect of both opening up NATO to new members and putting that prospect into the distant future. Volker Rühe commented that, with the endorsement of PFP at the January summit, new members could join the Alliance by the year 2000.[58] In contrast, British Defence Secretary Malcolm Rifkind argued that 'It would be a great mistake if some new line were to be driven through Europe.'[59] The PFP was, thus, essentially a NATO plan to solve NATO's internal problems – the arguments over enlargement within the Alliance, and within many of the governments of the Alliance.[60] This was vital, as the summit was taking on ever-growing importance. As George and Borawski noted at the time, 'All governments realise that unless the Summit succeeds in rejuvenating the Alliance after the perceived failure of its member nations over Yugoslavia and its slowness in adapting by deed as well as word to the new challenges of European security, support for the Alliance will wane on both sides of the Atlantic.'[61]

Again, NATO decisions on delaying enlargement were not well received in central Europe. It seemed that enlargement would be postponed in order to strengthen the position of Russian democrats. Vaclav Havel suggested that the success or failure of democracy in Russia was independent of NATO enlargement.[62] The Lithuanians indicated that they sought more than PFP by applying for membership.[63] President Walesa lectured President Clinton when the latter visited Prague in the aftermath of the Brussels summit in order to brief the central European leaders. 'It is difficult for me to hide my doubts and reservations,' Walesa said. 'The West today proposes for us a Partnership for Peace. This sounds fine. We wish to be partners, but in a partnership of independent and equal associates working for a specific goal, equal at every table and not only when prepared documents are signed. Today a balance for this initiative does not exist.'[64]

The criticism of PFP was widespread in NATO countries as well. For Martin Woollacott, 'The trouble is that there is no strategy here.'[65] Roger Boyes said: 'It is unacceptable, even absurd, for the west to allow Russia to set terms for NATO entry. It is reckless for the west to accept Moscow's own interpretation of its security needs. Yet President Clinton's soggy "Partnership for Peace" package does precisely that.'[66] Richard Perle condemned the 'vague, watertreading Partnership for Peace, the essence of which is that it does not admit East Europeans to NATO.'[67]

The essence of the criticism of PFP was that it continued the delaying policy. Inevitably, such a policy had to decay over time. To suggest that decay was inevitable does not suggest that the policy was necessarily inherently flawed, only that it would have a limited shelf-life.[68] And the actions taken to lengthen the shelf-life of the policy of delay – above all, PFP – also necessarily undermined the longevity of the policy. After all, PFP committed the Alliance to 'expect and ... welcome NATO expansion that would reach to democratic states to our east, as part of an evolutionary process, taking into account political and security developments in the whole of Europe.'[69] By not setting criteria for such expansion, the policy of delay was furthered. However, by formally accepting the evolutionary enlargement of the Alliance, pressure was placed upon NATO to define its criteria and thus to move away from the delaying policy.

Thus, the critical moment in the NATO enlargement debate took place in 1994 as pressure grew in the United States to move away from the policy of delay, and President Clinton's administration began to lead the Alliance on the issue. The Americans stressed that they were committed to NATO enlargement.[70] Many stated that in terms of enlargement, the issue was not 'if' but 'when'.[71] In January 1994, a 'sense of the Senate' resolution was passed in the US Congress by ninety-four votes to three, calling on the American government to argue for NATO enlargement. This was followed in April by the introduction of the NATO Expansion Act of 1994 in the US Congress, which called for the Visegrad states to become members by 1999. Pressure was increased in May when Republican Congressman Henry Hyde introduced the NATO Revitalization Act in Congress, which urged NATO 'to establish benchmarks and a timetable for eventual membership for selected countries', which were identified as the Visegrad countries and – particularly disturbing for Moscow – the Baltic states. President Clinton promised the Polish parliament in July 1994 that 'The expansion of NATO will surely come, and Poland's role as the first nation to participate in joint exercises with NATO troops makes Warsaw a prime candidate for inclusion.'[72]

But such a clear American lead on the issue was only possible owing to a bridging of the differences in the German government. In the period immediately after Chancellor Kohl's coalition was returned to power in the German elections, agreement was reached in Bonn that NATO enlargement should be pursued in parallel with the expansion of the EU. This kept Germany in line with the new American policy direction and also enabled Bonn to maintain a strong Franco-German policy line, given that Paris had been concerned that a speedy expansion of NATO would sideline European construction.

The new NATO position arrived at in 1994 was to end the policy of delay. This was revealed in the communiqué from the North Atlantic Council meeting on 1 December 1994. The ministers confirmed that they 'expect and would welcome NATO enlargement that would reach to democratic states to our East, as part of an evolutionary process ... part of a broad European security architecture based on true cooperation through-out Europe.'[73] The ministers confirmed that NATO enlargement would take place in parallel to the enlargement of the EU and that therefore there would be differentiation in the accession of new members. They also confirmed that no time frame for actual admission could yet be set. Under paragraph 6 of the communiqué, the ministers 'decided to initiate a process of examination inside the Alliance to determine how NATO will enlarge, the principles to guide this process and the implications of membership.'[74] Hence a study was authorised, under the Council, to include a significant input from the military authorities, particularly on the role of PFP in enlargement, to report the following year.

During 1994, PFP was stretched to the full and differences in interpretations of it became more obvious. While the central Europeans saw PFP as a waiting room for membership, the Russians saw it as the only means to prevent NATO expansion. As NATO policy in Bosnia became more assertive, Moscow withheld formal endorsement of PFP by not signing an agreement on a NATO–Russia PFP document. Then Moscow suggested that Russia should have a special arrangement with NATO, a special status, to recognise its importance. Russia signed a framework agreement on 22 June without achieving that special status, but problems emerged over finalising a second, more detailed agreement. The Russians condemned the new NATO position announced in December 1994, leading Moscow to refuse to sign their second, detailed, PFP document, with Yeltsin threatening the outbreak of a new 'cold peace'.[75] From this point, the break between NATO and Russia over enlargement became clear and deep.

Despite this, NATO continued to try to work with Moscow during 1995. Accordingly, the NATO Enlargement Study – which reported in September 1995 – did not provide a complex list of criteria for membership, and so did not identify potential new members, nor a timetable. Along with the needs of complying with the Washington Treaty and NATO operating and decision-making procedures (paragraph 70 of the Study report), the only criteria set out were commitments to: OSCE norms; 'promoting stability and well-being by economic liberty, social justice and environmental responsibility'; democratic and civilian control of the military (paragraph 72); and the prior resolution of conflicts (paragraph 6). This was an extremely permissive list, as virtually all the NACC states could argue that they fulfilled these criteria, or were on the road to doing so.

The Study avoided outlining three essential principles that had been agreed implicitly in the intra-NATO debate. First, the number of new members would be limited so that NATO's decision-making machinery would not be overloaded while the new members were being socialised into the Alliance *acquis*. This would also be a means of protecting the integrated military structure from the dangers of dilution. Second, new members would have a commitment to democracy and European integration (the latter ruling out Russian membership, as the EU did not intend to develop a Europe Agreement – see chapter 3 – with Moscow). Finally, the Alliance would not move directly to the border of Russia (with the exception of the Kaliningrad enclave bordering Poland), thus avoiding the issue of the candidature of the Baltic republics (which did have Europe Agreements with the EU). That these political limitations on the enlargement of the

Alliance were not stipulated in the document allowed the impression that all the NACC members might, in time, join NATO. However, it had been clear for some time that the first wave would be a very limited number of countries.

That NATO would move so far towards enlargement would not have been predictable in 1990 nor, indeed, in early 1994. Nearly all policy-makers and commentators were convinced that the high point for the enlargement issue had come and gone in August 1993, when in a matter of weeks Russia first agreed that Poland could join the Alliance, eliminating the most fundamental strategic drawback, and then withdrew that concession, raising Russian hostility to enlargement to an even more fundamental position. But in retrospect it seems that NATO's immediate solution to the dilemma – the PFP – was a holding operation for the Alliance to move beyond its policy of delay. For unless the PFP language and commitments were repudiated by NATO, the delaying policy had, very clearly, to be coming to the end of its existence. PFP thus played a pivotal role in the NATO enlargement debate, for it both maintained the delaying policy a little longer, and opened the way for a new policy to be developed, that of expansion.

The expansion policy was developed from the publication of the Enlargement Study in September 1995. It became manifest at the Madrid summit of the NATO heads of state and government in July 1997, when invitations were issued to Poland, the Czech Republic and Hungary to join the Alliance. From September 1995, NATO had become politically committed to enlargement. Had the Alliance delayed over the longer term from this point, or had it moved dramatically away from enlargement, then the whole credibility of NATO itself would have been brought into question. In short, NATO leaders had run out of ways of turning down the requests from central Europe for membership and had come to see enlargement as the primary rationale for the continued existence of an alliance that they believed was important for other reasons: notably as a counterweight to the Russians, for some to impede the development of a supranational Europe in the EU context, and for others to prevent the renationalisation of German defence policy.

Given that enlargement had, for the above reasons, become politically inevitable from the end of 1995, two important sets of issues had to be resolved: first, who was to be invited; second, how to deal with Russia. The question of invitations became very heated, particularly in early 1997. Five candidates emerged, and they could be placed on the following spectrum: Poland (with the most support), the Czech Republic, Hungary, Romania and Slovenia (with the least support). NATO enlargement without Poland was inconceivable: Poland was the largest state under consideration, had the greatest domestic support for NATO membership, and was strongly backed in Germany and the United States. But to enlarge by only one state was perceived as rather inadequate (hardly a strong endorsement of the value of the Alliance), while it would have focused Russian antagonism on Warsaw. And it was relatively easy to include the Czech Republic, with a government strongly committed to joining NATO; also, given the separation of the Czech and Slovak Federal Republic into its constituent parts, the country was now a long way from the Russian border. There were arguments against including Hungary, notably its lack of land border with any NATO state, but the US military had worked closely with the Hungarians over peacekeeping in the former Yugoslavia, and Hungary had become a liberal democratic state along with the other Visegrad states. In short, the United States supported the candidature of these three countries.

The Romanian case was supported by the French, who argued that Romania was an important state in terms of European integration. The counter-arguments were that the Romanian military was relatively unreformed and that the country would not bring any qualities to the Alliance at this point. These counter-arguments were also applied to the Slovenians, who had been backed by Italy. But in addition, it was also clear that there was a sense that raising the number of NATO states from sixteen to nineteen was manageable in one step, but that increasing it to twenty or twenty-one could seriously damage the integrated military structure.

The second set of issues requiring resolution revolved around dealing with Russia.[76] From the end of September 1995, NATO renewed its efforts to reach a diplomatic settlement with Russia over enlargement. This settlement was finally reached in Paris in May 1997, with the signing of the so-called Founding Act between NATO and Russia. The Act was the subject of long wrangling, notably over whether it should be politically or legally binding. It stipulated that Russia and NATO would work together to preserve stability, specifically through a new forum, the Permanent Joint Council. With this agreement, the looming political crisis over the decisions taken at the Madrid summit were circumvented.

But Madrid would not be the end of the story of NATO enlargement. NATO countries still had to go through a process of ratifying the enlargement decision. Russia demanded closer involvement in NATO decision-making through the Permanent Joint Council. Some NATO states openly backed the case for new members – notably for Romania and Slovenia. Some non-NATO states argued in favour of quick movement to a second wave of enlargement, notably the Baltic republics. In short, the Madrid summit, and the NATO Washington summit scheduled for May 1999, could not be seen as end-points on the road of NATO enlargement but, rather, as waymarks.

Conceptual problems

As has been seen in the last section, NATO policy has moved from initial hostility to the idea of enlargement, through operating a policy of deferral of decisions, to finally a formal decision on enlargement. This evolution of policy has moved through the above three stages as the balance of debate has changed over four conceptual issues, which will be examined in detail in this section. These issues are: relations with Russia; differentiation among the CEECs; the dilemmas concerning the double enlargement of the EU and NATO; and NATO's post-enlargement decisions.

Russia

In many ways the critical problem at the centre of the debate over NATO enlargement has been the Russian reaction, and the treatment and status of Russia. Could NATO enlargement include Russia? If not, could some compensation be given to Moscow that would offset the enlargement of the Alliance? And if there seemed to be no compensation acceptable to Moscow, should that mean that the Russians could effectively veto NATO enlargement?

The issue of whether Russia could conceivably join the Alliance was an important one in the period from the end of 1991 through to the middle of 1993. After all, at the end of 1991 President Yeltsin had sent a letter to the NACC participants in which he said, 'Today we are raising a question of Russia's membership in the NATO, however regarding it as a long term political aim.'[77] This statement reflected a western orientation in some elements of Russian policy and statements, with many senior officials apparently believing that Russia could and would integrate into NATO.[78]

Yet this initial pro-NATO orientation on the part of the Russians deteriorated over the next eighteen months to two years. In part this was due to a growing assertiveness in Moscow, as Russians began to identify specifically Russian foreign and security policy goals that might not be in line with NATO thinking. Although Yeltsin apparently accepted Poland's right to join NATO in a summit with Walesa in August 1993, this was repudiated in Moscow upon the President's return, with enlargement being portrayed as inimical to Russian interests. Perhaps a culmination of this trend was reached in the early winter of 1993. In November, the new Russian military doctrine was promulgated, specifying the acceptability and necessity of Russian troop deployments on the territory of other CIS states.[79] Later that month, an important Russian document was released by Yevgeni Primakov, Head of the Foreign Intelligence Service and later Foreign Minister, which set out Russian views on European security and explicit Russian opposition to the expansion of NATO. Primakov suggested that NATO was an old-style organisation which would damage European security if it expanded to central Europe.[80]

Some weeks after the release of this document, Yeltsin visited Brussels and, in the course of a meeting with Secretary-General Wörner, strongly emphasised Russian hostility to NATO expansion, suggesting that, were it to happen, Russia's strategic interests would be damaged and, thus, the partnership that Russia sought to develop with the west would be threatened.[81] At the same time, Foreign Minister Kozyrev stated that Russia sought partnership with, not membership of, NATO.[82] This greater Russian national orientation was strengthened in the aftermath of the Russian elections of 12 December 1993, which reflected the move to the right with the relative success of the ultra-nationalist Vladimir Zhirinovsky.

But if a part of the decline in interest in the idea of Russia becoming a member of NATO was due to increasing national assertiveness in Moscow, this should not camouflage the great disquiet in NATO countries about the prospect of Russian integration into the Alliance. Asmus, Kugler and Larrabee reported the view that 'Many Europeans believe that Russia is not a European country, is unlikely to become one and should not be allowed into core European institutions.'[83] This was well expressed by Lothar Rühl, for whom 'The more far-reaching idea forwarded by the former US Secretary of State, James Baker, that Russia should be integrated into NATO if it became democratic ... would ... definitely have one adverse effect: a loss of identity and cohesion for the alliance, since European Russia will not let itself be integrated.'[84]

However, there were some important counterpoints made. Joseph Kruzel, US Deputy Assistant Secretary of Defense for European and NATO Policy, argued that 'If Russia proves itself eligible for membership, then someday in the future they can be considered for membership.'[85] But these views were not taken at face value in Moscow, nor indeed within the Alliance, for it was clear that in diplomatic terms NATO, and especially the United States, believed that it was important not to be seen to be formally excluding Moscow. But the consensus view was that expressed by Klaus Kinkel, for whom Russia and Ukraine 'will not and cannot be members of the Alliance'.[86]

If the process of enlargement would not include the Russians, then would it be possible to devise some compensation package that would make enlargement into central Europe palatable to Moscow? When Volker Rühe argued that 'Russia's unmatched potential in almost every regard and its geostrategic situation will prevent it from becoming a full member of the European Union and of our alliances,' he had continued by saying that 'Our concept must compensate for this through intensified security cooperation.'[87] But the nature of that compensation was difficult to define.

Cooperation was a different issue, over which it was initially quite easy to make progress. The Russians had argued in 1994 that in return for Russian participation in PFP, Moscow should be given a special status in the Alliance's relationships in Europe. From that time a more formalised consultation process was developed into the so-called '15 + 1 format', enhanced by an agreement entitled 'Areas for Pursuance of a Broad Enhanced NATO/Russia Dialogue and Cooperation' in June 1995. In this context, the NATO countries and Russia discussed developments in the former Yugoslavia (where Russian troops served alongside NATO forces in the Implementation Force, IFOR, and later the Stabilisation Force, SFOR), the proliferation of weapons of mass destruction, the safe and secure dismantling of nuclear weapons, and the future of the CFE Treaty.[88]

However, cooperation was not compensation. From the end of 1995, Foreign Minister Primakov accepted that enlargement would happen and, therefore, that Russia had to try to negotiate a favourable deal under the circumstances. The only viable possibilities were that new NATO members would not be fully integrated into NATO's military command, or that they would not have foreign forces on their soil, possibilities allowed for by the NATO Enlargement Study. But although these gestures might lessen the hostility of Moscow's reaction to enlargement, could they really be described as compensation? As Dmitri Trenin put it, 'The expansion of NATO presents Russia, above all, with a psychological problem which is why it is practically insoluble in the near future.'[89] The Founding Act may be seen by some as compensation, but in Moscow it is seen more as an act of diplomatic wisdom, an act of crisis avoidance, rather than anything more grand.[90]

If compensation has been so difficult to define, and if it is unlikely to solve the Russians' 'psychological' problem with enlargement, the last alternative would have been to allow the Russians a *de facto* veto over the process. This certainly seemed to be the dominant position within NATO in the period of deferring decisions on enlargement from the end of 1991 to the beginning of 1994. Certainly, Russian hostility to enlargement could not be underestimated. In an issue of *Moscow News*, Foreign Minister Kozyrev stated that the expansion of NATO would 'lead to a kind of hidden confrontation and hence, ultimately, to instability.'[91] More explicitly, the deputy editor of the liberal *Moscow News*, Alexei Pushkov, argued that 'an expanded NATO may be used as an instrument for openly putting pressure on Russia. Particularly disturbing is that the concept of a new NATO implicitly or even explicitly includes intentions to play the Baltic countries and Ukraine against Moscow.'[92] Neil MacFarlane reported that he was told in interviews in Moscow that 'The extension of NATO membership to east European states without a comparable change in Russia's status would confirm the feeling in Moscow that Russia is being treated as a second-class citizen and would be cited by the right wing as confirmation that the west has a coordinated strategy of expansion at Russian expense.'[93] And these Russian reactions were greeted sympathetically by many in the west.[94] Owen Harries, for example, wrote that 'To ignore all this history and to attempt to incorporate eastern Europe into NATO's sphere of influence, at a time when Russia is in dangerous turmoil and when that nation's prestige and self-confidence are badly damaged, would surely be an act of outstanding folly.'[95]

Certainly, in central Europe there was a perception that NATO would allow the Russians to hold an implicit veto over the process. Lech Walesa said that Poland 'kept crying and shouting in 1939, but they only believed us when the war reached Paris and London. The situation is very similar today.'[96] The geostrategic nature of the threat to central Europe was echoed elsewhere in the region. For Istvan Gyarmati, in Hungary, 'The Soviet Union has always treated central Europe as its natural sphere of influence. There is no reason to believe that Russia will treat us differently.'[97]

But NATO policy was more sophisticated than simply being motivated by the not inconsiderable concern with Moscow's geostrategic response. Many in the NATO countries felt that to push ahead with enlargement would be to weaken the political position of the democrats in Moscow, and to strengthen the hand of the nationalists. Thus, at various times, NATO felt it had to be sensitive to domestic political events in Moscow: in the aftermath of the 1993 Duma elections; before the 1996 presidential elections; and at various other times when President Yeltsin seemed particularly vulnerable to domestic political pressure.

But the argument over supporting Russian democrats was not well received by the democrats in central Europe. Antoni Kaminski, former Director of Studies for the Polish Ministry of Defence, said: 'One wonders whether western tolerance of Russian imperialist policies serves the interest of democracy in this country and makes the world more secure and predictable or, on the contrary, it creates threats not only for the others but also for Russia.'[98] How would the expansion of NATO and the EU to central Europe, to support democratic and market reforms in the region, be damaging to Russian democrats? On the contrary, surely strengthening stability in central Europe – and providing concrete rewards for reform – would encourage those Russians committed to reform?

Yet others argued that enlargement was entirely independent of the Russian political debate. Either Russian democrats would succeed, in which case they would 'understand that NATO is not Russia's enemy but its partner, that the expansion of NATO would bring Russia closer to democracy and prosperity.'[99] Or, 'chauvinistic, Great Russian, crypto-totalitarian forces' would prevail, which would oppose the enlargement of NATO, and if NATO gave way to them, 'It would mean encouraging imperial ambitions.'[100]

Thus, the role of Russia has been pivotal to the discussions about NATO enlargement. Hopes that the Founding Act would serve to resolve NATO–Russian difficulties have, however, rather foundered on clearly differing interpretations of the nature of the Permanent Joint Council: while for

NATO the Council allows consultation, for Russia it is about joint decision-making.[101] Debate and decisions about a second wave of enlargement are likely to make these differences very obvious. Of course, at the heart of this have been concerns over differentiation. The central Europeans have sought to be differentiated by NATO favourably compared to the other post-communist states, in order to allow them to become members. The Russians have sought to reject that form of differentiation, but to have their great power status recognised through a special relationship with NATO. This debate over differentiation is the next section of the analysis.

Differentiation

From early 1991, when the central European states began to worry about threats from their east, it proved extremely difficult for NATO to arrive at an explicit conclusion, in any public forum, about which nations were important to the security of the Alliance and which were not, for the question was not solely about security, but also about identity. On this question, consensus within the Alliance proved very difficult, for it was hard to see how any open policy of differentiation could be other than against Russia. And, as seen above, it has been very difficult for NATO to decide on a clear policy acceptable to Russia. But the concern over differentiation has had two other important aspects.

First, in any open policy of differentiation, NATO would in effect be making decisions about identity that would have wide application. Those on the 'wrong side' of the line of differentiation would, in some senses, be 'non-west European'. When Romania's candidature was not accepted at Madrid in 1997, Bucharest's concerns ran very much along these lines. But this has another important dimension connected with identity. It is NATO, and therefore the American link, that is widely seen to be the key security forum in Europe. That is, setting out a new line of division in Europe, which would be the inevitable perception following any enlargement decision, would be seen to cut off those states on the 'wrong' side of the line from both European construction and from close partnership with the United States. Thus before and after Madrid, NATO has sought to manage this by talking about 'waves' of enlargement, to allow the perception to develop in eastern and south-eastern Europe that they may, in time, be NATO members. Not surprisingly, such talk is received with particular hostility in Moscow.

The second difficulty with differentiation was that NATO would lose influence in states in which it might actually be able to have the most impact. In any open policy of differentiation, Turkmenistan, for example, could never have been one of the beneficiaries. However, given the size and nature of the country, its military forces and its strategic questions, the Alliance might have been able to effect more change more quickly through its influence in such a state than in a country with a larger and more complex political and security environment.

NATO tried to ease the differentiation problem by putting responsibility on to the shoulders of the partner countries. This is yet another advantage of the PFP in bringing about a transition in NATO policy. While during 1990–1, and with the formation of the NACC, and throughout 1992 and 1993 NATO avoided discussing differentiation, this changed from the January 1994 Brussels summit. Under PFP, there was a move from non-differentiation to self-differentiation. Initially, this was disappointing for those states that wanted NATO to differentiate in their favour. As Max Jakobson put it at the time, for the central Europeans, 'the cup looks half empty.... Why was all this not figured out before hopes of NATO membership were raised? Now those nations which had expected membership feel let down, while the others resent being relegated to second-class status.'[102]

Yet, as seen above, in retrospect this judgement is much too harsh. PFP allowed central European countries to move much closer to the Alliance. Manfred Wörner had spoken of the possibility of self-differentiation in PFP working in favour of the Visegrad Group.[103] Developing this point, US Secretary of State Warren Christopher suggested that the PFP would give 'NATO the opportunity to evaluate their qualifications for membership ... to judge their conduct, judge their performance, judge their willingness.'[104] This was part of the nature of the PFP arrangement under which each partner nation would provide NATO with 'Presentation Documents' to identify the political goals of the individual partnership and the practical steps to be taken. Thus, in dialogue but also in clear agreements it became abundantly clear that NATO–Polish relations would be qualitatively superior to NATO–Turkmen relations – a very different rhetoric and reality compared to that surrounding the formation and operation of the NACC. From the middle of 1994 onwards, it was clear that non-differentiation would give way quickly to self-differentiation supported by NATO.[105]

But self-differentiation could only be a transitory phenomenon, as PFP had been a transitory strategy. At Madrid, NATO moved from self-differentiation to formal differentiation in opening accession negotiations with the Poles, Czechs and Hungarians. This could only heighten the desire of other states to follow this path, to move from self- to formal differentiation. But at Madrid, NATO took another step on the road to formal differentiation with the signing of a charter with Ukraine. This bilateral agreement between NATO and Kiev is of a lower standing than the Founding Act between Russia and NATO (there is, for example, no equivalent to the Permanent Joint Council), but Ukraine is the only state between the new members and Russia to be selected by NATO in this way, reflecting concern over Ukraine's future as an independent state and the argument that Ukraine is a strategic linchpin in Europe's security architecture.

As NATO moved from self-differentiation to formal differentiation, another key problem that had been debated for several years came to the fore: the dilemma of the double enlargement of the Western security organisations, NATO and the WEU.

Double enlargement

The debate over NATO enlargement could never be disentangled from that over EU and, as a consequence, WEU enlargement.[106] The development of closer links between the central Europeans and the WEU analysed in chapter 4 passed with very little negative comment from Moscow. Despite ideas about enlarging the EU and WEU before NATO – a concept that became known as the 'Royal Road' – consensus began to form during 1994 that this was not the best way forward. In its December 1994 statement, NATO's North Atlantic Council 'decided to initiate a process of examination inside the Alliance to determine how NATO will enlarge, the principles to guide this process and the implications of membership.'[107] Importantly, the ministers noted one vital parameter of that process of examination – that NATO enlargement should take place 'in parallel' with that of the EU. And NATO's Enlargement Study reported that 'all full members of the WEU are also members of NATO. Because of the cumulative effect of the security safeguards of Article V of the modified Brussels Treaty and Article 5 of the Washington Treaty, maintaining this linkage is essential.... The two enlargement processes should therefore be compatible and mutually supportive.'[108]

By the end of 1997, enlargement decisions had been taken by both NATO and the EU, which, broadly, could be said to be in parallel. Yet the policy of maintaining a parallel 'compatible and mutually supportive' process of enlarging NATO, the EU and WEU would not resolve all problems. As seen above, Russian hostility would not be minimised. Also, such a policy would lead to some tension between NATO, which privileged Ukraine with the charter, and the WEU, which, along with the EU, sees Ukraine on the 'wrong' side of any new dividing line (as Ukraine has no Europe Agreement with the EU). In addition, while such a solution might be made to work for the first round of the enlargements of NATO and the WEU (to the Visegrad countries minus Slovakia), it is easy to see it coming apart once other applications for membership enter the equation. Anti-European tendencies in the United States have been more apparent with applications from countries such as Slovenia that might seem to offer more to European construction than to US national interests; hence the United States was unwilling to add Slovenia to the list of invitees at Madrid. The Slovenian case will re-emerge on NATO's agenda, along with other dilemmas, in the aftermath of the first wave of enlargement decisions.

Post-enlargement decisions

The problems of enlargement most certainly do not end with the first-round enlargement decision in Madrid. An important post-enlargement issue will be how to deal with those states that wish to join the Alliance but that were not included in the first wave. The Berlin North Atlantic Council meeting in 1996 noted that fifteen countries had notified the Alliance that they were interested in becoming members; if all were to join, this would almost double the size of the Alliance.[109] Clearly, not all would be able to join in the foreseeable future, and hence policy had to be devised to deal with this. Would enlargement in fact be a process, or would the policy of deferral return? The NATO Enlargement Study stressed the importance of not shutting the door to future enlargements (see paragraphs 30 and 71), but doubts will remain.

Following the first decision on enlargement, a number of other states will seek to put pressure on NATO to speed the process of subsequent enlargements. Immediate and more determined efforts could be expected by the Baltic republics, Romania, Slovenia and perhaps Bulgaria. For these countries to be excluded from NATO in any selective expansion of the organisation would be to condemn them to the 'Russian' side of any new division of influence in Europe.[110] This fear was articulated by Romanian President Ion Iliescu, who spoke out against 'discriminatory' treatment of NACC members as early as October 1993.[111] And yet the Baltic republics will prove the key dilemma. On the one hand, having signed Europe Agreements with the EU, and having a good deal of political support in Scandinavia and in parts of the US establishment, they might expect to be thought about in a second wave of expansion. The EU has opened accession negotiations with Estonia. And yet any discussion of a second wave would be very unpopular in Moscow and would damage NATO–Russian relations further. Taking the Alliance on to the territory of the former Soviet Union, into countries bordering Russia and where there are still issues surrounding the treatment of Russian minorities would be diplomatically explosive.[112]

Thus the debate over NATO enlargement will not end after decisions on the first wave of enlargement; indeed, the debate over that first wave cannot end simply with grand statements on enlargement. The NATO enlargement debate has become a key part of the debate over Europe's future, and this is likely to remain the case for the foreseeable future. While NATO's ability to survive the end of the Cold War is impressive, it is also true that many of its prime supporters have not been its members, but rather the applicants for membership. Will their enthusiasm remain once they are members? And if many of those states are kept outside the Alliance for any period of time, will their commitment wane? And, of course, other factors could intervene to weaken the political strength of the Alliance, such as failures in peacekeeping activities. In any case, the deepening Europeanisation of the Alliance will mean that the NATO of the year 2000 will be fundamentally different in character from that of 1990, and indeed even that of 1995.

Some fear that the process of enlargement itself could undermine the cohesiveness of NATO. Holger Mey has warned that 'Poland should not expect too much security for itself from NATO membership as such. Most likely, the very reason why central eastern European countries seek membership in NATO (ie, that NATO is a strong military alliance), would fade away precisely because the issue of new membership would erode the very foundation of NATO and jeopardise consensus among its member states.'[113] Indeed, it has long been a fear that an uncontrolled enlargement could overwhelm the Alliance. Perhaps new members will not join in with NATO's system of compromise to reach consensus; perhaps they will bring national rivalries with them, and perhaps economic and social problems. Any of this could mean that the Alliance would face major problems. One solution could have been to have introduced some form of associate member status, which could have been used as a bridge to full membership, but which could also be used to demote problem full members. But this has never been seen to be politically acceptable by current members such as Greece and Turkey, let alone the applicants which seek to benefit from full membership and a strong guarantee of their security.

Conclusion

The debate over NATO enlargement has been a deeply controversial one, not only in NATO–Russian relations and in relations between NATO and the CEECs, but also in terms of the politics between NATO allies and, indeed, between different government ministries in the major Alliance states, the United States and Germany.

It is possible to map a picture of this disagreement by outlining the different theoretical positions that could have been taken over NATO enlargement and then assessing where each actor could be positioned. There are six theoretical positions that could be identified. These range on a spectrum from: first, no enlargement; second, a commitment to enlarge should a crisis occur; third, a longer-term enlargement following the expansion of the EU; fourth, a parallel process of EU and NATO enlargement; fifth, an immediate expansion based on the principle of differentiation; and sixth, an immediate 'big bang' enlargement of all interested states based on non-differentiation.

The first position was that NATO should not be expanded. Both the Russians and the French have argued for this option at various times since 1991. For the Russians, NATO enlargement would recreate bloc politics in Europe and, instead, they have favoured the strengthening of the OSCE.

This argument has found little favour in NATO, not only because few see the provision of security guarantees within that organisation as credible, but also because the Russians have sought the subordination of NATO to the new OSCE structures.[114] For the French, continued emphasis on NATO would be to the detriment of the construction of Europe, and so they favoured developments in the WEU. However, Paris began to move away from this position under the presidency of Jacques Chirac, and certainly by the time of the French announcement in December 1995 that they were moving closer to NATO structures. The 'no enlargement' option was, as seen above, NATO policy in the period 1989–91.

The second position is that which might be termed 'crisis expansion', by which it is meant that NATO would only expand were central European countries to be directly threatened by violence. Although this has not been propounded by any state, it has been highly popular in policy and academic circles in the United States.[115] However, many critics argued that such a policy would lack credibility throughout Europe, for to expand NATO in a crisis would be to exacerbate that crisis greatly; and it would also offer all of the disadvantages of formalising differentiation without any clear security or political gains.[116]

The third position – enlargement of NATO following that of the EU – was a position supported by Klaus Kinkel and the German Foreign Ministry in their argument with Volker Rühe before a consensus position was formed in the German government following Chancellor Kohl's re-election in the autumn of 1994. The argument was that by placing the enlargement in the longer term, Russian fears might be lessened, particularly given the non-reaction of Moscow to the creation of Associate Partnership in the WEU and that NATO enlargement would follow that of the WEU. However, this option produced many dilemmas and, as such, was widely seen to be flawed.

The fourth option was that of a parallel process of NATO and EU enlargement. However, it does not solve all of the problems by any means, even though this became NATO policy from the December 1994 meeting of the North Atlantic Council. After the 1997 NATO and EU enlargement decisions the practicalities of the enlargements may put even greater strains on any policy of parallelism.

An immediate expansion of NATO on the basis of differentiation is the fifth possibility. This position is the one that has been proposed and supported constantly by many of the CEECs since the violence in Lithuania and the Moscow coup in 1991, notably by the governments in Prague and Warsaw. This option would have placed NATO expansion before EU enlargement and, thus, would have allowed for an almost immediate enlargement of the Alliance, as NATO criteria for membership would have been much easier for the central Europeans to attain than EU criteria would be. This position was the one held for some time by Volker Rühe.

The sixth and final position is that all NACC members should be incorporated into NATO quickly, in a one-step 'big bang' expansion. However, this option has received little political support from within NATO, although it is a position supported by James Baker after leaving office as US Secretary of State. Such a process would, it was feared, totally destroy the consensus principle in the Alliance, undermine its military effectiveness and perhaps lead to a fusion of NATO and the OSCE. Yet, perhaps inevitably, the further one moves in central and eastern Europe from those states closest to NATO, the more sympathy one finds for these arguments.

Through outlining the nature of the debate over enlargement in this way, the dimensions of the divisions in Europe over the expansion of NATO become clear. Official NATO policy initially favoured the first option, that of no enlargement, but then went through a period of hiatus in which the Alliance did not clearly support any of the above positions. In this period, to 1994, a rough consensus was devised that allowed NATO to espouse the fourth option, that of a parallel enlargement of the Alliance and the EU. But that consensus position was a shaky one, with the British and French much less enthusiastic than the Americans and Germans. It was also a NATO consensus position that was not particularly popular in the wider Europe, from Bucharest to Moscow. By 1997, the fourth and fifth options merged, and NATO became committed to implementing enlargement, although tensions between these two variants may re-emerge over time.

Notes

1 On this, see J. Sedivy, 'From dreaming to realism – Czechoslovak security policy since 1989', *Perspectives* (published by the Institute of International Relations, Prague), No. 4, 1994–5, pp. 61–9.

2 S. Lunn, 'NATO in evolution: the challenges for 1994', *Brassey's Defence Yearbook 1994*, London: Brassey's, 1994, p. 118.

3 This excludes the enlargement of NATO to cover the territory of the former German Democratic Republic after the unification of Germany.

4 On the West German accession see, for example, A. Grosser, *West Germany from Defeat to Rearmament*, London: George Allen and Unwin, 1955; and E. Fursdon, *The European Defence Community: A History*, London: Macmillan, 1980. The Paris Agreements, which laid the foundation for West German accession, are reproduced in L. Freedman (ed.), *Europe Transformed: Documents on the End of the Cold War*, London: Tri-Service Press, 1990, pp. 33–42. On the Spanish accession, see P. Preston and D. Smyth, *Spain, the EEC and NATO*, Chatham House Papers 22, London: Routledge and Kegan Paul for the Royal Institute of International Affairs, 1984. The Protocols on the accession of the four countries to the Alliance are reproduced in *The North Atlantic Treaty Organisation: Facts and Figures*, Brussels: NATO, 11th edn, 1989, pp. 379–83.

5 'London Declaration on a Transformed North Atlantic Alliance', Brussels: NATO, 1990, p. 2.

6 Under the Brezhnev Doctrine, the Soviet Union and its socialist allies reserved the right to intervene in the socialist commonwealth under the principle of 'proletarian internationalism' to prevent counter-revolutionary forces from undermining communism. The

Prague Spring had been crushed by Warsaw Pact forces in 1968 under this principle. As implied in the title of Sinatra's song 'My Way', and popularised by the Soviet spokesman Gennady Gerasimov, under the Sinatra Doctrine the Soviet satellites would be allowed to develop along their own lines. See D. Mason, *Revolution in East-Central Europe*, Boulder, CO: Westview, 1992, especially p. 56.

7   For example, J. Urban, 'The Czech and Slovak Republics: security consequences of the breakup of the CSFR', in R. Cowen Karp (ed.), *Central and Eastern Europe: The Challenge of Transition*, Oxford: Oxford University Press for Sipri, 1993, p. 115; also, author's (Stuart Croft) interviews with officials in Prague, 1990 and 1991. For similarities in the Hungarian position, see P. Dunay, 'Hungary: defining the boundaries of security', in Cowen Karp (ed.), *Central and Eastern Europe*, p. 148. Also see A. Hyde-Price, 'Future security systems for Europe', in C. McInnes (ed.), *Security and Strategy in the New Europe*, London: Routledge, 1992, pp. 49–50.

8   On this, see A. Hyde-Price, 'After the Pact: East European security in the 1990s', *Arms Control: Contemporary Security Policy*, Vol. 12, No. 2, 1991, especially pp. 280–3.

9   Romania was the only state to do so. Soviet policy on this issue changed fundamentally after the Soviet coup. See L. Freedman, 'Gone but not forgotten', *The Independent*, 30 April 1991; and Hyde-Price, 'After the Pact'.

10 See J. Spero, 'Deja vu all over again?', *European Security*, Vol. 1, No. 4, 1992.

11 Polish, Czechoslovak and Hungarian leaders met at Visegrad in February 1991 to discuss cooperative approaches to their 'return to Europe'. They issued the *Visegrad Declaration on the Road to European Integration* and subsequently became known as the Visegrad states. On the Czechoslovak change in policy, see Urban, 'The Czech and Slovak Republics', p. 115.

12 'Partnership with the Countries of Central and Eastern Europe' is reproduced in *NATO Review*, Vol. 39, No. 3, 1991, pp. 28–9.

13 The text of the document is reproduced in an annexe to *Atlantic News*, No. 2345, 1991, pp. 1–2.

14 This became most explicit from the October 1991 summit of the Czechoslovak, Hungarian and Polish presidents in Cracow, when they declared that NATO membership was the only way to secure their countries in the face of state collapse – of the Soviet Union to their east and of Yugoslavia to their south.

15 Dienstbier is quoted in M. J. Faber, 'Good morning Europe!', in M. Kaldor (ed.), *Europe from Below: An East–West Dialogue*, London: Verso, 1991, p. 146.

16 G. Horn, 'Let's build the new interstate relations from brick to brick' (in Hungarian), *Tarsadalmi Szemle*, Vol. 46, No. 7, 1991, quoted in P. Dunay, 'Hungary: defining the boundaries of security', in Cowen Karp (ed.), *Central and Eastern Europe*, p. 150.

17 In September, it had seemed just possible that the Visegrad states might leap over the other former WTO countries into a special observer status at NATO. See, for example, 'Former foes may enter NATO fold', *Jane's Defence Weekly*, 28 September 1991, p. 545.

18 H. Kubiak, 'Poland', in Cowen Karp (ed.), *Central and Eastern Europe*, p. 95.

19 Cited in G. Gerosa, 'The North Atlantic Cooperation Council', *European Security*, Vol. 1, No. 3, 1992.

20 K. Karcagi, 'Nem teszünk visszautasithato javasloatot...' ('We do not make rejectable proposals...'. The address of Joszef Antall to the meeting of the North Atlantic Council), *Magyar Hirlap*, 29 October 1991, cited in Dunay, 'Hungary', p. 149.

21 However, this was also designed to leave two hours for discussion of central and immediate questions, notably the future of the Soviet nuclear arsenal. See 'Preparation of NACC', *Atlantic News*, No. 2345, p. 2.

22   J. Zielonka, *Security in Central Europe*, Adelphi Paper 272, London: Brassey's for the International Institute for Strategic Studies, 1992, p. 44.

23   E. Mortimer, 'Europe's security surplus', *Financial Times*, 4 March 1992.

24   *Ibid.*

25   *Ibid.*

26   J. Chipman, 'The future of strategic studies', *Survival*, Vol. 34, No. 1, 1992, p. 120.

27   On this, see S. Croft, 'Negotiations, treaty terms and implications', and 'Ratification of CFE and CFE 1A', both in S. Croft (ed.), *The CFE Treaty*, Dartmouth, 1994.

28   Such as high-level visits, staff talks, exchanges and participation in special and regular courses at the NATO school at Oberammergau. See the NACC Work Plan for 1992, reproduced in *NATO Communiqués 1992*, Brussels: NATO, undated, pp. 18–20. Also see W. Yerex, 'The North Atlantic Cooperation Council', in D. G. Haglund, S. N. MacFarlane and J. J. Sokolsky (eds), *NATO's Eastern Dilemmas*, Boulder, CO: Westview, 1994.

29   See, for example, 'NATO seminar on peacekeeping', *Atlantic News*, No. 2538, 1993.

30   C. Conliffe, 'The Alliance transformed: a skeptical view', in Haglund *et al.* (eds), *NATO's Eastern Dilemmas*, p. 33.

31   Yerex, 'The North Atlantic Cooperation Council', p. 186.

32   Also see H. Linnenkamp, 'The North Atlantic Cooperation Council: a stabilizing element of a new European order?', in H.-G. Ehrhart, A. Kreikemeyer and A. V.Zagorski (eds), *The Former Soviet Union and European Security: Between Integration and Re-Nationalization*, Baden-Baden: Nomos Verlagsgesellschaft, 1993, pp. 219–28.

33   For a counter-argument, see M. Rühle, 'NATO's evolving role in the New Europe', *European Security*, Vol. 1, No. 3, 1992, where he suggests that NACC 'is intended as a means to project stability into an otherwise potentially unstable part of the world.... Neither Switzerland nor Finland, for example, need this kind of help' (p. 269).

34   Cited in R. Baldwin, Jr, 'Addressing the security concerns of central Europe through NATO', *European Security*, Vol. 2, No. 4, 1993, p. 561.

35   This was the 1993 Alastair Buchan Memorial Lecture. The text is reproduced in V. Rühe's 'Shaping Euro-Atlantic policies: a grand strategy for a new era', *Survival*, Vol. 35, No. 2, 1993, pp. 134–5.

36   See K. Kinkel, 'NATO requires a bold but balanced response to the East', *International Herald Tribune*, 21 October 1993.

37   Once this had been leaked, however, the Bush administration disowned these ideas, and the final document was much more circumspect. See C. L. Glaser, 'Why NATO is still best', *International Security*, Vol. 18, No. 1, 1993, p. 11.

38   See Gerosa, 'The North Atlantic Cooperation Council', p. 289.

39   This was after the Defense Planning Council. Quoted in Baldwin, 'Addressing the security concerns of central Europe', p. 561.

40   Quoted in B. George and J. Borawski, 'Sympathy for the Devil: European security in a revolutionary age', *European Security*, Vol. 2, No. 4, 1993, p. 490.

41   One symbol of this was a paper on 'Russia's participation in peacekeeping operations in the countries of the former USSR', distributed by the Russians to NACC members on 28 June 1993, which spoke of a 'special responsibility' on the part of Russia for stability and human rights in the region, and that requests by other states were merely 'an important factor' in policy formation. This led to great concern among a number of NACC members, most notably the Baltic states, which protested that such a doctrine might legitimise the presence of the Russian army on their territory as peacekeepers. See George and Borawski, 'Sympathy for the Devil', p. 490.

42   See the report on the paper in F. Kempe, 'NATO: out of area or out of business', *Wall Street Journal*, 9 August 1993.

43   R. D. Asmus, R. L. Kugler and F. S. Larrabee, 'Building a new NATO', *Foreign Affairs*, Vol. 72, No. 4, 1993, p. 32. They also published a version under the title 'Time for a new US–European strategic bargain', *International Herald Tribune*, 28–29 August 1993.

44   See George and Borawski, 'Sympathy for the Devil', p. 488.

45 Quoted in A. Marshall, 'NATO moves to include former enemies', *The Independent*, 7 September 1993.
46 See W. Drozdiak, 'NATO family cool to taking in Warsaw Pact orphans', *International Herald Tribune*, 2 September 1993.
47 Quoted in Marshall, 'NATO moves to include former enemies'.
48 Quoted in A. Bridge, 'Courtship gets serious as NATO looks eastwards', *The Independent*, 10 September 1993.
49 Quoted in A. LeBor, 'Polish leaders cast doubt on entry to NATO', *The Times*, 21 September 1993. However, on 19 September, leaders of the three parties that won the Polish elections had stressed the need for Poland to join NATO 'as soon as possible'. See 'NATO enlargement', *Atlantic News*, No. 2561, p. 1. Despite this, doubt had already been created in many minds in the west.
50 This was made clear in a 'strictly personal' speech by Sir Richard Vincent, the British chair of NATO's Military Committee, in a speech to the Royal United Services Institute. Guarantees for central Europe had, unlike in the 1930s, to be backed up with political and military resolve. 'I do not see either of these seriously in prospect,' he commented. See D. White, 'Military chief fears for NATO expansion', *Financial Times*, 10 November 1993.
51 See, for example, D. White, 'Caution urged on NATO expansion', *Financial Times*, 23 September 1993; R. Boyes, 'Confusion in NATO ranks as left prepares for power in Poland', *The Times*, 16 September 1993; and R. Boyes, 'Bonn wants East in updated NATO', *International Herald Tribune*, 8 October 1993, which reported that French Foreign Minister Alain Juppé had suggested that the Balladur plan should be explored before NATO expanded its membership.
52 G. Wettig, 'Moscow's perception of NATO's role', *Aussenpolitik*, Vol. 45, No. 2, 1994, p. 127.
53 Yeltsin wrote to the Americans, British, Germans and French, apparently taking the 'two plus four talks' as a model for communication. Yeltsin suggested that the 'two plus four agreement' made NATO expansion illegal, a view rejected in the west. See 'NATO/East', *Atlantic News*, No. 2559, 6 October 1993, p. 3; and W. Drozdiak, 'NATO likely to slow East Europe's entry', *International Herald Tribune*, 6 October 1993.
54 See I. Traynor, 'Army success a blow to east's NATO ambitions', *The Guardian*, 6 October 1993.
55 R. Clement, 'North Atlantic Cooperation Council confronts eastern European problems', *German Tribune*, No. 1508, 20 March 1992, reprinted from the *Rheinische Merkur*, 13 March 1992.
56 At the National Press Club in Washington, DC, on 6 October 1993. Reproduced in M. Wörner, 'A new NATO for a new era', *Foreign and Commonwealth Office (London) Arms Control and Disarmament Research Unit Arms Control and Disarmament Quarterly Review*, No. 32, 1994, p. 9.
57 The PFP involved a formal agreement between each 'partner' and NATO. This agreement comprised two parts: first a framework agreement, and then detailed agreement on cooperative action.
58 See M. M. Nelson, 'NATO officials back plan for closer ties with ex-bloc', *Wall Street Journal*, 22–23 October 1993.
59 *Ibid.*
60 See, for example, 'The world sends NATO back to the drawing board', *The Economist*, 25 December 1993 – 7 January 1994.
61 George and Borawski, 'Sympathy for the Devil', p. 475.
62 In a speech to the opening session of the Czech parliament on 12 October, excerpted in V. Havel, 'Why NATO must not say no to the Czechs', *The Guardian*, 19 October 1993.
63 T. Barber, 'Lithuania knocks on NATO's door', *The Independent*, 5 January 1994.

64 SHAPE Central and East European Defence Studies, 'An initial look at reaction to Partnership for Peace', 14 January 1994.

65 M. Woollacott, 'Gate-crashing NATO's exclusive club', *The Guardian*, 5 January 1994.

66 R. Boyes, 'Clinton must not appease Yeltsin', *The Times*, 7 January 1994.

67 R. Perle, 'NATO wastes an opportunity', *International Herald Tribune*, 12 January 1994.

68 However, the authors would argue that it was flawed on the grounds that enlargement has been inevitable since the very early 1990s, and that it would have been much easier at that time than in the late 1990s.

69 'Partnership for Peace Invitation', Brussels: NATO, 10 January 1994, p. 1. Article 10 of the Washington Treaty reads: 'The Parties may, by unanimous agreement, invite any other European State in a position to further the principles of this Treaty and to contribute to the security of the North Atlantic area to accede to this Treaty. Any State so invited may become a party to the treaty by depositing its instrument of accession with the Government of the United Sates of America. The Government of the United States of America will inform each of the Parties of the deposit of each such instrument of accession.' Source, *NATO Handbook*, Brussels: NATO, 1994, p. 145.

70 See, for example, President Clinton's speech to the French National Assembly, 7 June 1994.

71 See, for example, Warren Christopher, cited in 'Christopher', *Atlantic News*, No. 2631, 11 June 1994, p. 3.

72 Cited in 'Enlargement of NATO', *Atlantic News*, No. 2639, 8 July 1994. The Republican's proposed 'NATO Revitalization and Expansion Act' in 1995 suggested that the Visegrad states should accede to NATO in one group. See, for example, D. Priest and D. Williams, 'Clinton draws line against Republicans on national security', *International Herald Tribune*, 16 February 1995.

73 North Atlantic Council communiqué, 1 December 1994, reproduced in *Atlantic News*, No. 2676 (annex), 3 December 1994.

74 *Ibid.*

75 See M. M. Nelson, 'Yeltsin's sharp attack on the US casts a cloud over CSCE's agenda', *Wall Street Journal*, 6 December 1994; A. Marshall, 'Russia warns NATO of a "Cold Peace"', *The Independent*, 6 December 1994.

76 See D. Averre, 'NATO expansion and Russian national interests', *European Security*, forthcoming.

77 Reproduced in *Atlantic News*, No. 2382 (annex II), 21 December 1991. See also T. L. Friedman, 'Yeltsin says Russia seeks to join NATO', *New York Times*, 21 December 1991.

78 On this, see the comments of the chair of the Russian Supreme Soviet Security Committee, Sergei Stepashin, recorded in *FBIS-SOV-91-202*, 18 October 1991, p. 64, cited in S. N. MacFarlane, 'Russia, the west and European security', *Survival*, Vol. 35, No. 3, 1993, p. 23.

79 Basic Provision of the Military Doctrine of the Russian Federation, Presidential Decree 1833, 2 November 1993. For reaction, see 'NATO opening to east is likely, Wörner says', *International Herald Tribune*, 27 November 1993.

80 Published in *Izvestiya*, 26 November 1993, cited in Wettig, 'Moscow's perception of NATO's role', pp. 127–8.

81 See W. Drozdiak, 'A blunt new Yeltsin warning to NATO', *International Herald Tribune*, 10 December 1993.

82 On 10 December; see T. Garton Ash, M. Mertes and D. Moisi, 'Engagement in Europe, partnership with Russia', *International Herald Tribune*, 3 January 1994.

83 Asmus, Kugler and Larrabee, 'Building a new NATO', p. 32.

84 L. Rühl, 'European security and NATO's eastward expansion', *Aussenpolitik*, Vol. 45, No. 2, 1994, p. 122.

85 'Partnership for Peace initiative explained', comments of J. Kruzel in an interview on 7 December, *Wireless File 233*, 8 December 1993, p. 6.

86 Kinkel, cited in 'NATO Council', *Atlantic News*, p. 1.

87 Rühe, 1993 Alastair Buchan Memorial Lecture, 'Shaping Euro-Atlantic Policies', pp. 134–5.

88 On this, see 'Ministerial meeting of the North Atlantic Council in Berlin', 3 June 1996, final communiqué: NATO press communiqué M-NAC-1 (96)63, paragraph 16.

89 D. Trenin, 'Avoiding a new confrontation with NATO', *NATO Review*, No. 3, 1996, p. 18.

90 Author's interviews in Moscow, September and December 1997.

91 A. Kozyrev, 'What are we supposed to do with NATO?', *Moscow News*, 24 September 1993.

92 A. Pushkov, 'Building a new NATO at Russia's expense', *Moscow News*, 24 September 1993.

93 See MacFarlane, 'Russia, the west and European security', p. 19.

94 See, for example, C. W. Maynes, 'No, expansion eastward isn't what NATO needs', *International Herald Tribune*, 21 September 1993. Others thought that NATO was being distracted by the focus on the east. In outlining six roles for NATO, T. Greenwood notes the function 'to facilitate the dialogue and cooperation with Central and Eastern European states' as only number six. T. Greenwood 'NATO's future', *European Security*, Vol. 2, No. 1, 1993, p. 5. Still others felt that NATO as a whole had outlived its usefulness. For J. Clarke, 'The United States should seek to replace NATO with what Christopher [Warren Christopher, the US Secretary of State] has called a continent-wide security structure.' J. Clarke, 'Replacing NATO', *Foreign Policy*, No. 93, 1993–94, p. 22.

95 O. Harries, 'The collapse of the west', *Foreign Affairs*, Vol. 72, No. 4, 1993, p. 43.

96 Cited in T. Barber, 'Lithuania knocks on NATO's door', *The Independent*, 5 January 1994. Also see M. Fletcher and M. Binyon, 'Walesa fears NATO snub could revive Soviet bloc', *The Times*, 5 January 1994.

97 I. Gyarmati, a Hungarian diplomat, quoted in *NRC Handslsblad*, 21 September 1991, and cited in Zielonka, *Security in Central Europe*, p. 35.

98 A. Kaminski, 'East-central Europe between the east and the west', *European Security*, Vol. 3, No. 2, 1994, p. 311.

99 Speech opening the new session of the Czech parliament on 12 October, excerpted in Havel, 'Why NATO must not say no to the Czechs'; see also 'Enlargement of NATO', *Atlantic News*, No. 2562, 15 October 1993, p. 1.

100 Havel, 'Why NATO must not say no to the Czechs'.

101 For an account of the first meeting of the Permanent Joint Council, which involved procedural wrangling and a one-day delay, see K.-H. Kamp, 'The NATO–Russia Founding Act: Trojan Horse or milestone of reconciliation?', *Aussenpolitik*, No. 4, 1997, pp. 323–4.

102 M. Jakobson, 'Only NATO membership will soothe their fears', *International Herald Tribune*, 9 November 1993.

103 'NATO Council', *Atlantic News*, No. 2577, 4 December 1993, p. 1.

104 Quoted in C. Goldsmith, 'NATO hails plan to offer East Europe "Partnerships"', *Wall Street Journal*, 3–4 December 1993.

105 See the defence of PFP on the grounds of the value of 'self-differentiation' in M. Rühle, 'NATO is realistic about Russia and enlargement', *International Herald Tribune*, 9 February 1994.

106 On this, see S. Croft, 'Security dangers of double enlargement: the expansion of NATO and the WEU', *Welt Trends*, No. 10, March 1996, pp. 31–44.

107 North Atlantic Council communiqué, 1 December 1994, reproduced in *Atlantic News*, No. 2676 (annex), 3 December 1994.

108 The two Article 5s refer to security guarantees. The quotes from the NATO Enlargement Study are from 'NATO/enlargement', *Atlantic News*, No. 2753, 30 September 1995.

109 Paragraph 13; Berlin North Atlantic Council.
110 See, for example, L. Rühl, 'European security and NATO's eastward expansion', pp. 115–16.
111 See the remarks in 'Enlargement of NATO', *Atlantic News*, No. 2562, 15 October 1993, pp. 1–2.
112 On this, see R. D. Asmus and R. C. Nurick, 'NATO enlargement and the Baltic states', *Survival*, Vol. 38, No. 2, 1996, pp. 121–42.
113 H. H. Mey, 'New members – new mission: the real issues behind the new NATO debate', *Comparative Strategy*, Vol. 13, No. 2, 1994, p. 227.
114 See, for example, 'NATO enlargement', *Atlantic News*, No. 2636, 28 June 1994, p. 1. Also see A. Migranyan (a member of the Russian Presidential Council), 'Partnership for Peace: no, Russia is too big for this exercise', *International Herald Tribune*, 24 June 1994.
115 The clearest exponent of the crisis enlargement approach is M. E. Brown, 'The flawed logic of NATO expansion', *Survival*, Vol. 37, No. 1, 1995. See the reference to such ideas in F. Kempe, 'The answer to Europe's German question', *Wall Street Journal*, 16–17 September 1994. One might detect support for crisis expansion in F. Bonnart (editor of *NATO's Sixteen Nations*), 'Give NATO realistic tasks and don't enlarge', *International Herald Tribune*, 11 January 1994. Bonnart suggested that the central European states 'are not under threat, and there is no sense in committing NATO to security guarantees against currently nonexistent dangers.' More explicitly, Anatol Lieven wrote that 'If Zhirinovsky or someone like him does come to power, then NATO should certainly be expanded.' A. Lieven, 'Don't bait the Bear', *The Independent*, 6 December 1994.
116 Criticism of crisis enlargement can be found in P. M. Nielsen, 'Enlargement of NATO is necessary', in W. Goldstein (ed.), *NATO and European Security in the 1990s*, London: Brassey's, 1994.

3

The enlargement of the European Union[1]

Introduction

The contrast between the Europe of the early 1980s with that of the late 1990s is truly remarkable. The EU was in a state of semi-paralysis (or 'Eurosclerosis') in the early 1980s, having been brought to a halt by acrimonious internal conflicts over its budget and the reform of its common agricultural policy (CAP). There were no signs of the impending, dramatic events in eastern Europe and the status quo of a divided Europe seemed set to continue indefinitely. Within western Europe, while the EU and European Free Trade Association (EFTA) were moving closer together, there was absolutely no indication that the members of EFTA were willing to abandon their preference for intergovernmental cooperation and embrace EU membership. In the Mediterranean, Malta continued to be ruled by an essentially anti-EU Labour government and Turkey and Cyprus were clearly beyond the pale of EU membership (or even an active Association Agreement). Prospective enlargement to the south quite clearly did not extend beyond Spain and Portugal (and they were regarded as difficult). Thus, ten or so years ago, a significant enlargement of the EU appeared to be an unlikely prospect. Virtually every potentially eligible European country that had not already joined was excluded by political constraint (membership of the Soviet bloc), by deliberate decision (membership of EFTA) or by their internal situation (Turkey, Malta and Cyprus).

However, in the late 1980s the unthinkable began to happen and, over the next few years, eighteen aspiring members emerged and went on to submit formal applications. These eighteen countries divide into three distinct groups:

- the EFTAns – Austria, Finland, Norway, Sweden and Switzerland (although Norway ultimately decided not to join and the Swiss application is effectively suspended);

- the CEECs, of which the front runners have always been Poland, Hungary and the Czech Republic, subsequently joined by Slovenia and, very recently, Estonia, the other 'contenders' being Slovakia, Bulgaria, Romania, Latvia and Lithuania (however, this list may grow to include, for example, Croatia and Albania);
- the Mediterranean applicants – Turkey, Malta and Cyprus – whose applications were among the earliest.

Turkey was the first to apply (in April 1987), followed by Austria (July 1989), Cyprus and Malta (both in July 1990), Sweden (July 1991), Finland (March 1992), Switzerland (May 1992), Norway (November 1992), Hungary (March 1994) and Poland (April 1994). There was then an avalanche of applications in 1995 – Romania and Slovakia (both in June), Latvia (October), Estonia (November) and Bulgaria and Lithuania (both in December) – and finally the Czech Republic and Slovenia applied in 1996, in January and June, respectively.

In fact, although it has rarely, if ever, dominated EU affairs for prolonged periods in the past, the issue of enlargement has been on the EU's agenda almost since its inception. Indeed, for virtually its whole existence the EU has been reacting to applications to join, negotiating accession with prospective members or absorbing new members through their transition periods. Thus, for the EU, unlike the other institutions examined in this book, enlargement is not so much a discrete issue as an ongoing process. As a result, the EU has considerable experience of enlargement and the process of enlarging has a degree of normality and acceptability. Indeed, the EU had doubled in size by 1986 – from six to twelve members[2] – and the new members were quite diverse across a range of characteristics: in terms of wealth/gross national product (GNP) per capita (from the UK/Denmark down to Greece/Portugal), size (from the UK/Spain down to Ireland) and political 'outlook' (with Spain, Portugal and Ireland relatively in tune with the aspirations of the original six members and the UK and Denmark rather less so).

However, whether the EU can draw much from its history other than the observation that absorbing new members is difficult is the fundamental question. There is clearly a debate about the value of the experience of previous enlargements – more specifically, the question as to whether the characterisation of the enlargement process as the traditional, 'classical' method[3] is likely to be appropriate – and thus past experience is a helpful guide – or whether enlargement post-1989 is better described as 'adaptive',[4] with the implication that much of the future enlargement process will involve much more adjustment of the EU itself (and its institutions) than in the past. The presumption that the 1995 accession of Austria, Finland and Sweden may be the last 'classical' enlargement rests on the assertion that future enlargement will differ from previous ones both quantitatively and qualitatively:

- In terms of numbers, the European Commission has proposed[5] (and the European Council agreed[6]) that the next wave of enlargement should involve the same number of new members (six – Poland, Hungary, the Czech Republic, Slovenia, Estonia and Cyprus) as the EU accepted in its first thirty years. Indeed, if the other six active applications (on the part of Slovenia, Bulgaria, Romania, Latvia, Lithuania and the now reactivated Maltese application) are pursued in a subsequent wave then the EU would have twenty-seven members – more than double its size in 1989.
- The EU also has to cope with absorbing countries that are significantly different to its existing member states. Most obviously, the prospective members are much poorer and, in the case of Cyprus, much smaller (Luxembourg excepted) than any of the present membership. However, more fundamentally, virtually all the countries seeking membership have, in recent years, neither experienced parliamentary democracy nor operated as market economies.

All this has two general implications: first, the post-1995 enlargements will be more difficult than anything the EU has experienced so far; and second, for the first time, not only the new members but the EU itself will have to adapt and adjust; in particular, it is highly unlikely that the present institutional structure – which is essentially a 'stretched' version of what was in the 1957 Treaty of Rome – can survive in its present form.

Nevertheless, many of the questions raised by previous enlargements remain central to the EU and the accessions and subsequent performance of the nine countries that have joined the EU since its creation may shed some light on the ultimate resolution of these issues. Moreover, there are some general lessons that can be learned from the EU's history and, further-more, at least two elements of past enlargements are certainly carrying over into the future: the procedure by which enlargement takes place, and the use of qualifying criteria (some of which were applicable to pre-1989 enlargements, some of which have been added since).

A history of EU enlargement

By the mid-1990s, the EU had experienced three 'waves' of enlargement:

1 the first 'northern' group – the UK, Denmark and Ireland joined in 1973;
2 a Mediterranean group became members in the 1980s – Greece in 1981 and Spain and Portugal in 1986;

3 the second 'northern' wave – Austria, Finland and Sweden – acceded in 1995.

Of course, Norway negotiated accession in both 1973 and 1995 but elected not to join on each occasion, after the terms of membership had been rejected in a popular referendum.[7]

In fact, the process of economic integration within the EU had barely begun before it was being courted by prospective new members. In a dramatic change of mind, the aloofness of the 1950s was forgotten and the UK applied to join in 1961, having recognised reluctantly its reduced status in the world (although the application was by no means unanimously supported within the UK). British interest was also based on the perceived economic benefits of membership, even more so at the time of the second application, in 1967. This became progressively more the case thereafter as the debate within the UK on EU accession increasingly focused on potential economic advantage, taking as its starting point the realisation that the British rate of growth was lagging behind that of the EC Six.[8] Thus the British change of heart was primarily driven by the lack of alternatives to EU membership and the pursuit of economic advantage. The British application triggered those of Denmark, Norway and Ireland and their decisions to seek EU membership arguably also stemmed from economic self-interest, specifically their close links with the UK, rather than from the pursuit of any vision of an integrated Europe.

However, political factors were much to the fore in the second, 'Mediterranean' round of enlargement, although in a very specific way, relating to the applicant states rather than the EU itself. Greece, Spain and Portugal all applied to join the EU in the mid to late 1970s on their emergence from periods of authoritarian rule.[9] Acceptance of their membership bids was largely due to the EU's desire to support and help them consolidate their newly established democracies. This decision ignored their economic weaknesses and the economic impact of their accessions – indeed, the Commission actually advised that Greece should not be allowed to join the EU at that time[10] – although French and Italian farm interests did protest and delay the Iberian accessions for some years.

The most recent enlargement, in which Austria, Finland and Sweden took the EU's membership from twelve to fifteen in 1995, has been the quickest and the most complex to date. Initially, there were five applicants from EFTA – in fact, only the two smallest members (Iceland and Liechtenstein) did not apply. However, the Swiss application was effectively withdrawn after the electorate rejected membership of the European Economic Area (EEA) in a referendum in December 1992 and, in their referendum on EU membership in 1994, the Norwegians chose not to join (again, and by a similarly narrow margin to that of 1972).[11]

There are a number of observations that might be made about the experience of the EU relating to features that might be expected to carry over to post-1995 enlargements. Specifically:

- The EU drives a hard bargain and is adept at protecting 'its' own interests, which can tend towards the lowest common denominator.
- The attitude of existing member states can be critical. The most notorious case is provided by the French veto of the British application in the 1960s but, equally, it was French support for the Greeks in the 1970s that enabled a doubtful Commission opinion to be overturned. Similarly, in the post-1995 enlargement negotiations, the Baltic states will receive support from Denmark, Sweden and Finland, and Cyprus from Greece, for example.

Clearly, aspiring members should take note of these tendencies but there is arguably a more important lesson they should embrace: EU accession does not provide an instant solution to all their problems and, in particular, does not, in itself, guarantee economic success. EU membership is what new members make of it. It offers a chance to attract foreign investment and EU financial aid, and to use this to generate economic development and enhanced growth, but this opportunity can be grasped only with appropriate national economic policies. This much is clear from a comparative examination of the performance after accession of countries that have joined the EU (particularly Greece and Spain[12]). Consequently, prospective members of the EU would do well to consider accession as a beginning as well as an end.

Finally, while politics have played an important part in various aspects of the enlargement process, it is the economic bottom line that has dominated the negotiations over the accession terms. The latest statement of EU policy intentions – 'Agenda 2000'[13] – may imply that this will be different post-1995 but, as in the past, the political considerations may play a largely permissive role, with economic issues continuing to dominate the detail. The primacy of economics in the negotiations and the associated assessment of net benefit have been characteristic of previous EU enlargements: it is agriculture, the absorption of 'sensitive' industries, effects on trade, likely claims on the structural funds and more general budgetary issues that have quickly become the principal considerations. The financial bottom line of an applicant country's wealth and level of economic development can either facilitate or frustrate its accession. Thus the (rich) EFTA countries were regarded by the EU as relatively easy to assimilate but the (poorer) Mediterranean and central and eastern European applicants provoke uneasiness.

Procedures and accession criteria

There is a formal procedure for joining the EU which begins with an application being made, in writing, to the Council of Ministers. The Council may then decide to reject the application (as it did with the Moroccan application in the late 1980s) or request an opinion ('avis') from the Commission. The Commission's opinion has been accepted by the Council in nearly every case so far[14] and it can be:

- positive (for example, Austria, Finland and Sweden), in which case negotiations will begin;
- negative (for example, Turkey), in which case the application is rejected but an alternative is offered to soften the blow – a customs union in the case of Turkey – and a subsequent reapplication is not precluded;
- conditional (for example, Malta, Cyprus, Slovakia, Bulgaria, Romania, Latvia and Lithuania). This is where the EU is not prepared to enter negotiations at the present but, instead of rejecting the application, indicates the changes the applicant country has to make to be considered more favourably. In practice, there appears to be two different kinds of conditionality, which might be termed 'conditional conditionality' and 'unconditional conditionality'. The conditional version was applied to Malta and Cyprus, where (respectively) economic and political conditions were expressed in the opinions and EU help was offered to fulfil them but the movement from being conditionally to unconditionally accepted is not automatic and has no timetable. 'Unconditional conditionality' seems to be what has been given to those five of the ten current applicants from central/eastern Europe excluded from the first post-1995 wave of enlargement. They not only have a timetable but also their shift from 'conditional' to 'unconditional' is to some extent automatic. Specifically: 'In order to review ... [the] progress [of these countries] .... the Commission will submit an annual report to the European Council, beginning at the end of 1998.... When an applicant country is judged to have fulfilled the necessary conditions to enter into accession negotiations, the Commission will forward a recommendation to the Council to that effect.'[15] This could be interpreted as reissuing the opinion each year until the Commission feels it can say 'yes'.

If the opinion is positive (or becomes so) then the Council has to agree unanimously to proceed and the approval of the European Parliament has also been required since the Single European Act came into effect in 1987. Negotiations take place between the government of the applicant state and the Council (represented by the presidency) assisted by the Commission.

The EU negotiates with individual applicants rather than groups, although parallel negotiations take place when several countries apply simultaneously.

However, the EU does tend to group countries and, consequently, finds it difficult to offer significantly different terms to two or more countries joining at the same time – what is given to one applicant sets a precedent for what can be offered to others. On timing, countries negotiating in parallel have previously joined together even if this causes delays for some; for example, the Portuguese felt that their accession was delayed because it was linked to the more problematic case of Spain.[16] The treaty of accession that emerges for each prospective member from the negotiations then has to be ratified in the European Parliament and the parliaments of the EU member states and that of the applicant (usually after a referendum).

The accession procedure is thus long and drawn out, with ample scope for difficulties to arise and for individual member states and EU institutions to delay or even sabotage the process. Moreover, a difficult political tightrope has to be walked, in that while the treaty of accession must reflect the reality of what accession entails, both for the new member and the EU itself, the terms of entry have to be sufficiently attractive to allow the government of the prospective member to 'sell' them to its electorate in a referendum. Finally, the actual time that each stage (and hence the whole process) takes is variable and is determined by the enthusiasm within the EU for the applicant country in question and the extent of the problems raised by the application. The period from making a formal application to actually joining has ranged from two years and eight months (Finland) to eight years and ten months (Portugal); on average, the nine countries that had joined by 1995 had taken five years and nine months.[17]

In order to be acceptable as members, applicant countries have to fulfil a number of criteria. Only one of these was laid down in the Treaty of Rome – that new members should be 'European'. In fact, there is a little ambiguity because what the Treaty actually says is that 'any European nation can apply' (Article 237), which is not quite the same as saying only European states can apply. Indeed, this ambiguity has been amplified by the Commission, which explicitly chose not to define 'European' in the context of enlargement in a submission to the Lisbon summit in mid-1992.[18] Other criteria 'evolved' during the course of the first EU enlargement and subsequently, notably the need to be a democracy and respect human rights and to adopt the *acquis communautaire* – the latter refers to all the existing rules, regulations and agreements of the EU; in short, a new member cannot attempt to unravel existing EU laws. In the early 1990s, the European Council extended the criteria further to include a 'functioning and competitive market economy ... [and] an adequate legal and administrative system in the public and private sector.'[19] In addition, new members are required to subscribe to the emerging *acquis politique*, that is, the developing common foreign and defence policy, and to the *finalité politique* (the long-term objective of European union).

These criteria were stated in the 'Agenda 2000' document:[20]

- the applicant country must have achieved stability of institutions guaranteeing democracy, the rule of law, human rights and respect for and protection of minorities;
- it must have a functioning market economy, as well as the capacity to cope with competitive pressure and market forces within the EU;
- it must have the ability to take on the obligations of membership, including adherence to the aims of political, economic and monetary union.

This list of criteria may seem to give a precise indication to prospective members of what they need to do to become eligible for EU membership. However, few (if any) of the criteria represent clear hurdles to be jumped and, in practice, much will come down to interpretation. There is ample scope for 'fudges' of the kind all too familiar in EU decision-making. Objectivity may well be in short supply and decisions on the order and timing of the accessions of the current (and any future) applicants may be determined by politics – that is, by the extent to which an aspiring member has friends (within the EU) and influence. It may also be dependent, to some extent, on the EU's internal agenda.

Origins of and motivations for the EU enlargement 'boom'

The rush in applications for EU membership from 1987 onwards was driven by three main factors. The first of these was the regeneration of the EU itself, the catalyst for which was the Cockfield White Paper on the creation of a single EU market.[21] The momentum continued with the (Maastricht) Treaty of the European Union (TEU) and, more recently, the Amsterdam Treaty. This rejuvenation of the EU had two principal effects:

1 The EU's pre-eminence and its position as the embodiment of 'Europe' was established beyond doubt. On the one hand, the 'Eurosclerosis' of the early 1980s was forgotten as the EU rediscovered its original dynamism while, on the other, the alternative European 'clubs' faded away: Comecon ceased to exist and EFTA lost most of its (always limited) attraction.
2 It became clear that developments within the EU were taking place so rapidly that there were actually costs incurred by not joining it. Consequently, European countries which were not members had to re-examine their relationships with the revitalised EU, especially the economic aspects. In particular, they were concerned to ensure continued market access to the EU as some feared that it was seeking to establish a 'fortress

Europe'. In fact, it was not just the costs of exclusion that concerned non-members, but also the fact that they would not participate in the benefits of being part of the EU's single market.[22] The deepening of the EU entailed by the TEU extended these fears of exclusion beyond the economic sphere into the fields of politics and security. Thus, by the early 1990s, and in some cases earlier, most European states outside the EU had decided that the costs of non-membership had become so high that any reservations about joining were more than offset.

The second development occurred in Europe but outside the EU: there were momentous changes among the CEECs that had transformed the economic, political and strategic balance of the continent. After over forty years, the old post-war certainties vanished and a range of new possibilities and alternative scenarios opened up. Most important of all, Europe was once more a whole, or at least potentially so. The hitherto unimaginable prospect of EU membership attracted many former Soviet bloc countries, some of which did not even exist as separate nations until very recently. However, there have also been important effects in western Europe, most obviously the relaxation of the security constraint for the EFTA countries, in particular for Austria initially, and subsequently Finland.

The third factor was global rather than European. The tortuous negotiations of the Uruguay Round and the difficulties in bringing them to an amicable and speedy conclusion gave two signals regarding EU membership to non-members:

1 It indicated their impotence in world economic affairs. The Uruguay Round was essentially a debate between two main players – the United States and the EU; the rest (including non-EU European countries) were reduced to operating at the fringes.
2 As the Uruguay Round dragged on and, at times, appeared close to failure, there was speculation that the world might degenerate into (protectionist) trade blocs. This was fuelled by the creation of the US-led North American Free Trade Area. Faced with this prospect, non-member European countries increasingly perceived membership of the nearest 'bloc' – in their case, the EU – as essential.

Thus the Uruguay Round generated both internal (to Europe) and external pressures on non-members to join the EU.

What is striking about these forces driving the majority of European states into the arms of the EU is that they are based on a combination of opportunistic and negative factors. There is obviously a positive element in the shape of the attraction of the perceived 'success' of the EU, particularly economic success. However, it is unlikely that there are many among the current applicant states who share the federal aspirations of the EU's founders. There are three aspects of this 'negative' motivation for EU membership.

First, there is the fear of exclusion from the European mainstream and particularly the single market. As suggested above, this is not based solely on the rather crude 'fortress Europe' concept, but also reflects fears of non-participation in the setting of technical standards, exclusion from EU public procurement markets, and loss of investment (both domestic and foreign) as this is diverted into the EU's single market – in short, not obtaining the wider benefits of being part of the EU's internal market. An additional basis for feeling a sense of exclusion stems from the growing perception that the EU represents 'Europe'.

Second, EU accession is considered attractive because it provides applicant states with a useful additional channel for pursuing domestic objectives. The objectives may be either economic or political. In general terms, the EU is a useful scapegoat: EU objectives can be 'blamed' for the adoption of unpopular policies which are required for primarily domestic purposes. More positively, all the current applicants (and most likely future applicants) are poor compared with the EU member states. Consequently, they all equate EU membership with increased economic prosperity, in the short term through access to the EU's structural (and agricultural) funds and in the long run through the higher economic growth associated with EU membership (although the precise mechanism by which the latter leads to the former is never specified). On the political front, all prospective members also see EU accession as directly beneficial to internal objectives: the CEECs see it as reinforcing their newly established democracies and market economies, while Turkey wishes to confirm its 'European vocation', and the (Greek) Cypriots see EU accession as a catalyst for resolving the 'Cyprus problem'.

The third essentially negative factor is that countries are seeking EU membership because there is no suitable alternative. EU dominance within Europe and the implied need for some attachment by non-members means that the real issue has become what form that attachment should take. Short of full membership, what the EU offers is 'association', which is actually a rather ill-defined concept originally specified in very broad terms as 'creating ... reciprocal rights and obligations, joint actions and special procedures.'[23] Consequently, association has effectively been defined by practice and has taken three forms:

1 the original, pre-1989, *ad hoc* form of association made available, on a country-by-country basis, to those countries which might ultimately aspire to EU membership – Greece in 1961 and Turkey in 1963, and subsequently extended to Malta in 1970 and Cyprus in 1972;
2 the EEA – an EFTA–EU agreement which basically allows EFTA participation in the EU's single market;

3 the 'Europe Agreements', which were a specific arrangement, designed in the 1990s, to meet the aspirations of the emerging CEECs in the short to medium term; in fact, these are not dissimilar to the original Association Agreements and, indeed, in a sense amounted to a reinvention of the earlier form of association, which had become discredited (for reasons outlined below).

All of these suffer from (similar) drawbacks and few, if any, non-member countries have regarded them as suitable frameworks for a long-term relationship with the EU.

The first-generation Association Agreements consisted of the following elements:

- either a free trade area or a customs union (for trade in industrial goods), to be achieved in stages;
- some (limited) concessions for agricultural exports from the associate to the EU;
- a financial protocol (EU financial aid);
- association institutions at Council and Parliament level;
- some (relatively weak) provision for coordination or alignment of economic and related policies.

The Agreements became progressively more modest and proved difficult to negotiate and implement in practice. It is true that in all four cases developments within the associates effectively wrecked the Agreement but also the EU has often seemed ambivalent and unenthusiastic about the whole concept of association. Indeed, the benefits to the associates have been consistently undermined by safeguard clauses, the exclusion of agriculture and other sectors, and the effective erosion of benefits as similar concessions are given to non-associates under the EU's Generalised System of Preferences.

The second alternative – the EEA – is essentially a mechanism by which the four freedoms of movement (goods, services, people and capital) have been extended to non-members (all ex-members of EFTA) to allow them to participate in the EU's single market. However, while the EEA is much more than the original concept of association, it is still unsatisfactory from the perspective of participants on the non-EU side, particularly because all decisions to determine the rules, regulations and technical standards of the EEA are taken in the EU's Council of Ministers; therefore, members of the EEA who are not also members of the EU play only an indirect (and effectively advisory) role in the decision-making process.

The third form of association – the Europe Agreements – are a special category of association devised specifically for the emerging CEECs. They are essentially an updated and extended version of the original Association Agreements: they contain all five of the elements listed above with the fifth element (coordination of economic and related policies) much more developed and two additional elements – political and cultural cooperation. However, they suffer from similar drawbacks to the original Agreements (and the EEA) and, in any case, particularly with the publication of 'Agenda 2000', the Europe Agreements have become a stepping stone towards, rather than an alternative to, full membership of the EU. Therefore they are not available on demand to non-EU members.

Moreover, beyond delaying inevitable membership bids, the EU often appears to have no clear idea as to what the role of association should be; in short, the EU has only a negative and no positive view of association. It is therefore not surprising that association has become an increasingly unattractive option and that all three forms of association have essentially the same disadvantages: non-participation in decision-making, exposure to safeguard clauses, limited concessions from the EU in key sectors such as agriculture, steel and chemicals, and erosion of benefits as the EU makes agreements with other countries. In reality, there is no feasible substitute for EU membership and the halfway houses of association and the EEA offer no guarantee of eventual accession. Moreover, as the EU develops at speeds and in directions that make future accession increasingly difficult, countries seeking membership would be well advised to join as soon as they can.

The lack of alternatives means that, as with the fear factor and the pursuit of EU accession to achieve domestic objectives, prospective EU members may increasingly be joining for the 'wrong' reasons; their motivation is not positive – they lack the desire to pursue the vision of Europe of the (more federalist) existing members – but is essentially negative – they simply do not want to be left out. They are faced with what has been characterised as an 'integration dilemma':[24] they have to choose to join the EU and consequently lose a significant element of their sovereignty, with the danger of being 'entrapped' within European integration, or to remain independent, which carries the risk of being 'abandoned' and isolated from the integration process; the problem is that isolation (non-membership of the EU) is not costless.

This is not a dilemma for prospective members joining the EU for 'positive' reasons, since they actually wish to be 'entrapped' within European integration and, indeed, see this as a benefit. However, most EU members have joined for 'negative' reasons. Thus the British pursued EU membership largely as a matter of economic and political expediency.[25] Greece, Spain and Portugal were driven towards the EU by the need to nurture and sustain their restored democracies. Most recently, it was clearly the fear of 'isolation' (especially from the single market) which motivated most EFTA members to pursue EU membership in the 1990s. These countries did not suddenly change their minds and switch their (long-time) preferences away from intergovernmental cooperation to a supranational approach. They were driven by the realisation that they had more to lose by staying out of the EU than going in. Their referenda campaigns and results (including – perhaps especially – Norway's) are clear evidence of this.

It seems probable that the next wave of EU members – from central, eastern and Mediterranean Europe – will be similarly ambivalent about European integration and equally pragmatic in their reasons for pursuing membership. It will be interesting to see how the CEECs react to the inevitable (and potentially growing) loss of a significant part of their newly created independence implied by EU membership. As for the Mediterranean, Turkey is simply pursuing its 'European vocation' (and economic benefits) while Cyprus and Malta are too small not to join the EU, and are both pursuing internal political agendas; in none of these countries is there much evidence of the pursuit of a vision of Europe. This implies that as the EU grows (and, indeed, has grown), it becomes an increasingly broad church within which it is progressively more difficult to determine a common sense of direction. In fact, ultimately, the EU may reach a size at which it is impossible for member states to reach agreement. It is not just economic convergence but also political convergence that is important.

It may seem that this argument is undermined by the 'successful' outcome of the TEU but:

- much remains to be implemented;
- some of the TEU is not specified in detail and it remains, to some extent, an agenda;
- the two more 'politically divergent' member states – the UK and Denmark – were allowed to 'opt out' of key areas;
- there were difficulties in ratifying the TEU.

More generally, the TEU was, in a sense, a defensive device whereby the EU sought to 'deepen' before it 'widened' and thereby compel later members to accept the 'deepening' as part of the *acquis communautaire*. The TEU does, indeed, mark a crossroads for the EU, but one at which it has stopped, not passed through.

In fact, the relative failure at Amsterdam may well be more indicative of what lies ahead. The essential problem is that having admitted political 'dissidents', the EU has to live with them – and they are a growing band whose presence has critical implications for the future development of the EU. They may seek to redirect the EU, possibly along more intergovernmental lines, or may even seek to reverse some of the existing policies. If this proves to be unacceptable to the EU's founding members,

then some form of division or 'differential integration' may be the only way forward. These matters are addressed further in the conclusion.

The 'issues', 'problems' and 'challenges' of enlargement

The post-1995 enlargement of the EU will be the most challenging yet, and will be more 'adaptive' than 'classical'. It therefore raises a number of 'issues' (if one wishes to be neutral), 'problems' (if pessimistic) or 'challenges' (if optimistic) that are of a greater order than those raised by previous enlargements or that are 'new' (in that they were either not raised or, more typically, evaded in the past). These issues fall into three broad categories:

1 institutional;
2 financial;[26]
3 policy – either specific (for example, the common foreign and security policy) or general (the future direction of the EU).

The EU was supposed to resolve the institutional issues at Amsterdam but failed to do so. The financial issues are addressed in the 'Agenda 2000' document and the policy questions are likely to be ongoing and only resolved over time.

Institutional issues

The institutional changes prompted by the 1995 and earlier enlargements were essentially numerical adjustments and involved increasing numbers in line with the 'weight' of the new members. This was relatively uncontentious until 1995, when there was a dispute over the decision to increase the number of votes in the Council of Ministers required to form a blocking minority. This was opposed by the UK (and initially Spain) and resolved in a temporary and rather unsatisfactory way – the Ioannina compromise. This provides for a 'reasonable delay' if there is a blocking minority equal to the 'old' level (twenty-three votes) or more, but less than the 'new' level (twenty-six votes), during which the Council presidency will try to broker an agreement. The difficulties encountered in 1995 do not augur well for any future efforts to introduce the much more radical institutional changes that may lie ahead.

The formal debate over the reform of the institutional system began in the Reflection Group, established in July 1995 to prepare for the 1996/7 intergovernmental conference. The Group's first report[27] flagged the broad issues: the size of the Commission and the Parliament and, for the Council of Ministers, the reform of the voting system. The common factor linking the main issues is the uneasy balance of representation in the institutions between the large and small EU member states. However, little progress was ultimately made at Amsterdam and institutional reform remains an ongoing and highly contentious question.

At one level there is no problem for the Commission because it represents the 'Community' (EU) interest and therefore its size and the nationality of the individual commissioners is irrelevant. However, the political reality is that each member state jealously guards its right to appoint its commissioner(s). The implicit assumption underlying the argument that the Commission needs reform is that efficiency dictates that it should not grow beyond a certain size and that it is already too big. Reform designed to 'slim down' the Commission could take two forms (which are not mutually exclusive):

1 one commissioner per member state (implying the larger members should lose a commissioner);
2 smaller members should share a commissioner.

This puts the issue of over-representation of smaller countries in the EU institutions in sharp relief. Both these reforms are politically controversial and will not be easy.

Beyond these highly political issues, the enlargement process also creates a variety of more pragmatic difficulties for the Commission's internal working processes. Staying with the top tier of the Commission, it becomes progressively more difficult to create enough meaningful portfolios as the number of commissioners increases. Moreover, even if portfolios can be found for everyone, they are not balanced: some are clearly more important than others and this leads to there being 'first-class' and 'second-class' commissioners. This undermines the collegiality of the Commission by creating a hierarchy of commissioners. Furthermore, it is not only the number of commissioners that increases but also that of directorates-general, which only serves to increase the complexity of the Commission's activities. Any enlargement also brings with it the need to take on new staff from the acceding countries quite rapidly, and the absorption of a relatively large number of new recruits will not be easy when they lack experience in dealing with EU affairs and may have quite different administrative practices and traditions; moreover, it could play havoc with the career prospects of existing staff (with consequently adverse effects on morale). Finally, there is concern in the Commission about the proliferation of official languages (which is also a problem for the other institutions).[28]

Just as the Commission is becoming too big, it is, similarly, widely presumed that the European Parliament is rapidly approaching its optimum size. The number of Members of the European Parliament (MEPs) is already close, at 646, to what it already considers to be its maximum size (700), but if current levels of representation were extended to the twelve states expected to join the EU in the medium term, then the result would be more than 1,000 MEPs. This is clearly unworkable. However, the implication of controlling the growth of MEPs is fewer MEPs for existing members. Not only would a reduction in principle be difficult to introduce, but the large-member/small-member issue might also emerge in any debate about the sharing out of the reduced number of parliamentary places among the EU's existing members. There is also the question of the democratic deficit, which will loom even larger in an enlarged EU.

More fundamentally, the problems for the Parliament raised by enlargement are likely to extend well beyond mere adjustments in size. At the present time, a German MEP is elected by over thirteen times the number of voters (800,000) than an MEP from Luxembourg (60,000). It is difficult to envisage how this particular circle can be squared in a single chamber. A solution may be a bicameral system along US lines, where the states are (equally) represented in the Senate and population differences are reflected in the composition of the House of Representatives. Any change of this kind in the EU would clearly be a major step.

While such changes would involve profound reforms, even more momentous issues are raised by the prospect of differential integration (which may be the inevitable consequence of further enlargement). It is possible that the Commission, as the 'voice' of the EU, and the Council, with appropriate variations of the voting system, may cope with this scenario, but not the Parliament. The European Parliament has gradually evolved into an intricate and sophisticated working parliament with a genuinely supranational remit and operations. Breaking this down to reflect an EU operating as a multi-tier organisation would be difficult, and for an EU on an *à la carte* basis may be impossible.

Finally, the Council of Ministers remains the most difficult institution to reform, essentially because this is where decisions are ultimately taken and hence where the power lies. There is no debate over numbers as such, since every member state must obviously be represented, but the implications of a Council of twenty-seven or more ministers (in terms of time, manageability and working procedures) are a source of concern. However, the two principal issues relate to the voting system – first, the adjustment of the size of the blocking minority and, second, the possible reform of the weighting system to address the situation where a qualified majority might be mustered by a group of small countries representing only half the EU's population. As already indicated, the former caused problems in 1995 and was resolved only by the rather unsatisfactory Ioannina compromise. At that time, the UK objected to any attempt to increase the size of the blocking minority in absolute terms, since this would decrease its power to block policy developments. The UK may be joined by others as the absolute size of the required blocking minority grows in line with the enlarging EU, as it would grow if the (so far) less controversial practice of maintaining the relative size of the minority (at approximately 30 per cent) were to be continued.

If the pattern of weighting were to be changed then there is a whole range of possibilities. Table 1 summarises this range by presenting two feasible extremes. Column 1 indicates the population (in millions) of the existing fifteen EU member states plus the ten CEECs aspiring to join, plus

Table 1. Weighting systems for voting in the Council: two feasible extremes

	Population (millions)	Weight of vote: present system	Weight of vote: revised system
Current members			
Belgium	10.1	5	2
Denmark	5.2	3	1
Germany	81.5	10	15
Greece	10.4	5	2
Spain	39.2	8	9
France	58.0	10	12
Ireland	3.6	3	1
Italy	57.3	10	12
Luxembourg	0.4	2	1
Netherlands	15.4	5	3
Austria	8.0	4	2
Portugal	9.9	5	2
Finland	5.1	3	1
Sweden	8.8	4	2
UK	58.5	10	12
Prospective members			
Poland	38.3	8	9
Czech Republic	10.3	5	2
Slovakia	5.3	3	1
Hungary	10.3	5	2
Slovenia	2.0	3	1
Bulgaria	9.0	4	2
Romania	22.8	7	5
Lithuania	3.7	3	1
Latvia	2.6	2	1
Estonia	1.5	2	1
Malta	0.3	2	1
Cyprus	0.7	2	1
Total	478.2	134	104
Qualified majority	–	95	74
Blocking minority	–	40	31

Source: See notes 29 and 30.

Cyprus and Malta. Column 2 extends the present weighting system to the twelve prospective members and is based on the work of Edwards.[29] Column 3 postulates a revised system based on population and is an extended version of a calculation by White;[30] it assumes a maximum weight of fifteen and a minimum of one.[31]

Column 2 indicates the dilemmas raised by continuing and extending the present system. It would be possible for the small countries (those with two to five votes) voting together with one large country (Italy) and two 'near-large' countries (Romania and Poland) to engineer a qualified majority with a combined population (50.4 per cent) of barely half the EU total. Perhaps even more unacceptably, small member states (those with two to four votes) could together muster a blocking minority of forty votes on the back of a population of less than 12 per cent of the EU total, whereas Germany voting with two of France, Italy and the UK, and either Spain or Poland, with a combined population of approximately half the EU total (49.2–49.6 per cent) could not. This would produce an uncomfortable, if not unacceptable, situation for larger member states.

Column 3 provides a weighting system based on population but with upper and lower limits which still produce a bias in favour of the smaller countries (otherwise Germany would have 240 times as many votes as Malta, the UK 39 times more than Estonia, and so on). This essentially removes the 'anomalies' described above. The fourteen small countries that could form a blocking minority under the present system could only muster just over half (seventeen) the votes required under this revised system. Conversely, it would take only three of the large countries, or even two of them and one 'near-large' country, to produce a blocking minority.[32] This would have a degree of political legitimacy, since these various combinations would always represent at least 32 per cent (and up to 41 per cent) of the EU's population.[33] However, it may arguably redress the balance too far in favour of the large member states and would be politically unacceptable for small members, particularly the Benelux countries.

Between these two extremes are various compromise positions. For example, it might be possible to have a variable qualified majority that was set higher for the more politically contentious issues. An alternative approach might be to require a double majority (and presumably a double blocking minority): in terms of the weighted voting system (the current version) and of population. Ultimately, of course, none of this might matter because the Council tends to work by compromise and consensus and, to that extent, qualified majority voting is an irrelevance. However, whether current procedures will continue in a much larger, more diverse EU is debatable, and it certainly cannot be relied upon.

Finally, there are a number of issues relating to managing the presidency of the Council of Ministers (and the European Council) that are essentially a manifestation of the small-country/large-country issue. In an EU of twenty-seven members, the large (and, indeed, all) countries would have to wait thirteen years between presidencies but, more importantly, certain countries – particularly the smaller ones – may have neither the credibility nor capability (in terms of officials) to run a competent presidency. This issue has been effectively recognised by the EU by the decision taken to reorder the sequence of presidencies up to 2002 so that the troika[34] always contains at least one large country. However, if the old alphabetical order were to be reinstated, then the prospect of troikas of Romania, Slovenia and Slovakia, and Malta, Latvia and Lithuania may well cause concern. An obvious 'solution' would be to ensure the presence of a large (or near-large) member in the troika at all times, but this would clearly have serious implications for the balance between large and small members. Moreover, it ignores the fact that there has not always been a strongly positive correlation between size and efficient administration of the EU in the past.

Financial issues

The argument over the financial aspects of post-1995 enlargement of the EU has perhaps generated the most heat in the enlargement debate but, in many ways, has shed the least light. There are simply too many unknowns – for example, with regard to the timing of the accessions of the CEECs and the course of any future reform of the CAP – to make precise calculations. However, what is clear is that all the current 'live' applicants (the ten CEECs, Cyprus and Malta) will be net beneficiaries from the EU budget. Moreover, while they may well receive a disproportionately high share of EU expenditure in virtually all policy areas, they will receive most of their funds via the CAP and the EU's structural funds, which account for 50 per cent and 30 per cent, respectively, of the EU's budget.

The dependency of the prospective members on agriculture is very marked. In the mid-1990s they employed (proportionately) over four times as many people in agriculture as the EU (22.5 per cent of the total workforce compared with 5.3 per cent) and agriculture contributed over three and a half times as much to gross value added (8.6 per cent of total gross value added compared with 2.4 per cent). Poland is the country most often singled out, but agriculture in the second largest CEEC – Romania – is even more predominant, accounting for a third of employment and a fifth of total gross value added.[35] The financial implications of extending even the current, 'semi-reformed' CAP to these countries are huge – up to 12 billion ECU for the Visegrad Four alone;[36] moreover, it is clearly undesirable to extend the economic inefficiencies of the CAP to yet more countries and the reaction to any attempt to do so from outside the EU – particularly in the United States – would be very negative, and possibly aggressive.

However, a simple extension of existing policy is probably the least likely scenario. There has never been any genuine momentum – that is, based on a desire to 'improve' the policy for its own sake – behind the EU's efforts to reform the CAP. Reform has always been driven by factors external to agriculture – specifically, budget constraints and pressure from third countries, most recently through the Uruguay Round. Enlargement to the east triggers both these forces and will, therefore, inevitably lead to more CAP reform.

The cost of bringing the new members into the CAP will depend on two things: how far the reform goes and precisely how the CAP is extended to new members. Josling[37] identifies three potential future scenarios for the CAP:

1 minimal/no changes in the CAP – in short, the previous policy of adopting a reactive rather than a proactive approach;
2 modest reform – basically, a gradual continuation of the reforms begun in 1992;
3 rapid/maximum reform, designed to make EU agriculture competitive on the world market as soon as possible.

Josling likewise sees three possible speeds of adjustment:

A exclusion of CEECs (along the lines of the EEA, which excludes agriculture);
B a long transition period (possibly up to fifteen years);
C immediate incorporation of CEEC agriculture into the CAP, or after a very short transition period.

Table 2 provides a grid showing the various possible combinations of CAP development and transition periods for the CEEC's agricultural sector. In fact, anything in the first row (1A, 1B, 1C) is unlikely to be feasible economically and anything in the first column (1A, 2A, 3A) unlikely politically. Exclusion of CEEC agriculture would render the EU's internal market incomplete, require the continued use of border posts, create a new layer of red tape with associated administrative problems (depending on precisely how the exclusion was made effective[38]) and provide a rather unfortunate precedent. This would be bad enough, but exclusion is a political nonstarter anyway, because the CEECs would regard it as making them 'second-class' members of the EU. It would amount to the introduction of a multi-tier or *à la carte* EU, which is perhaps not an impossible scenario but, in practice, the CEECs will want at least the fig leaf of a long transition period for their agriculture.

Minimum reform could work only with exclusion (1A) and is feasible only in the short run; in the longer term, external pressures from the EU

Table 2. Combinations of future scenarios for the CAP and possible transition periods for the incorporation of CEEC agriculture

	Exclusion	*Long transition*	*Short/no transition*
Minimum reform	1A	1B	1C
Modest reform	2A	2B	2C
Maximum reform	3A	3B	3C

budget[39] and from the World Trade Organisation would force a shift in policy up to the level of modest reform (at least) and a policy of inaction is inherently unsatisfactory anyway. Minimum reform with incorporation of CEEC agriculture would make the CAP too expensive eventually (1B) or immediately (1C); this would raise questions about the feasibility of the EU enlarging to the east, require drastic increases in funds – through, for example, national financing of the CAP, or would necessitate a hurried shift to maximum reform. Much the same might be said of the combinations of modest reform and incorporation (2B and 2C). The timescale for the impending crisis would be longer and CEEC accession might not be threatened but the end result would be the same: either more money for or more reform of the CAP. This leaves maximum reform and incorporation (3B and 3C) as the only feasible long-term options. The adjustment period should be short – it would be undesirable to raise the expectations of CEEC farmers by offering them high EU prices which were about to be reduced to world levels – and possibly inversely related to the speed of introduction of reforms.

The contention here is, therefore, that while it might be in character for the EU to try to pursue minimum reform (1A or 1B, depending on how the CEECs react), maximum reform (3B/3C) is inevitable if eastward enlargement is to proceed satisfactorily, although it may be possible to pursue modest reform (probably 2B rather than 2C) as an interim measure. If this is the case, then the financial implications of future enlargement for the CAP are not serious because any payments made to farmers in new members of the EU would be at least offset by the reduced level of payments to farmers in existing member states.[40]

The contentious bottom line is, of course, that existing members have to accept lower receipts from the CAP, and this is also the key to the structural funds' accommodating further enlargement. In fact, the structural funds were the source of some initial, alarmist predictions about the costs of enlargement. Hughes has gathered together seven estimates (from academic, member state government and EU sources).[41] They are not directly comparable because they cover different groups of CEECs and use different methodologies, but are nevertheless broadly in agreement: the increase in the structural funds required to enlarge to the east is around 25 billion ECU for the Visegrad Four and 40–45 billion ECU for all ten CEECs. These calculations are all essentially based on the assumption that the grant of structural fund monies per head (400 ECU) to the EU's two poorest countries – Greece and Portugal – in 1999 would simply be extended to the ten CEECS. This then gives the level of increase that would be required for 'unreformed' structural funds. It would imply that they would more than double – a prospect which is politically unacceptable.

Fortunately, it is not economically feasible either: such a level would imply that CEECs would have to absorb exceedingly high amounts of capital, equivalent to a fifth of their GNP in three of them and over a third in three others (Table 3, column 1). While there is no shortage of deserving investment projects in central and eastern Europe, such high rates of absorption are not realistic. Table 3 illustrates an alternative approach that recognises this: column 3 estimates CEEC receipts of structural funds on the assumption that they are equal not to the absolute amount per capita that the poorer EU member states currently receive, but to the same proportion (approximately) of their total GNP that they currently receive. This produces a much more manageable figure of 8.49 billion ECU – roughly a quarter of current structural fund expenditure. Moreover, it

Table 3. The cost of extending the structural funds to CEECs

	Structural fund receipts:		
	at 400 ECU per capita (% of GNP)	at 400 ECU per capita (ECU bill in billions)	capped at 4% of GNP (ECU bill in billions)
Poland	19.7	15.44	3.12
Czech Republic	13.5	4.12	1.21
Slovakia	20.3	2.12	0.41
Hungary	11.8	4.12	1.39
Slovenia	6.7	0.80	0.47
Bulgaria	39.0	3.36	0.34
Romania	36.0	9.08	1.00
Lithuania	33.6	1.48	0.17
Latvia	22.0	1.08	0.19
Estonia	15.3	0.60	0.15
Total	n/a	42.2	8.49

Source: K. Hughes, 'Managing the costs of enlargement: the structural funds', paper given at the conference Enlarging the European Union: The Way Forward, Birmingham, 1–2 July 1997, table 2.

should be remembered that the ten CEECs will not all join together, that the first wave may not join until as late as 2005 and that full access to the structural funds may not be immediate if there is a transition stage. Thus there will be ample time to 'phase in' the increase and to 'persuade' the Spanish and other current beneficiaries from the structural funds that they will have to accept a declining share.

Thus the key elements of the financial transfers to CEECs acceding to the EU would seem to be the contributions from the common agricultural fund and the structural funds. It has been argued above that the amounts involved may not be as high as initially expected and, indeed, are quite manageable. The main issue raised by enlargement for the overall EU budget therefore becomes not the increase in its size – since this is relatively small – but rather the redistribution of it. If the new members of the EU are to receive their fair share (and they will all be net beneficiaries), then this implies one of two changes (or some combination of both): either current net contributors pay more, or current net beneficiaries receive less (possibly to the point of becoming net contributors). Neither of these alternatives will be easy to agree and it is probably just as well that the extended nature of forthcoming enlargement will give the EU several years in which to reach agreement.

The Commission's response to these financial issues[42] would seem to support this interpretation. Its approach to the CAP is to advocate 'deepening and extending the 1992 reform through further shifts from price supports to direct payments'. This is certainly not 3C (maximum reform and short transition) nor even 3B (maximum reform and long transition) in Table 2, which were identified as the only feasible long-term options for the CAP, if enlargement to the east is to proceed satisfactorily. However, it could well approximate to 2B (modest reform and long transition), which was put forward as a practicable interim measure.

With regard to the structural funds, the Commission proposes that transfers 'should not exceed 4 per cent of the GNP of any current or future Member State', thereby avoiding absorption problems in the CEECs and keeping the cost of enlargement down to a manageable level. This allows the Commission to suggest maintaining the 'budget for economic and social cohesion at 0.46% of Union GNP' – the level it reaches in 1999 – for the whole period covered by the next financial perspective (2000–6). (This will, of course, allow total expenditure to increase as GNP will grow because of economic growth.) The share of existing, 'poorer' member states will decline but the Commission hopes to soften the blow (and facilitate agreement): 'a phasing-out mechanism must be defined' for Objective 1 regions which lose their status, and similar regions in Objective 2 'should continue to benefit during a transitional period from support which is limited financially'.[43] The amount to be made available to the CEECs will total 45 billion ECU over 2000–6, an average of 6.43 billion ECU a year. This is in line with the 8.49 billion ECU put forward in Table 3 (column 3), especially bearing in mind that the latter refers to full membership for all ten CEECs, whereas the former figure covers a period in which a maximum of five (plus Cyprus) will join and the other five CEECs will not be fully eligible for structural fund assistance but will receive only 'pre-accession' aid (one billion ECU per year in total).[44]

The projected development of the overall EU budget therefore appears to be within manageable limits. The Commission is suggesting that the 'own resources' ceiling (the maximum amount the EU is permitted to spend) of 1.27 per cent of EU GNP should, and can, be maintained, and will allow additional expenditure of up to 20 billion ECU by 2006. Within this, the growth of CAP expenditure can be held to a maximum of 74 per cent of GNP growth, and structural fund spending held at 0.46 per cent of GNP (as indicated above). Other expenditure should grow at roughly the same rate as GNP. The bottom line is that the EU budget should grow 'by 17% from 1999 to 2006 in real terms which is less than the expected growth of GNP (24% ...) ... [which] would leave a large margin .... to cover [any additional] ... requirements ... and also to prepare for the completion of the transitional arrangements applying to the first countries to join and for the accession of the other applicants.'[45] The Commission further considers the present 'own resources' system of funding of the budget is adequate and that although 'new accessions will inevitably mean a deterioration in the budgetary position of the current Member States, ... this cannot give rise to demands for compensation.'[46] This would appear to set the scene for the political battleground described above.

Policy issues

There is a wide range of specific policy issues raised by enlargement besides agriculture and structural/regional policy, which have already been covered. EU policy with regard to security and defence will clearly be affected by enlargement. This still leaves a wide range of other specific policies, which have been, or are in the process of being, examined elsewhere.[47] The effects are wide ranging and important but, provided the institutional and financial issues can be resolved, these are a matter of detail and do not represent fundamental difficulties that could delay or even prevent further enlargement. However, there are a number of central policy issues (or, perhaps better, attitudes or philosophies) on which the accession of the CEECs and the Mediterranean applicants could have a significant impact.

The first of these issues concerns the implications for the whole internal agenda of the EU in terms of its content and the timing of its implementation. This is the old 'widening versus deepening' dilemma, which goes back at least as far as the first EU summit at the Hague in 1969, since when it has continued to cause concern intermittently. However, it has become particularly acute in the 1990s because of the sheer scale of both widening (in terms of numbers of aspiring members) and deepening (the Maastricht agenda) that is currently proposed. There are three channels of potential conflict between widening and deepening. First, there are the practical effects on the EU's institutions: these would include the short-term impact of diverting energy away from deepening to negotiating the accession of new members and, more fundamentally, the long-term reper-cussions of a large influx of new members on the day-to-day functioning of the institutions (discussed above). Second, widening may impose strains on particular aspects of EU policy; for example, it may lead to temporary (and possibly very long) derogations from certain aspects of the single market and the accession of so many economically divergent states may impede the programme to implement economic and monetary union. Third, these new members may also be politically divergent and may seek to question further deepening of the integration process, or at least question its direction, content and, indeed, very nature. There is a view that this aspect of the potential conflict between widening and deepening is fanned by the attitudes of some existing EU members (particularly the UK).

Fundamental conflict about the course of future integration is much more likely as the EU embraces a progressively larger and more diverse membership. This leads on to the second central policy issue raised by enlargement: will all the new members-to-be accept the (ultimately federalist) agenda of the founders of the EU? In short, in an increasingly diverse EU, it becomes more and more difficult to be certain of the com-mitment of new members to deepening. At the very least, some prospective members may press for British/Danish-style opt-outs once they have become full EU members. More fundamentally, they may seek to redirect, inhibit or even reverse the present course of European integration.

It may seem (and some would encourage the view) that a federalist agenda is implicit in the *finalité politique* that all new members of the EU have to accept on joining. However, this is rather disingenuous. It is difficult to assert that any of the nine countries that have joined the EU since its inception were attracted by the opportunity to participate in a federal project, nor is this likely to be the case with any of the current candidates for EU membership; in fact, it seems more likely that the majority of them will be at best either neutral or favour intergovernmental cooperation. Their motivation for joining the EU has been or is essentially pragmatic and stems from the 'integration dilemma' (outlined above): the choice for those on the fringes of the EU is either EU membership and economic and political benefits, or staying out, with the consequent exclusion and disadvantages (the costs of non-membership). Virtually all on the periphery have decided to pursue the former.

While there will inevitably be some individuals in the aspiring members with positive attitudes and visions of a federal Europe, or even some alternative grand design, the majority have probably given little thought to the long-term future of the EU; their ambitions extend little beyond accession (and the associated economic and political benefits which they expect). When they do address the future they may well have a much more constrained and limiting perception of the future shape of the EU than its founders.

It might be argued that prospective members tend to 'go native'[48] once they join the EU and that, despite having more 'new' than 'old' members, the EU has continued to deepen, but the history of enlargement does not support this. The new (actually or potentially) 'dissident' members have been persuaded to accept the (somewhat limited) federalist trend within the EU through a variety of devices:

- the UK and Denmark have been bought off with 'opt-outs';
- Ireland, Spain, Greece and Portugal have been 'bribed' with receipts from the EU budget;
- Austria, Sweden and Finland are still feeling their way to some extent, although the outcome of the 1996/7 intergovernmental conference and Amsterdam (or lack of it) may be indicative of future foot-dragging tendencies.

The truth is that the critical step from an ambivalent to an overt and undeniably federal programme has yet to be taken. 'Maastricht' was an agenda and 'Amsterdam' failed to make it any more than that. Consequently, the uneasy truce between the federal and intergovernmental camps within the EU continues.

In short, no enlargement, past or future, has or is likely to increase the practical implementation of federalism through institutional or policy development. Indeed, the most visible institutional change in the EU since 1958 has been the formalisation and elevation of summits – the European Council – an essentially intergovernmental body; and the main policy development has been the emergence of structural/regional policy, which is *communautaire* in principle but, in practice, is there to provide economic benefits to those (mainly) poorer countries that joined the EU before 1995. The strains caused by the forthcoming enlargement of the EU may make a real debate inevitable and raise the question as to what happens if member states' differences are irreconcilable? The answer may lie in differential integration. This leads on to the third central policy issue: is further enlargement compatible with the continuation of a single-tier, single-speed EU?[49]

The concept of variable geometry is not new[50] but it has become a more likely scenario in the 1990s. The 1995 enlargement extended the northern

(Anglo-Nordic) 'dissident' bloc and tensions will increase – as the EU enlarges to the east and the south – between those who favour a more deeply integrated EU and those who prefer a much looser, intergovernmental arrangement. Coexistence within a single-speed, single-tier EU will become progressively more difficult. The only way to resolve the disagreement may be for an inner group to break away and pursue fast-track integration without the participation of all EU member states. Somewhat surprisingly, such a development was outlined in a proposition from Germany in 1994[51] that suggested a hard core of five countries (the original six minus Italy), which must 'participate as a matter of course in all policy fields', should give 'the Union a strong centre to counteract the centrifugal forces generated by constant enlargement', and 'must be open to every member state willing and able to meet its requirements.'[52] This would appear to be a contingency plan for the kind of situation being envisaged in the analysis above.

However, the problem is moving from principle to practice. The terms 'differential integration' and 'variable geometry'[53] are widely used but rarely (if ever) defined. The precise form that integration – differential or not – takes is of great importance. There would seem to be a number of possibilities:[54]

1 A single-speed EU is where every member state participates fully in every stage in every policy. (The EU has actually not been single speed since 1973, when it began to enlarge, because, for most of the period since then, there have been one or more new members in a transition stage with a variety of temporary derogations. More fundamentally, the EU has pursued a number of multi-speed policies in which, by design, not all members participate fully; the most obvious example is economic and monetary policy, which has always been envisaged as a multi-speed policy – the 'Snake' in the 1970s, the European Monetary System in the 1980s and the plan within the TEU.)

2 A single-tier EU is where every member state is pursuing the same group of policies, which correctly describes the EU until 1992, when the British and Danes were given opt-outs from various aspects of the TEU. (Of course, while a single-tier EU may also be single speed, it is equally possible to have a single-tier, multi-speed EU;[55] in fact, the latter is an accurate characterisation of the EU over 1973–92.)

3 A multi-speed EU is where every member is included in every policy in principle but, in practice, each member is moving at a different speed. In practice, this is already happening in the EU and arguably is merely an expedient device for maintaining unity at a time when some members are better able to press ahead than others.

4 A multi-tier EU (or EU of concentric circles) is where all members do not pursue all policies. Instead, members are grouped into tiers,[56] and

are 'signed up' to progressively fewer EU policies; only the tier at the centre – the 'hard core' – participates in all EU policies. In short, it is not simply a question of different speeds but of different destinations.

5 An EU of intersecting 'Olympic rings' is a variation of (4) in which there are several overlapping 'hard cores' or, alternatively, a number of 'tiers' that are overlapping rather than arranged in concentric circles.

6 A Europe *à la carte* or Europe with opt-outs is where each member state chooses to opt into or out of each policy; in effect, each country is in a tier of its own and, although there may well (in practice) be a 'hard core' at the centre, such a system lacks order.

Clearly (1) and (2) are not controversial and (3) has become accepted practice in a (limited) number of areas. The contentious scenarios are provide by (4), (5) and (6), which raise the fundamental difficulty as to how the EU's institutions – particularly the European Parliament – and decision-making procedures could be suitably adapted. However, while (5) and (6) may not be workable, (4) may provide a way out of the coming impasse in which an enlarged EU may find itself:

- It provides an amicable framework within which the 'hard core' can press on while the weaker and less enthusiastic among the membership can lag behind or opt out.
- It is a more transparent mode of organisation than the various rather 'messy' alternatives.
- It provides a practical framework within which the federalist and inter-governmental wings of the EU can reconcile their positions.
- It would facilitate enlargement and allow the aspirations of applicant states to be accommodated, especially if there is free movement between tiers (subject to prospective members being willing and able to fulfil the requirements of the tier they wish to join).

However, in addition to the difficulties for the institutions, there is another potentially problematical issue: in a multi-tier EU the concept of 'membership' becomes variable. This has radical implications for aspiring EU members of the late 1990s and beyond. On the one hand, this may not seem unattractive, as it could allow new members to opt out of the aspects of EU membership that do not suit them; on the other hand, past experience of the EU's attitudes and negotiating stance suggests that a more likely scenario is that the existing EU membership will dictate the nature of the 'membership' that is on offer. If that is the case, then a multi-tier EU would be in a position to offer a lower tier of membership that amounted to little more than association.[57]

Challenges or problems?

It is possible to adopt a positive ('challenges') or negative ('problems') approach to enlargement. However, this largely misses the point. Enlargement will take place because the political reality within Europe dictates that it must. The central questions concern the terms on which enlargement will be realised and the adjustments to the workings and policies of the EU, and the *finalité politique*, that might be necessary to accommodate the new members. Enlargement will accentuate the internal divisions within the EU and lines will be drawn between different groups of EU member states within the three areas highlighted above:

1 institutional issues will divide large and small countries;
2 financial issues will split the rich (northern) states, which are net contributors to the EU budget, and the poor (southern) states, which are net beneficiaries;
3 policy questions and the issue of the future direction of the EU will divide the EU into its federalist and intergovernmental camps (broadly defined).

The scene is thus set for a period of conflict within the EU of a very complex nature with a different division of members for different issues. On the one hand, this may create the opportunity for many trade-offs and therefore agreement but, on the other, it may make agreement impossible, thereby causing the EU to grind to a halt. If the latter is the case, then the only way to square the circle may be differential integration.

Conclusion

This chapter has highlighted a range of issues raised by enlargement. It has argued that enlargement must, will and, indeed, can take place but that the EU may have to adapt its structure and embrace 'flexibility'. It has gone on to examine various forms of 'flexibility' and identified one of them – a multi-tier arrangement – as being the most feasible. Nevertheless, the EU resisted enlargement in the late 1980s and early 1990s. In part, this was an attempt to deepen before widening, by getting as much deepening as possible embedded within the *acquis communautaire* in advance of enlargement: first, the single market had to be completed, then the Delors II budget package had to be agreed, and then the TEU had to ratified. However, there was also genuine reticence about enlargement, not to say downright opposition, as evidenced by the EU's efforts to keep any reference to eventual accession out of the Europe Agreements. Moreover, there is clearly ambivalence about certain individual cases – for example, Romania, in the short run, and Turkey, even in the long run.

Indeed, the EU has never adopted an 'open door' to new members. Just as the motivation for many of the applications for membership in the 1990s has been based on negative factors, similarly the EU's motivation for accepting them has also been negative. Specifically, just as the applicant countries are concerned about the costs of non-membership, so the EU perceives substantial costs of not enlarging: first, there would be an economic cost, directly, through a lost opportunity to expand the single market, and indirectly, through the effects of migration (legal or otherwise) from the excluded countries of the former Soviet bloc into western Europe; second, this latter effect could trigger a rise in nationalist sentiment, with consequent political unrest, and there would be obvious direct political costs in the shape of an unstable and politically explosive region on the EU's immediate borders.

The EU therefore has actually no choice but to enlarge and the real issue comes down to the questions of what kind of Europe do the different (current and future) member states want and what kind is practical with a membership of twenty to thirty. There are two aspects of this: the organisational structure (most importantly multi- or single-tier/speed?) and the organisational 'philosophy' (supranational/federal or intergovernmental?). The divisions within the EU make agreement to go forward in a single-tier, single-speed framework unlikely. Therefore, a multi-tier structure, facilitating the accommodation of several 'philosophies' (and evading the need to agree on only one), may provide the most practicable means of managing the increasing diversity of the EU membership.

Ultimately, there are broadly three scenarios for the future enlargement of the EU:

- *Smooth progression.* The EU simply continues as a single-tier, single-speed organisation, with the exception of a few concessions to the 'slower' members along the lines of those that already exist (derogations during transition periods for new members, the temporary exclusion from the third stage of economic and monetary union of countries until they meet the convergence criteria and a few *ad hoc* arrangements like the Schengen Accord). In an ideal world, enlargement would take place according to the 'classical' model, with adjustment rather than change of EU institutions and policies.
- *Paralysis.* The EU would simply grind to a halt under the weight of number of members and the increase in political dissidence and divergence.
- *Adaptation*, most probably differential integration. This could take a number of forms (catalogued above) but the most ordered (and therefore feasible) variation is probably a multi-tier arrangement.

The first of these is unrealistic and the second undesirable, leaving only the third. 'Variable geometry' (or 'differentiated integration' or 'flexibility') will not be an easy option but it may be the inevitable consequence of enlargement. Acceptance of the federalist agenda that underpins much of the debate and writing on the EU will come increasingly under question as the EU enlarges further. Indeed, there is some recognition of this in the Amsterdam Treaty, which provides for 'closer cooperation' among a subset of EU members, albeit in a rather constrained form.[58] It is always easy to criticise proponents of 'flexibility' as advocates of a 'quick fix' that is badly specified and not practical. However, to ignore the tensions between the federalist and intergovernmental camps within the EU, to assume that the federal agenda can remain unquestioned and to 'hope in due course for a more positive attitude'[59] from the British and others may ultimately be even less practical. Whatever happens, enlargement will force the EU to address a range of critical issues, many of which it has been evading for some time. In the long term, this can only be a good thing for the future of European integration.

Notes

1 Strictly speaking, one should refer to the European Coal and Steel Community (ECSC) from 1951 to 1957, the ECSC plus the European Economic Community (EEC) plus the European Atomic Energy Community (EAEC or Euratom) from 1958 to 1967 and the European Communities (or Community) from 1967 until 1993. The name 'European Union' became valid only after the ratification of the (Maastricht) Treaty of the European Union. However, for the purposes of simplicity, the term 'European Union' shall be used throughout this chapter, and elsewhere in this book, even for periods during which it is technically incorrect.

2 For a comprehensive account of this process see F. Nicholson and R. East, *From Six to Twelve: The Enlargement of the European Communities*, Harlow: Longman, 1987.

3 C. Preston, 'Obstacles to EU enlargement: the classical Community methods and the prospects for a wider Europe', *Journal of Common Market Studies*, Vol. 33, No. 3.

4 For an explanation of the concept of 'adaptive' enlargement and a comparison with 'classical' enlargement, see J. Redmond, 'Mediterranean enlargement of the European Union', in P. Xuereb and R. Pace (eds), *The State of the European Union*, Malta: University of Malta Press, 1996, and J. Redmond and G. Rosenthal (eds), *The Expanding European Union: Past, Present and Future*, Boulder, CO: Lynne Rienner, 1998, Introduction.

5 European Commission, 'Agenda 2000: for a stronger and wider Europe', press release IP/97/660, Strasbourg/Brussels: European Commission, 16 July, p. 9.

6 Agence Europe, 'Luxembourg European Council: Presidency conclusions', *Agence Europe Daily Bulletin*, No. 7121, 14 December, point 27, p. 8.

7 In addition, a number of countries sought association with, or 'associate membership' of, the EU, particularly in the early 1960s. Greece (1961) and Turkey (1963) were successful but of the six other countries that explored association at that time – Austria, Sweden, Switzerland, Spain, Portugal and Cyprus – only Cyprus went on to conclude an agreement (in 1972). Malta also secured an association (in 1970).

8 A survey of extracts from the original contemporary debate is reproduced in J. Barber and B. Reed (eds), *European Community: Vision and Reality*, London: Croom Helm, 1973, pp. 235–88 (section 5, 'Growth and the British economy'). The contemporary sources represented include *The Economist*, *The Times*, *Financial Times*, *The Observer* and *New Statesman*.

9   Greece was ruled by a military junta from 1967 to 1974; democratic elections in 1976 followed Salazar's regime in Portugal; and the death of Franco in Spain in 1975 opened up the way for the emergence of democratic government there.

10 European Commission, 'Opinion on the Greek application for membership', *Bulletin of the ECs*, Supplement 2/76, 1976.

11 For a detailed account of the third EU enlargement see J. Redmond (ed.), *The 1995 Enlargement of the EU: Negotiations, Issues, Accessions and Rejections*, Aldershot: Ashgate Publishing Company, 1997.

12 For a comparison of Spain and Greece (and Portugal) see D. Ethier, *Economic Adjustment in New Democracies: Lessons from Southern Europe*, London: Macmillan, 1997.

13 European Commission, 'Agenda 2000'.

14 The one exception has been the opinion on Greece, which was essentially negative but was overruled by the Council, which decided to embark on negotiations that eventually led to Greek accession in 1981.

15 European Commission, 'Agenda 2000', p. 9.

16 However, this may change if the Commission's assertion in the 'Agenda 2000' document – 'that a decision to open accession negotiations simultaneously with these ... [five] countries does not necessarily imply that they will be concluded simultaneously' – is carried through.

17 A summary table is provided by F. Grannell, 'The first enlargement negotiations of the EU', in Redmond, *The 1995 Enlargement of the EU*, table 3.1, p. 37. See also G. Avery, 'The European Union's enlargement negotiations', *Oxford International Review*, Vol. 5, No. 3, 1994, tables 1 and 2.

18 Agence Europe, 'European Commission report on the criteria and conditions for accession of new members to the Community', *Agence Europe Europe Documents*, No. 1790, 3 July, paragraph 7. The Commission considered that it was 'neither possible nor opportune' to do so.

19 *Ibid.*, paragraph 9.

20 European Commission, 'Agenda 2000'.

21 Commission of the ECs, *Completing the Internal Market: White Paper from the Commission to the European Council*, Luxembourg: Commission of the ECs, June 1985.

22 The value of these benefits for an average EFTA country has been estimated as being two to three times as large as that for an average EU member. See V. D. Norman, 'EFTA and the internal European market', *Economic Policy*, No. 9, 1989, p. 449.

23 Treaty of Rome (EEC), Article 238.

24 See M. Kelstrup, 'Small states and European political integration', in T. Tiilikainen and I. Petersen (eds), *The Nordic Countries and the EC*, Copenhagen: Copenhagen Political Studies Press, 1993, pp. 136–62.

25 See, for a recent example, M. Holland, *European Community Integration*, London: Pinter, 1993, p. 166.

26 This category contains the key economic areas – agriculture, the structural funds and the EU – but does not include all economic aspects. A more comprehensive list would also have to address trade effects, migration and economic aspects of environmental and social policy.

27 'Progress report from the chairman of the Reflection Group on the 1996 intergovernmental conference, September 1995', reproduced in *Agence Europe Europe Documents*, No. 1951/2, 27 September 1995. For a Commission view, see European Commission, *Intergovernmental Conference 1996: Commission Opinion: Reinforcing Political Union and Preparing for Enlargement*, Luxembourg: European Commission, pp. 19–22.

28 The issues raised in this paragraph are discussed in more detail in D. Dinan, 'The Commission and enlargement', in Redmond and Rosenthal (eds), *The Expanding European Union*, pp. 21–30.

29 G. Edwards, 'The Council of Ministers and enlargement', in Redmond and Rosenthal (eds), *The Expanding European Union*, tables 3.2 and 3.3, pp. 59–60.

30 R. C. A. White, 'Reforming and adapting the institutions', paper presented at the Twenty-Eighth UACES Annual Conference, 5 January 1998, Leicester. White's calculation has been extended by the author to include Bulgaria, Romania, Latvia, Lithuania and Malta.

31 Turkey is excluded from these calculations, as it was by Edwards and White, as Turkish accession is considered unlikely in the short run. However, Turkey should really be included for completeness and, if it were, it would presumably command a similar weight to that of Germany. Similarly, it would be possible to include a number of smaller countries – such as Croatia and Albania – and they would have similar weights to the 'small' countries. Their inclusion would reinforce some of the points being made here.

32 In fact, Germany could produce a block without the support of any of the other large countries if both Spain and Poland were to vote with it.

33 In fact, the smallest group in terms of population would consist of the fourteen smallest countries (seventeen votes under the revised system) – those with two, three or four votes under the current system – plus the five countries with five votes under the current system (ten in the revised system) plus Romania (five in the revised system), giving a thirty-two votes and a combined population of 130 million, 27.2 per cent of the EU total. This would seem to be a sufficiently high proportion to be acceptable as a blocking minority, even though all the large and near-large countries would have voted in favour of the policy in question.

34 The 'troika' consists of the previous, current and next presidencies. The current presidency manages Council business with the assistance of the other two.

35 The data in this paragraph are taken from European Commission, 'Agenda 2000', p. 138.

36 S. Tangermann and T. Josling, 'Pre-accession agricultural policies for central Europe and the European Union', report prepared for the European Commission (DG I), Luxembourg: European Commission, 1994.

37 T. Josling, 'Can the CAP survive enlargement to the east?', in Redmond and Rosenthal (eds), *The Expanding European Union*, pp. 96–103.

38 The obvious method of implementation would be through quantitative restrictions on CEEC agricultural exports to the EU, or through a border tax/subsidy system similar to the monetary compensation amounts used to operationalise the green currency system. The difficulties associated with administering quotas and monetary compensation amounts are well known.

39 The cost of extending an unreformed CAP to the CEECs is calculated as being in a broad range from 4–8 billion ECU (on the assumption that CEEC production levels are unchanged) to 12–40 billion ECU (if CEEC farmers were to react to higher EU prices by increasing production). For brief survey, see J. Rollo, 'Economic aspects of EU enlargement to the east', in M. Maresceau (ed.), *Enlarging the European Union*, London: Longman, pp. 262–4.

40 This is admittedly simplistic since it implicitly refers primarily to the budgetary implications of reducing levels of price support. Clearly, to the extent that direct income support for farmers replaces price support, then subsidisation of European agriculture would be redirected through the EU budget and away from the market place; hence the direct expenditure on the CAP would increase. However, unlike price support, income support in a reformed CAP would not be paid universally, thereby reducing its (EU) budgetary impact and so, ultimately, managing the cost of income support is just another part of the CAP reform jigsaw that has to be completed if enlargement is to be viable.

41 K. Hughes, 'Managing the costs of enlargement: the structural funds', paper given at the conference Enlarging the European Union: The Way Forward, Birmingham, 1–2 July

1997, table 1: 'Structural funds: costs of enlargement'. There are four academic sources, two government (UK and Denmark) and one Commission.

42 European Commission, 'Agenda 2000'.

43 Objective 1 (underdeveloped) regions and Objective 2 (declining industrial) regions are the principal beneficiaries of the EU's structural policy and are mainly located in the less wealthy EU states.

44 European Commission, 'Agenda 2000'.

45 *Ibid.*, p. 11.

46 *Ibid.*, p. 12.

47 See, for example, C. Preston, *Enlargement and Integration in the European Union*; Redmond and Rosenthal (eds), *The Expanding European Union*; J. Redmond and L. Miles, *Enlarging the European Union*, London: Macmillan, forthcoming; plus various chapters in a wide range of general texts on the EU. See also the Commission's 'Agenda 2000' and related documents.

48 They 'go native' in the sense of becoming enthusiastic (once they join the EU) and taking on the attitudes and ambitions of the existing membership (that is, the federal agenda of the EU's founders); part of the argument is that once you join an organisation you take on a vested interest in it succeeding.

49 Strictly speaking, the EU is already multi-speed in some respects.

50 See F. de La Serre and H. Wallace, 'Flexibility and enhanced cooperation in the European Union: placebo rather than panacea?', *Research and Policy Papers* (published by the Groupement D'Etudes et De Recherches 'Notre Europe', Paris), No. 2 (revised version, September), 1997, p. 6.

51 'Reflections on European policy', reproduced in K. Lamers, *A German Agenda for European Union*, London: Federal Trust, 1994.

52 *Ibid.*, p. 17.

53 Other expressions include 'flexibility' and 'enhanced cooperation'.

54 The following inventory draws heavily on Redmond, *The 1995 Enlargement of the EU*, pp. 179–80. See also A. C.-G. Stubb, 'A categorization of differentiated integration', *Journal of Common Market Studies*, Vol. 34, No. 2, 1996, pp. 283–95; and de La Serre and Wallace, 'Flexibility and enhanced cooperation in the European Union'.

55 Similarly, it is possible to have a multi-tier, single-speed EU in the sense of having a number of tiers of membership, pursuing different subsets of EU policies, but with all the members within each tier implementing their group of policies at the same speed.

56 Obviously, the tiers could all be single or multi-speed or some could be single and some multi-speed.

57 Another alternative form of cooperation (which is not really a form of variable geometry) is parallel cooperation. This takes place alongside the EU's activities; it is not part of the EU but can include some or all of the EU membership. There is no agreement as to what extent this is ultimately intended to be incorporated into the EU. Some member states see parallel cooperation as a means of accelerating the process of European integration, while others see it as an alternative. Examples include the Schengen Agreement and the WEU.

58 See de La Serre and Wallace, 'Flexibility and enhanced cooperation in the European Union', pp. 39–41; and A. Duff (ed.), *The Treaty of Amsterdam: Text and Commentary*, London: Federal Trust, 1997, pp. 181–4.

59 Duff, *The Treaty of Amsterdam*, p. 197.

4

The enlargement of the
Western European Union

Introduction

The major European organisations outlined in this book were all created for specific purposes during the Cold War but, with its demise, they have faced the question of whether their original missions continue to be relevant. Some organisations have been faced with the task of modifying and adapting their roles in the light of new demands, while others have had to confront a more fundamental reorientation. The issue of whether to enlarge the membership of the organisations has had to be placed within a broader context of changing roles and missions.

However, the WEU has differed from other institutions, in that its actual role during the Cold War had been imprecise. Although created as a collective defence organisation, its Article 5 guarantee had been left to NATO to operationalise. It had served as a modest European identity in defence and as a discussion forum, but great care was taken to ensure its complementary nature to the Atlantic Alliance. With the ending of the east–west confrontation, it was necessary to determine a role for the WEU before the enlargement of the organisation could be justified. Consequently, the debate about the addition of new members to the WEU was linked fundamentally with defining its post-Cold War mission and relevance.

Such a view is substantiated by the history of the organisation. The foundation for the WEU, the Brussels Treaty, was signed in March 1948: partly as a way to justify an American commitment to the defence of the continent and partly as a means to concert a European defence effort.[1] It succeeded in both of these endeavours and the immediate result was the signing of the Washington Treaty and the establishment of the Atlantic Alliance. Yet, in the longer term, the second objective of concerting the defence effort of the European powers failed, because of the inability to agree upon its institutional framework, the European Defence Community (EDC). This would have been a supranational defence structure with a European Minister of Defence and integrated armed forces. In 1954 the French failed to ratify the EDC and it collapsed, raising a question mark over the future of the American role in Europe.

This led to the modifying of the Brussels Treaty and the creation of the WEU. It was designed as a facilitating mechanism to allow the Federal Republic of Germany to rearm and to enable the Atlantic Alliance to serve as the dominant defence framework for the western half of Europe. Henceforward, European states came to rest under the nuclear protection and to rely upon the leadership of the United States. The WEU fulfilled functions of secondary importance, such as promoting collaborative efforts in armament production, but it gradually fell into disuse, to the extent that by the latter part of the 1970s it was almost moribund.

In the early 1980s, the WEU experienced a modest renaissance. Because of its limited membership, it was able to reflect specifically European priorities at a time when superpower tensions were rising and there were renewed fears of an east–west conflict. The WEU, as the European identity within NATO, was shaken from its slumber in 1984 to discuss matters of European concern.[2] As a forum, it had unique strengths in being able to bring the key European countries together on defence matters but without the United States being involved. As such, it enabled the Europeans to respond to US pressures for a more equitable distribution of burdens between the two sides of the Atlantic. It also served to air French views on security at a time when Paris remained semi-detached from NATO's military structures. In 1987, the 'Hague Platform' delineated the principles upon which the organisation was based. It specified that the WEU would remain compatible with the existing defence obligations of its members.[3]

Nevertheless, despite providing a meeting place for European foreign and defence ministers, the powers of the WEU were narrowly circumscribed. The WEU had only a small, London-based secretariat and a tiny budget. Furthermore, it possessed no command structure like that of NATO, nor did it have military forces under its control during times of conflict. Its only operational experience was in 1987, when it acted as a coordination body for the European navies that were ensuring freedom of navigation and mine clearance duties in the Persian Gulf during the Iran–Iraq War.[4] The WEU remained an organisation, up until the end of the Cold War, that lacked a clearly defined role.

Yet, viewed from a different perspective, the historical weakness of the WEU could be interpreted as a source of strength in the post-Cold War environment. Unlike the Atlantic Alliance, the WEU was not tarred with the brush of bloc confrontation and consequently there was no constituency that was advocating its abolition. Providing that its member states shared a common vision, there was the opportunity for the WEU to make a clean start. It had considerable potential, because the UK, France and Germany were all among its members. There was no doubt that in the WEU these states possessed a highly malleable organisation that was capable of adapting to a variety of new demands. It was grounded upon a strong treaty base that gave it the right to be involved in defence issues, unlike other organisations, such as the EU or the Council of Europe.

Thus, in 1990, the enlargement of the WEU depended upon the answers to two questions. First, what would be the position of the WEU in the European architecture? This would depend, to a significant extent, upon its relationship with the other institutions, the most important of these being NATO and the EU. How these organisations would adapt themselves to the new situation – what roles they would relinquish and what new ones they would assume – were likely to be vital determinants in the development of the WEU. In fact, the very viability of the WEU could be assessed only in relation to these other organisations.

Secondly, and related to the above, was the question of what tasks the WEU would be expected to fulfil. It was clear that with the Cold War over, the essence of security in Europe had undergone a profound transformation. The threat of large-scale, inter-state war had diminished markedly, but in its place was an increasing risk of ethnic and civil conflicts on the periphery of western Europe. The WEU was well suited to taking on these 'out-of-area' tasks, as the Brussels Treaty did not confine its activities to the territories of its member states.[5] If, as a result of undertaking these tasks, the WEU was to become the focus of a meaningful European defence identity, then CEECs, as well as states from southern Europe, would be eager to join. If, however, the WEU remained an organisation of minor importance, then its attractiveness to new aspirants would be negligible.

The WEU's position in the institutional architecture

The relationship between the WEU and the other security and defence organisations in Europe was a highly charged political issue. NATO had been the primary western defence organisation during the Cold War and had been built upon strong transatlantic cooperation. The WEU represented the European identity in defence, but to have increased its power would have brought it into conflict with NATO. It would also have meant finding the political will among the Europeans to act in a cohesive manner on defence issues, something that had not been attempted seriously since the EDC. There was no denying the fact that the WEU had been a much less capable military actor than NATO during the Cold War. However, in a post-confrontation Europe, there appeared to be less justification for preserving the remnants of the old east–west bloc structure.

This logic was championed by countries in western Europe that had long chafed under American leadership in defence and security matters. France, for example, had consistently argued that US domination of NATO had served the United States' own interest and that the Europeans had paid an unnecessarily high price for its involvement. Now the opportunity existed to construct a new European agenda that no longer reflected the interests of extra-continental powers. With the removal of the Soviet threat, a specifically European-focused defence effort was conceivable. Although the French government did not call for the immediate termination of the Atlantic Alliance, it sought to limit its role to guaranteeing the territorial integrity of the sixteen members.[6] Paris expressed considerable anxiety lest the Alliance begin a process of adapting its functions and thereby perpetuating American domination in Europe.

Concurrently, there was pressure to forge ahead with the process of integration within the EU, a desire to complement the momentum of economic integration with political integration. This was launched in April 1990, when President Mitterrand and Chancellor Kohl called on the other member states to advance towards political union. The motivation was both a perceived need to constrain German power and a belief that the time was propitious for Europe to assert a stronger identity on the world stage. One element of political integration would involve the EU extending its competencies into the areas of foreign and defence policy. Foreign policy cooperation had hitherto been handled intergovernmentally, through the mechanism of European political cooperation,[7] while the issue of defence had deliberately been eschewed. The possibility of involving the EU in defence led to the WEU being hailed as the natural candidate to carry out this role on its behalf. In time, it was envisaged that the WEU might be collapsed into the EU as a way of bringing defence issues within the EU's framework.

Yet there were member states within the WEU that did not share such a vision. Countries such as the UK and the Netherlands were reluctant to sacrifice the proven record of the Atlantic Alliance in assuring continental stability, in order to invest in an untested European framework. They pointed to the limited military capabilities at the disposal of the WEU members, as well as the diversity of their defence interests. Because the WEU could act only on the basis of unanimity, they held a veto over its development. The UK advocated a more modest enhancement of the WEU's operational capabilities that was designed to ensure its compatibility with NATO. While France and Germany set about creating dedicated military forces for the WEU in the shape of the 'EuroCorps',[8] the UK supported only the 'double-hatting' of forces it had already declared to the Alliance.

The TEU represented a compromise in determining the WEU's relationship to NATO and the newly created EU. Agreement was reached by which the WEU retained its autonomy of action, but it was institutionally linked with the two larger organisations. The Declaration on the WEU that accompanied the TEU stated that the WEU was to be both the putative defence component of the EU and the European pillar of NATO.[9] It was unclear how this would work in practice and much depended on the political will of the European states, after the TEU was ratified, to carve out a meaningful defence capability. Therefore, the WEU was destined to sit, for the foreseeable future, in a position between the EU and NATO.

As for the WEU's relationship with the process of European integration, the TEU limited the purview of the EU common foreign and security policy (CFSP) to action in the field of 'soft' security issues. This, it was agreed, ought to include matters such as arms control, the CSCE (later renamed the OSCE) and nuclear proliferation. The WEU was given the role of representing the defence dimension of the EU and was declared to be 'an integral part of the development of the Union'.[10] The European Council had the power only to 'request' the WEU to act, thereby turning the WEU into a subcontractor on its behalf.

The most immediate problem following the signing of the TEU was how to resolve the question of overlapping memberships between the WEU, the EU and NATO. Its resolution was recognised as important for a number of reasons: it would assist in harmonising the WEU's work with both NATO and the EU, and would enable all three organisations to approach the issue of enlargement in a complementary fashion. As a consequence of these considerations, full membership of the WEU was offered only to those states that were already in the EU and NATO. An important signal was sent in this way to aspirant states that WEU membership would be contingent upon membership of the other organisations.

New types of association were created for those states that were already members of the EU but were unwilling to join the WEU. They had to be brought into a closer relationship with the WEU because of its new-found status as the EU's defence arm. The status of 'Observer' was created for the states of Denmark and the Republic of Ireland. This category accorded them the right to attend all those WEU Council meetings that were not restricted to the ten full members. They were given the right to attend meetings of the WEU working groups, at the invitation of the members, and were allowed to participate in arms collaboration programmes conducted under the aegis of the WEU. In this regard, the Independent European Programme Group had been taken over by the Western European Armaments Group in December 1992.

In addition, the status of 'Associate Member' was created for Iceland, Norway and Turkey, reflecting their membership of NATO but not of the EU. Turkey was a particularly difficult case because of its ardent and long-standing desire to join the EU and the WEU. The government in Ankara felt that it was the victim of discrimination because its arch-rival, Greece, had been granted the right of accession. Associate Membership proffered similar rights to those of Observers, but it also allowed participation in the activities of the WEU Planning Cell, thereby increasing the likelihood of involvement in future military tasks. The only limitation placed upon Associate Members was that they were unable to block a decision taken by all of the full members in the Council. These arrangements were duly accepted at the Rome meeting of the WEU in November 1992.

The experience of creating various levels of membership between 1991 and 1992 proved to be instructive when, in 1995, the EU was enlarged with the entry of Austria, Finland and Sweden. There was much to commend these former EFTA states to the WEU, as all three were prosperous nations, with stable governments and strong civilian control over their armed forces. They did not bring with them any significant disputes or tensions with their neighbours. In the light of these strengths, they could have been expected to contribute usefully to the WEU as well as to the wider stability of the continent. A precondition of their accession into the EU was adherence to the TEU, which included the CFSP and the aspiration to develop a common defence.

Nevertheless, the former EFTA states presented a problem for the WEU because they were not members of NATO and because of their traditions of armed neutrality. The absence of NATO membership made them ineligible to be offered full membership of the WEU. As for neutrality, this was incompatible with the collective defence provisions of the WEU. The ability to activate the Article 5 collective defence clause of the modified Brussels Treaty, however unlikely in practice, was regarded as a solemn and binding legal commitment. For countries such as the UK, the existence of neutral states in the EU was an important justification for preserving the separate status of the WEU. As a result of these obstacles, Sweden, Finland and Austria were granted Observer status in the WEU.

Whether the issue of neutrality is likely to remain an obstacle in the long term is open to question.[11] The sorts of military operations in which the WEU may be involved are unlikely to be Article 5 tasks but rather peacekeeping activities and low-intensity conflict. Amid these scenarios, military involvement is likely to become more variable for states, and formerly neutral states would, as a consequence, have the option of non-participation. Furthermore, many of these states would find no difficulty in being involved in peacekeeping operations; a state such as Sweden has a proud history of involvement in UN missions. Nevertheless, it would be desirable, as far as the WEU is concerned, if these states made efforts to move away from a declaratory attachment to the status of neutrality in order to make it possible for them to become full members.

The WEU's missions and capabilities

The second question that preceded enlargement was the sort of tasks that the WEU would be expected to execute: this would have a vital bearing on the organisation's future stature and its attractiveness to new members. The TEU had left deliberately vague the development of the EU as a defence actor. It declared the aim of moving towards a common defence policy, which 'might lead to a common defence'.[12] This appeared to envisage a process involving successive stages and those countries that opposed such an objective were reassured that no timetable was specified. Subsequent attempts to sketch out the concepts that would be part of a common European defence policy have experienced little progress. Discussions have focused on drawing up an agreed set of defence interests as part of a White Paper[13] but this has exposed a broad range of differences within the thinking of the national governments on defence issues.

In the Declaration on the WEU that accompanied the TEU, it was announced that the practical capabilities of the organisation would be improved. Provision was made to transfer its headquarters from London to Brussels, which would assist in greater communication between the WEU, the EU and NATO. A Planning Cell was created, consisting of some fifty staff, whose job was to draw up generic plans for possible military operations.[14] In order to underpin these plans with tangible military capabilities, it was decided that member states should be able to earmark forces to the WEU in much the same way as had always been done with NATO. This resulted in the 'Forces Answerable to the WEU' concept. Improvements since then have included the establishment of a Political–Military Group to pass expert advice to the Council, a Situation Centre to provide around-the-clock monitoring of a crisis and an Intelligence Cell.[15]

As far as the military tasks of the WEU were concerned, it was acknowledged as premature for the organisation to be responsible for the territorial defence of its members. The member states would have needed to increase their defence spending at the very time when they were seeking to achieve post-Cold War savings. Neither was there the political will evident among the WEU states to render the defence guarantees of the Brussels Treaty credible. As a result, it was difficult to see how defence guarantees could be extended to those CEECs that aspired to join the organisation. To extend guarantees to the east would have required the capacity to project military power, and the WEU was incapable of performing this task on the required scale.

In the absence of being able to offer territorial defence commitments, the WEU was left to consider what lesser tasks might lie within its range of capabilities. At the 1992 Petersberg meeting of the WEU Council, it was agreed that three new types of task would be accorded priority:

humanitarian assistance, peacekeeping operations and the employment of combat forces in crisis management.[16] Focusing on these tasks offered four sorts of benefit. First, these were the most likely types of problem to arise in the near future. Second, as they involved predominantly low-intensity operations, they would be within the capabilities of the WEU to carry out. Third, they offered the benefit of occurring outside the traditional area of NATO responsibility, which reduced the risk of institutional overlap. Finally, such operations offered the possibility for the CEECs to participate. It was judged that states aspiring to join the organisation might be able to contribute troops and resources to a WEU-led operation and that such cooperation would offer practical experience for adapting the militaries of the CEECs. For example, the three Baltic states took the opportunity of collaborating in the assembling of a Baltic Battalion (BALTBAT), designed to contribute to peacekeeping operations.[17]

However, in practice, the opportunities for the CEECs to engage in WEU-led military actions have been few, for the simple reason that the WEU has been involved in only a small number of operations. The conflict in the Balkans offered the greatest scope, but the WEU member states were reluctant to engage in activities that could have drawn their organisation into competition with NATO. Thus, when peacekeepers from the Baltic states, Poland and Hungary were sent to the former Yugoslavia, they operated under the auspices of the Atlantic Alliance rather than the WEU. In the Adriatic Sea, the WEU became involved in monitoring the UN-designated embargo[18] but this was later subsumed within the larger NATO operation. The WEU was involved in the extension of the embargo to the River Danube and this enabled states such as Romania, Bulgaria and Hungary to cooperate with the organisation. Lastly, the WEU was called upon to organise the policing of the divided Bosnian city of Mostar, at the request of the EU.

Defenders of the WEU have argued that these missions, although falling short of major military operations, have demonstrated the adaptability of the WEU and its willingness to undertake unconventional tasks. Yet critics have derided these missions as evidence that the WEU lacks a meaningful role. They have pointed to more recent examples, such as the Albanian crisis in 1997, when large-scale civil disorder broke out and the WEU failed to show the necessary will to intervene (although the WEU subsequently provided a Multinational Police Element). The fact that the WEU has drawn back from conducting military operations and has acted only in policing functions has supported the argument that the WEU's limited capabilities and its political association with the EU have deterred its members from employing it for important tasks.

The creation of the Combined Joint Task Force (CJTF) concept in 1994 reinforced the point that the WEU was militarily dependent on the Atlantic

Alliance. In order to avoid duplicating NATO's assets and command arrangements, it was agreed that the WEU would be able to borrow from the Alliance's inventory.[19] In the event of the WEU being accorded the leadership of a future mission, it would be able to request the provision of military capabilities from NATO. This was not formally agreed until June 1996, but it confirmed a veto power for the United States over operations in which the WEU acted independently. Although lauded as a new opportunity for the WEU, the CJTF arrangement symbolised its subordination to NATO and confirmed the impression for the CEECs that the Atlantic Alliance remained the dominant defence actor on the continent.

Learning from earlier enlargements

Like other organisations in Europe, the prospect of enlargement has led the WEU to recall the lessons of earlier experiences of institutional expansion. The WEU has in fact increased its membership on several occasions. To the five states that originally signed the Brussels Treaty (Belgium, France, Luxembourg, the Netherlands and the UK) were added Italy and West Germany, which joined in 1954. In 1988, Spain and Portugal were brought into the fold and Greece was admitted as the tenth full member after the signing of the TEU. Thus, on the face of it, one could argue that enlarging the WEU with the CEECs would be the continuation of an established process and should not be treated as of special significance. However, this would be to misunderstand the nature and the circumstances of the prior enlargements of the WEU.

The 1954 expansion, undertaken at a time of considerable post-war sensitivity, was an expedient measure to bring about the rearmament of West Germany. Due to the need to obtain German forces for continental defence, the western powers searched for an institutional framework to facilitate that country's entry into NATO. This was eventually found in the form of the WEU. At the same time, the WEU provided a vehicle for exercising restraints over the types of armaments procured by Germany:[20] namely atomic, biological and chemical weapons. There were also strict limitations on the range of its military aircraft and the tonnage of its submarines and warships.

The only lesson from this period applicable to the enlargement issue in the 1990s was the precedent of allowing differentiation within the WEU. The Federal Republic of Germany was unique in the extent of the constraints that were placed upon its military programmes and it was not until 1984 that the limitations were formally lifted. It could be argued that such a policy of differentiation provides a pretext for withholding the full range of benefits of WEU membership from aspiring states in central and eastern Europe. In such a way it might be possible to extend the politically important symbol of membership without taking on the burden of security guarantees to those states in the most sensitive regions of Europe, close to the Russian Federation. Yet this has been an approach that has not been adopted by the WEU, on the grounds that it would accord new members a second-class status, which would be politically unacceptable.

The next WEU enlargement decision, to include Spain and Portugal, was taken at a ministerial meeting in November 1988 and formally came into effect in March 1990. In one sense, the admission of Spain and Portugal provides an important lesson because the offer of membership was perceived, at the time, to be a way of supporting democratic government, particularly after the Franco regime in Spain. This has parallels in the current debate about eastern enlargement, where important aims include the reinforcement of stability and the encouragement of nascent democratic structures. Yet the comparison is imperfect, because by the time Spain and Portugal entered the WEU, they had been offered membership of NATO and they had each joined the EU. Therefore, their pro-western orientation and legitimacy had already been firmly established and the significance of membership of the WEU was much reduced.

In the 1990s, the major difference has concerned the environment in which the debate about eastern enlargement has occurred. Without the backcloth of the Cold War, the justification for allowing states entry into western institutions on the grounds of denying them to an adversary has no longer sufficed. The WEU would benefit little from the accession of the CEECs; rather, it would be enlarging in order to contribute to their stabilisation. Following the collapse of the Warsaw Pact and the subsequent disintegration of the Soviet Union, what might be described as a security vacuum has existed in the eastern half of the continent. The CEECs have been searching for anchors for their foreign and defence policies and the WEU, in the light of its relationship with the EU, has been viewed as a useful symbol of integration into the west.

Another difference has been that previous enlargements of the WEU involved only a few states. Never were more than two states in the process of being considered for membership simultaneously. As a consequence, the WEU was able to absorb new members with relative ease and was not forced into a reassessment of its own role in the continent's security architecture. Earlier enlargements of the WEU, therefore, had not forced the organisation to modify itself significantly in order to absorb the new entrants. The WEU was able to remain a relatively homogenous group of European states and a core grouping in relation to defence issues.

By contrast, in the current situation, up to a dozen states have been seeking admission to the WEU. This has raised fundamental questions about the impact upon the organisation if some or all of them were allowed to enter. Inevitably, the nature of the WEU, its procedures and process of decision-making by consensus would be altered by such an influx. The accession of these states might risk altering the cohesion and the unity of the organisation, as each state would bring to the WEU its own particular vulnerabilities and security perceptions. Most would be incapable of making substantial contributions to the collective effort and would be net consumers of security. Such factors as these have caused member states within the WEU to approach the enlargement question with caution.

From the Forum for Consultation to Associate Partnership

In post-Cold War Europe, it was understandable that the CEECs were un-clear about how their security could best be assured. They found themselves disorientated, without the old frameworks of the WTO or the Comecon and sandwiched between an ailing Soviet Union and a collection of bewildered western governments. Some initially considered neutrality, but this was swiftly rejected. Others, such as Hungary, floated the idea of central European states forming their own regional defence arrangement, but there was too much diversity and too little trust between them. The CSCE also received much interest, from states such as Czechoslovakia, as it did not evoke the negative memories of the east–west divide and seemed to offer the prospect of a pan-European structure.

Yet the attitude of the CEECs began to change as the Soviet Union showed itself to be willing to use force to further its aims. In January 1991, Moscow resorted to violence against Lithuania, thereby signalling that it was willing to act ruthlessly to protect its interests. Furthermore, the collapse of the Soviet Union at the end of the year raised the spectre, for the CEECs, of long-term instability on their eastern borders. Such experiences had a galvanising effect and they switched rapidly from advocating the creation of new continental security structures to seeking admission to existing western security institutions that could offer defence guarantees.[21]

As a result, the ambiguity as to how the WEU would develop in relation to NATO and the EU presented the CEECs with considerable difficulties. Determining the future importance of the WEU and what it could offer new members, at a time when there was a lack of clarity about the WEU's own status, was problematic.

Nevertheless, there remained certain attributes of the WEU that made it an attractive institution for the CEECs. First, the WEU was a manifestation of a European identity. This in itself was a desirable objective for some CEECs, as they felt that their own European identity had been forcibly suppressed during the Cold War era. The WEU consisted of a core grouping of west European states on defence issues. Joining such an inner circle would give states such as Poland, Hungary and Romania grounds for claim-ing that they were part of the western club and had 'returned to Europe'.

It would confer legitimacy over their domestic reform programmes and signal to any hostile neighbour that they were in the process of being integrated into the western community.

Second, the linkage of the WEU to NATO was seen by the CEECs as providing useful insights into western security thinking. It offered them a forum in which to acquaint western states with alternative perspectives on security issues and possibly even speed up the process of their accession into NATO. Some conceived of the WEU as a pre-accession route into NATO, serving to resolve the problems of the CEECs before granting them admission into the Alliance. In return, the WEU's relationship with NATO provided a mechanism by which western countries could encourage their central European neighbours to respect their international obligations, address intra-regional tensions and discourage the dissemination of destabilising military technologies.

Third, the CEECs were attracted by the WEU's linkage to the enormous economic strength of the EU. With the CEECs struggling to reorientate their economies from command to capitalist market systems, suffering in the process from varying levels of decline, the EU offered significant benefits, including access to the single European market, financial assistance and long-term inward investment. Additionally, the EU offered association with its CFSP, which represented a means by which the CEECs could tackle the plethora of 'low-security' issues that had emerged with the end of the Cold War.

Contact was established between the WEU and the CEECs as early as the beginning of 1990.[22] The objective was to initiate a dialogue that could inform both sides about the views of the other. The Secretary-General of the WEU, Willem van Eekelen, paid a series of fact-finding visits to the capitals of the Visegrad states, Romania and the three Baltic republics, in order to demonstrate the interest of the organisation in responding to their needs.[23] This formed the basis for a decision within the WEU that a new forum was required for the conduct of a regular dialogue with the CEECs. This was duly built up through the rest of the year and a meeting in Bonn, in 1991, announced its formalisation. At the Petersberg meeting, the WEU established the Forum for Consultation.

The Forum was innovative in that it was specifically targeted on a group of just nine countries. This approach was an important departure from that of NATO, which attempted to reach out to all its former adversaries. The Forum sought to acquaint some of the CEECs with western thinking on such issues as the promotion of stability, the CSCE and arms control.[24] In return, it provided a consultative framework for the CEECs to express their opinions on security matters, as well as a multilateral mechanism for resolving tensions with their own neighbours. Although there was no explicit reference to the possibility of membership of the WEU, the fact that nine states were invited to join the Forum carried the implicit message that these were the most eligible for future accession.

Those offered membership of the Forum were states that had entered into Europe Agreements with the EU (see chapter 3). The Visegrad states of Poland, Hungary, the Czech Republic and Slovakia[25] were regarded as automatic candidates for inclusion. They had enjoyed historically close ties to western Europe, their level of democratic and economic development was among the most advanced and their civil societies were firmly rooted. But others, such as Romania and Bulgaria, were economically and politically less advanced and were less obvious partners. Where the WEU was at its most innovative was in its inclusion of Latvia, Lithuania and Estonia. Having regained their independence in 1991, the Baltic states nonetheless remained a sensitive issue in the eyes of the new Russian government. They were, however, offered access to the Forum for Consultation as part of a strategy of including them in the EEA, despite the fact that the WEU would be unable to extend security guarantees to them.

The WEU's choice of states was guided by two considerations. First, it had to comprise countries that were acceptable to the EU.[26] Second, it had to contribute to the separate defence identity of the WEU. In its invitations to accede to the Forum, the organisation was expressing a view of its own particular place in the European security architecture. The WEU continued to be viewed as a potential competitor to NATO and by the time the Forum was inaugurated, the Alliance had taken the step of creating the NACC (see chapter 2). The Forum was deemed to be a similar development to the NACC, as both were only consultative bodies, but they were symbolically important because they were part of the process of expanding NATO and the WEU.

The CEECs that were invited into the Forum for Consultation expressed misgivings about the limited scope of the initiative. In the light of the perceived threats to their security, they regarded the Europe Agreements as overly focused on economic and technical issues. In the absence of a coordinated western position on enlargement, the CEECs recognised that they possessed the opportunity to play off the major security organisations against one another. Yet, in the light of the uncertainty surrounding the future role of the WEU, this was recognised to be a high-risk strategy. Tying themselves too closely to the WEU could have proved foolish when the WEU was unsure of its future mission.

The WEU was sensitive to the criticism that the Forum for Consultation was inadequate for the needs of the moment, but it was constrained by disagreement among its members over its relationship to the EU and NATO and by fears of alienating the United States. Efforts were made to enhance the relationship with the CEECs, but before any substantive progress was achieved, NATO announced a major initiative, the PFP programme that was unveiled at the Alliance's Brussels summit in January 1994 (see chapter 2). The PFP marked a significant departure for NATO, as it offered states a means of self-differentiation. Henceforth, states could help to determine the speed at which they drew closer to the Alliance and thereby improve the chances of their accession. Combined with the determination of the United States to lead the process, this placed NATO firmly in the vanguard of the enlargement debate. By contrast, the WEU continued to insist on approaching all nine of its Forum members as a collective group rather than differentiating between them. A decisive point had been reached in the enlargement of European organisations and it was clear that in the future the WEU was to play only a secondary role to that of the Atlantic Alliance.

When the WEU decided to increase cooperation with its eastern neighbours, it elevated the status of all nine states to that of Associate Partners. This was agreed at the Kirchberg meeting of May 1994, and the Forum for Consultation was duly superseded.[27] This new level of relationship was an echo of the Associate Member status that had been accorded to Turkey and Iceland.[28] Associate Partners were accorded the right to attend and play a full part in meetings of the Permanent Council;[29] they were able to maintain liaison arrangements with the Planning Cell and nominate forces for the conduct of Petersberg tasks (the first opportunity to do this arose with the police contribution in Albania in 1997). The only substantive power that Partners lacked was the ability to veto decisions taken by full members in the Council. In effect, the WEU granted Associate Partners the highest possible level of cooperation, short of giving them full membership.

This led to criticism that the WEU was risking its own homogeneity. The decision both to create various levels of membership and to open up its decision-making to such a range of states was regarded by some as misguided. Unlike NATO, which preserved the exclusivity of its North Atlantic Council, the WEU granted Associate Partners a voice in the inner sanctum of its organisation. For example, the Kirchberg meeting[30] of the WEU in May 1994 initiated a study by the Permanent Council of the formulation of a common European defence policy, which had been raised in the TEU. As a mark of their enhanced status, the Associate Partners were invited to play a part in discussing these ideas. This demonstrated the value to the Partners of being included in WEU activities, as it gave them a voice in policy-making. Yet critics countered that, with Slovenia becoming the tenth Associate Partner in 1996, there was now a total of twenty-eight states represented in the levels of WEU membership and this made it an unwieldy body that would struggle to find consensus.

Nevertheless, an important element in creating the status of Associate Partners was to enable the CEECs to make effective contributions to military tasks. At the Birmingham Ministerial Council meeting, it was agreed to 'keep under review ... enhancing the Associate Partners' involvement in the ... operational role of WEU'.[31] This approach was regarded as a way forward for all parties concerned: aspirant states would gain experience through cooperating with the organisation, while the WEU would be able to draw upon a wider range of military resources. Gaining a reservoir of additional personnel for military tasks was an important consideration for west European states that had been reducing the size of their armed forces since the end of the Cold War and many were switching from conscript to smaller, professional armies. Yet as far as the Associate Partners were concerned, participation in Petersberg tasks was a secondary, rather than a primary, goal. What these states wanted above all else was territorial defence guarantees and NATO was the only organisation in the foreseeable future that would be in a position to offer such assurances.

The WEU chose, by its creation of Associate Partner status, to move in advance of the EU. Not until October 1994 did the EU give states with Association Agreements the right to meet periodically with its Council of Ministers and to participate in some of its working groups. In addition, the three Baltic states, which cooperated in their approach to the WEU, became Associate Partners before they signed Association Agreements with the EU, in June 1995.[32] In this way, the WEU gave the appearance of taking a leadership role in the enlargement process. However, the CEECs were justified in remaining sceptical about the WEU's relative importance. Its overriding limitation as a defence organisation, in their eyes, was the absence of the United States as a member. The experience of Russian actions in regions such as Moldova and Chechnya led the CEECs to believe that Moscow might still contemplate employing intimidation or even force against them. In the light of these assumptions, only the presence of the United States would serve as a sufficient counterweight to deter Moscow and this refocused CEEC attention on the Atlantic Alliance.

Furthermore, there was still a credibility problem with the WEU because of its limited military capabilities. Throughout the early 1990s, the WEU struggled to generate even rudimentary operational capabilities based on the Petersberg missions. In the case of actual military crises, it was evident that the WEU lacked the requisite strength to act and that its members were unable to muster the political will for its employment. Proposals to use the WEU as an intervention force in the former Yugoslavia in the latter part of 1991 came to nothing[33] and when the UK and France took the lead in assembling the Rapid Reaction Force in Bosnia in 1995, they did so without recourse to the WEU. By contrast, NATO, under US leadership, was the organisation that took decisive action. NATO aircraft were responsible for implementing the 'no-fly zone' over Bosnia and for the selective use of force against the Serbs when the UN-declared 'safe areas' were violated. It was also under NATO auspices that 'Operation Deliberate Force' compelled the Bosnian Serbs to sit at the negotiating table. Such lessons were not lost on those states in central Europe that were eager to join western institutions. It was obvious that compared with NATO, the WEU did not enjoy unqualified support, even of its own members.

The Russian Federation and Ukraine

Because of its historically low profile, the WEU was a relatively unknown actor to the Russian government. In the 1990s, this Russian indifference towards the WEU was exacerbated by Moscow's continuing predilection to view security issues through a power politics lens. When approached from this perspective, the WEU does not appear to be very significant. On the one hand, this has been a source of opportunity for the WEU for, unlike NATO, it has not been perceived as an inherently hostile institution to Russian interests. But on the other hand, it has been more difficult for it to be taken seriously by Russia. Having less to offer than NATO, the WEU has tended to let it take the lead in relations with the Russian government, particularly as the United States has been eager to guide policy towards that country.

This is not to say that Russia has remained completely ignorant of the WEU as its role in European security has evolved. First, the fact that the TEU explicitly linked the WEU with European integration increased its attractiveness because the WEU became associated with the economic assistance programmes of the EU. Second, the linkage of the WEU to the development of the CFSP provided a form of reassurance to Russia. The CFSP concentrated on a broad range of security issues and therefore diminished the traditional focus on Russia as a residual military threat. Finally, the EU–WEU relationship pointed towards an integrated security model for the continent and reduced the likelihood of countries, such as Germany, returning to nationally inspired defence priorities.

As for Russian attitudes towards the enlargement debate, Moscow has demonstrated sensitivity to the prospect of any of the CEECs entering western organisations. Its foremost opposition has always been to NATO expansion, but it has shown no enthusiasm for the WEU either – especially as the enlargement of the WEU might be a precursor to NATO admitting new members. Russia has made it clear that it favours the OSCE becoming the central security framework in Europe, because of its pan-European nature. Consequently, the raising of CEECs to Associate Partner status by the WEU, as well as the inclusion of the Baltic states, has increased Russian concern about the organisation's chosen path. Former Russian Foreign Minister Andrei Kozyrev stated his disapproval of the WEU's Associate Partner initiative, noting that it was contrary to his government's objective of building up a collective security system embracing the whole continent.[34]

However, the Russian response was not entirely negative, perhaps in light of the more objectionable alternative of NATO enlargement. The integration process in western Europe did at least offer the prospect of exporting greater stability into central Europe and providing an additional forum for communication between Russia and the CEECs. With this view in mind, one leading Russian writer commented that, 'the West European integration center could be for [Central and Eastern Europe] a ... more efficient channel of interaction ... and guaranteed security'.[35]

The potential for increased tension between the WEU and Russia does exist. Although the WEU's linkage to the economic strength of the EU has been seen as a benign factor in Moscow, this attitude could change if the WEU were to be absorbed into the EU and the latter were to be successful in creating a common defence policy. The transformation of the EU from a politico-economic into a defence actor could bring it into confrontation with Russia, particularly if the ten Associate Partner states were granted full membership. In such a scenario, the EU could find itself attempting to fulfil security guarantees to states on Russia's border, such as Latvia and Estonia. With such a possibility in mind, the Russian government might become more vociferous in opposing the entry of the CEECs into the WEU. The fact that its opposition is currently muted may reflect a Russian assessment that the risks of such a scenario being realised are low.

Nevertheless, despite the potential for friction, Russia remains interested in improving relations with the WEU. The image of the WEU has been improved by the 1996 NATO Berlin agreement over the implementation of the CJTF concept.[36] The endorsement by the United States of the WEU taking the lead in certain low-intensity operations may have encouraged the Russian government to treat it more seriously. At the WEU Madrid Council meeting, in November 1995, it was agreed that the organisation needed to find ways to deepen its relationship with Russia.[37] One example of this has been the contract signed between the WEU Satellite Centre and the Russian state company Rosvoorouzhenie for the provision of commercial satellite imagery.[38] Another has been the potential for cooperation between the two sides on peacekeeping operations, in which the Russian Federation is becoming more active.

As for Ukraine, the WEU has long recognised its pivotal yet delicate position in European security, with Russia on one of its borders and the CEECs, eager to join western institutions, on the other. In the early 1990s, there was comparatively little interaction between the WEU and Ukraine. This was because there were perceived to be few issues on which the WEU and Ukraine could cooperate, resulting in a situation where NATO dominated relations with the government in Kiev. But from the middle part of the 1990s onwards, there has been an attempt on behalf of both the WEU and Ukraine to find new areas for dialogue and cooperation.

In July 1996, President Kuchma of Ukraine addressed the WEU Assembly in Paris and outlined his strategy for drawing his country, in practical ways, closer to western Europe. In the month following that speech, its Foreign Minister sent a request to the WEU for Ukraine to be considered for Associate Partner status.[39] The Ukraine has come to regard the WEU as a structure that would cause less concern to the Russian government than NATO, and would therefore be more politically acceptable for their country to approach. Tangible evidence of this improved relationship has been flourishing political contacts between the WEU and Ukrainian officials at a variety of levels, as well as an agreement by which the WEU might lease Ukrainian transport aircraft for the execution of Petersberg missions.[40]

The WEU in relation to NATO and the EU

The issue of WEU enlargement has remained inseparable from the wider debate about the expansion of NATO and the EU. Following the signing of the TEU, the WEU created various levels of membership within its own organisation in order to ensure its compatibility with NATO and the EU. Yet the more fundamental issue was that since its creation, the WEU had relied upon NATO to operationalise its Article 5 territorial guarantee. Without the resources of NATO, the WEU was unable to enact the core provision of the modified Brussels Treaty. Even though some commentators argued that it would be preferable to de-link the enlargement of the WEU and NATO,[41] there was no avoiding the fact that the Alliance possessed an effective veto over WEU expansion.

Furthermore, the United States made clear its view in NATO that it was unwilling to see the Alliance being enlarged via the 'backdoor' as the result of the extension of military guarantees through the WEU. In the words of Sturmer, 'It would be unwise ... for the Europeans to promise more through the WEU than the US might be willing to honour.'[42] There was also the risk that if the US Senate was made to feel that the WEU had forced upon the United States the extension of security guarantees before the appropriate time, then the whole process of NATO enlargement could be derailed.

Thus, although there had been speculation after the creation of the Forum for Consultation that the WEU might enlarge before NATO, it gradually became clear that this would not happen. The NATO PFP programme, of January 1994, signalled a more concerted effort within the Alliance towards enlargement and drew the focus of attention of the CEECs from the WEU. With the Americans spearheading the process, NATO emerged as the actor that was going to enlarge first and in October 1996 President Clinton announced in Detroit that the first wave of new members would enter the Alliance in 1999.[43] As a consequence, the issue of WEU enlargement slipped down the political agenda. There was speculation that the

WEU might serve as some form of compensation for those states that were excluded from the first wave of NATO enlargement, but it was difficult to see what the WEU could offer such countries. Having already created the status of Associate Partners, there was little more for the WEU to offer.

As NATO emerged as the pace setter in the enlargement debate, the preoccupation of the WEU turned to its relationship with the EU. Enlarging the WEU remained contingent on the prior expansion of the EU. This was a more complex issue even than NATO's enlargement, because the EU was responsible for such a broad array of issues. Taking new members into the EU was likely to prove to be a very drawn out process. For example, the economies of aspirant states had to converge with those of the existing EU members and the extensive legal *acquis* of the EU would have to be adopted. Such factors had made it very difficult to determine the way forward and contributed to turmoil within the EU over the question of expansion.

A further complication was that the EU was undergoing its own process of internal change and adaptation. With a majority of states supportive of closer political and economic integration, the EU had committed itself, within the TEU, to reassess its own situation in a second intergovernmental conference (IGC). This IGC duly took place between March 1996 and June 1997. Although enlargement was not designated as an issue for discussion, it was nevertheless a vital matter and one that the EU was scheduled to address six months after the IGC concluded. It was also widely acknowledged that unless major reforms of the EU were achieved within the IGC, such as rationalising institutional structures and speeding up the decision-making mechanisms, then the subsequent enlargement of the membership would result in the organisation's paralysis.

The IGC also threw under the spotlight the future relationship between the WEU and the EU. In the lead up to the IGC, a majority of states supported the proposed integration of the WEU into the EU. Nine out of the ten WEU members endorsed this view at the November 1995 WEU Ministerial Council meeting in Madrid. Only the UK opposed this objective, with the result that the communiqué released at the end of the meeting discussed several options for the future of the WEU.[44] The British ambassador to the WEU justified his country's obstruction by arguing that: 'Encumbering the Union with military responsibility would do nothing to enhance the ... [the EU's] contribution ... to ... security.'[45] The UK was willing to see no more than a strengthened partnership between the WEU and the EU, with contacts between the organisations improved at all levels. Its ability to wield a veto made it an obstacle that its allies were unable to circumvent.

The prospect of ending the autonomy of the WEU had important ramifications for those CEECs desirous of entry into the EU, as the latter would be based on a powerful defence guarantee. Although greater institutional simplicity would have been achieved, two difficulties were evident. First, accession into the EU by the CEECs would have been rendered more problematic, as these countries would be expected to sign up to the various defence obligations embodied within the EU. Second, there would need to be the confidence within the EU that it could operationalise the modified Brussels Treaty. It would not have been able to rely upon NATO to carry out Article 5 tasks, as the WEU had formerly done. This might have increased the EU's caution with regard to admitting new members.

In the Treaty of Amsterdam that concluded the IGC, the autonomous status of the WEU was preserved. Although Article 17 called for progress towards a common defence policy and for the fostering of closer relations between the two organisations, the WEU was not collapsed into the EU and there was no legal requirement for the WEU to act on the EU's behalf. The inclusion of the Petersberg tasks into the CFSP was the only substantial change in defence terms over what had been agreed at Maastricht. The result has been that the EU has not undertaken the substantial reforms that proponents argued would be a necessary precondition to its enlargement.

The WEU has been left in a position of limbo in the expansion process. By the time the EU enlarges, it is not clear whether those states that want to see the WEU merged with the EU will have succeeded in their objective. It has also not been clear whether states granted entry into the EU will be offered simultaneous accession to the WEU. When the EU offers admittance to its first new members, these states will probably already have been made members of NATO. As such, they will be eligible to seek accession to the WEU. A further problem could emerge if NATO enlarges to only some of the CEECs, but declines to admit the Baltic states. If Latvia, Lithuania and Estonia were then admitted to the EU, the WEU would be in the awkward position of having to perpetuate their Associate Partner status and defer their transition to full membership. In such circumstances, NATO would continue to exercise a veto over the enlargement of the WEU.[46]

Conclusion

The process of enlargement has witnessed a careful balancing act by the WEU. It has sought, on the one hand, to link itself closely with the EU by developing relations with a particular group of CEECs. This has accorded the WEU a particular identity that has distinguished its approach from that adopted by NATO. On the other hand, it has been careful to avoid making commitments that it would be incapable of fulfilling. Thus, it has sought to engage with prospective members but without entering into firm defence obligations. Its earliest initiative was the creation of a dialogue with the CEECs in the shape of the Forum for Consultation. This was later enhanced with the creation of Associate Partner status, which gave aspirant states the right to participate in the inner functioning of the organisation. Yet there the WEU was forced to stop, unable to offer states full membership.

What emerged from the institutional interaction between the WEU and NATO was the recognition that the enlargement of the WEU was less significant than that of the Alliance. The WEU became subordinate to the process of NATO enlargement once the Alliance took the political decision to admit new members. Early on, when NATO was unclear about its objectives, there was speculation that the WEU could emerge as a serious competitor to the Alliance. But this optimism rapidly faded as the greater strength of NATO became apparent. Countries such as the UK that were members of both organisations refused to allow the WEU to rival the Alliance.

Because of its linkage with the EU, set out in the TEU, the WEU has been forced to await its larger partner's chosen pattern of expansion. Although the WEU's linkage to the economic strength of the EU has been a source of attraction to the CEECs, it has not served to quicken the pace of WEU enlargement. Rather, the complexity of increasing the membership of the EU has acted as a brake upon the progress of the WEU. In addition, the future status of the WEU has been thrown into doubt by the reform process in the EU and the debate about whether the autonomy of the WEU should be preserved in the long term.

Furthermore, in addition to its institutional relegation, the WEU has been unable to clarify its functions. The Petersberg meeting went some way to defining low-level missions for the organisation, but, in practice, there has been an inability on the part of the members to let the WEU take the lead in an actual operation. Whether in the case of the Rapid Reaction Force in Bosnia or the crises in Rwanda or Albania, the WEU remained inert. In fact, the modest role that the WEU and the EU performed in the conflict in the former Yugoslavia undermined the high expectations that had previously been invested in them. The grandiose hope that the WEU would embody a dynamic European defence identity was revealed to be empty. The CEECs, not surprisingly, chose to focus their attentions on NATO, whose power to act was so evidently displayed in the events leading up to the Dayton agreement.

Even now, when NATO has taken steps to admit new members, the position of the WEU remains unclear. Accession into NATO will inevitably diminish the perceived value of the WEU. Its remaining importance will be its representation of a uniquely European expression in security matters and its potential to facilitate closer integration in the field of defence.

Notes

1   A well established debate has existed over whether the Brussels Treaty should be interpreted as an attempt to create a 'third force' between the superpowers or merely

evidence of sufficient European effort to justify a US commitment to the continent's security. See J. Kent and J. Young, 'British policy overseas: The "Third Force"' and the origins of NATO – in search of a new perspective', in B. Heuser and R. O'Neill (eds), *Securing Peace in Europe 1945–62: Thoughts for the Post-Cold War Era*, Basingstoke: Macmillan in association with St Antony's College, 1992.

2 See A. Cahen, *The Western European Union and NATO: Building a European Defence Identity Within the Context of Atlantic Solidarity*, Brassey's Atlantic Commentaries No. 2, London: Brassey's, 1989.

3 Communiqué from the WEU Council of Ministers, 'The Platform on European Security Interests', The Hague: WEU, 27 October 1987.

4 W. van Eekelen, 'WEU and the Gulf Crisis', *Survival*, Vol. 32, No. 6, 1990, pp. 519–31.

5 Article 8 specifies that the WEU Council should convene 'with regard to any situation which may constitute a threat to peace, in whatever area this threat should arise.' Treaty of Economic, Social and Cultural Collaboration and Collective Self-Defence, signed at Brussels, 17 March 1948, as amended by the Protocol Modifying and Completing the Brussels Treaty, Paris, 23 October 1954.

6 France acknowledged that NATO offered residual reassurance in relation to German unification.

7 For an authoritative survey of the development of European political cooperation, see S. Nuttall, *European Political Cooperation*, Oxford: Clarendon Press, 1992.

8 The EuroCorps was officially announced at the Franco–German summit meeting at La Rochelle in May 1992: it was to be a force about 50,000 strong and was subsequently joined by Belgium, Spain and Luxembourg.

9 'Declaration on Western European Union', in the TEU, Maastricht, 1992.

10 Title V, Article 4.2 of the TEU.

11 In the view of Ian Gambles, for example, neutrality is likely to fall gradually into disuse. See I. Gambles, *European Security Integration in the 1990s*, Chaillot Papers No. 3, Paris: WEU Institute for Security Studies, 1991.

12 Title V, Article J.4,1 of the TEU.

13 WEU Council of Ministers, 'Noordwijk Declaration', Holland, 14 November 1994.

14 B. Rosengarten, 'The role of the Western European Union Planning Cell', in A. Deighton (ed.), *Western European Union 1954–1997: Defence, Security, Integration*, Oxford: European Interdependence Research Unit, St Antony's College, 1997.

15 For further details see G. W. Rees, *The Western European Union at the Crossroads: Between TransAtlantic Solidarity and European Integration*, Boulder, CO: Westview Press, 1998, pp. 61–2.

16 WEU Council of Ministers, 'The Petersberg Declaration', Bonn, 19 June 1992.

17 E. Bajarunas, 'Lithuania's security dilemma', in P. van Ham (ed.), *The Baltic States: Security and Defence after Independence*, Chaillot Papers No. 19, Paris: WEU Institute for Security Studies, 1995, pp. 22–4.

18 'Operation Sharp Vigilance' involved the WEU in the naval monitoring of the UN embargo from July 1992. This was combined with the NATO monitoring activity in the following year and was renamed 'Operation Sharp Guard'.

19 C. Barry, 'NATO's Combined Joint Task Forces in theory and practice', *Survival*, Vol. 38, No. 1, 1996.

20 See Cahen, *The Western European Union and NATO*.

21 J. Spero, 'The Budapest–Prague–Warsaw triangle: central European security after the Visegrad summit', *European Security*, Vol. 1, No. 1, 1992, p. 67.

22 W. van Eekelen, 'Western European Union – the European security nucleus', *NATO's Sixteen Nations*, No. 3, 1993, p. 14.

23 Further details can be found in W. van Eekelen, *Debating European Security 1948–1998*, The Hague: Centre for European Policy Studies, in association with Sdu Publishers, 1998.

24 WEU Council of Ministers, 'Extraordinary meeting of the WEU Council of Ministers with states of central Europe', Document No. 1322, Bonn, 19 June 1992.

25 The state of Czechoslovakia divided into two in January 1993.

26 Through its linkage to the EU, the WEU avoided the thorny issue of establishing explicit entry criteria. At its Copenhagen summit in June 1993, the EU declared its intention to enlarge and laid down the conditions upon which it would offer membership to new states. The WEU has been able to draw upon these criteria while avoiding the opprobrium of defining its own guidelines.

27 Sir R. Johnston, 'Information report', WEU Assembly, Fortieth Ordinary Session, Part II, France: Imprimerie Allenconnaise, March 1995, p. 38.

28 'Declaration on Western European Union'.

29 Henceforth, the Council would meet in alternate weeks with its permanent members and then with the addition of the Associate Partners.

30 WEU Council of Ministers, 'Kirchberg Declaration', Luxembourg, 9 May 1994.

31 WEU Council of Ministers, 'Birmingham Declaration', United Kingdom, 7 May 1996.

32 I. Gambles (ed.), *A Lasting Peace in Central Europe*, Chaillot Papers No. 20, Paris: WEU Institute for Security Studies, 1995, pp. 72–3.

33 P. Wood, 'France and the post-Cold War order: the case of Yugoslavia', *European Security*, Vol. 3, No. 1, 1994, pp. 134–6.

34 J. Baumel, 'WEU's relations with Russia', WEU Assembly report, Document No. 1440, 10 November 1994.

35 D. Danilov, 'Development of Russian–Western European Union relations', *Nezavisimaya Gazeta* (in Russian), 27 December 1995, p. 7.

36 Press release from the Ministerial Meeting of the North Atlantic Council, Berlin, 3 June 1996.

37 Press release from the WEU Council of Ministers, 'The WEU contribution to the EU intergovernmental conference', Madrid, 14 November 1995.

38 R. Tibbels, 'WEU's dialogues with Russia and Ukraine', *NATO's Sixteen Nations*, special supplement, 1998, p. 45.

39 R. Antretter, 'The eastern dimension of European security', WEU Assembly, Document No. 1542, Paris, 4 November 1996.

40 WEU Council of Ministers, 'Erfurt Declaration', Germany, 18 November 1997.

41 See Sir Dudley Smith's comments to the Defence Select Committee, *Western European Union*, fourth report, Session 1995–6, House of Commons, London: HMSO, 8 May 1996, p. 27.

42 M. Sturmer, 'Beware of soft options for security', *Financial Times*, 12 January 1995.

43 B. Knowlton, 'Clinton targets '99 for NATO growth', *International Herald Tribune*, 23 October 1996, p. 1.

44 WEU Council of Ministers, 'WEU contribution to the EU intergovernmental conference of 1996', Madrid, 14 November 1995.

45 J. Goulden, 'The WEU's role in the new strategic environment', *NATO Review*, Vol. 44, No. 3, 1996, p. 24.

46 Antretter, 'The eastern dimension of European security'.

5

The enlargement of the Organisation for Security and Cooperation in Europe

Introduction

Before 1990, the body then known as the CSCE operated in a rather unique manner. A child of détente, the CSCE was inaugurated in 1973 with the express purpose of facilitating communication and discourse across the Cold War divide. As a consequence – and unlike NATO, the WEU, the COE and the then European Economic Community (EEC) – the CSCE from its very inception embraced a pan-European membership and agenda. The Helsinki Final Act, concluded in 1975 after two years of discussions within the CSCE, outlined principles of inter-state behaviour and political commitments in a number of fields of activity (or 'baskets'). Such breadth did occasion considerable scepticism at the time – the CSCE being seen as subordinate to the central security arrangements organised by the two alliance systems of NATO and the Warsaw Pact and as incapable of maintaining a meaningful dialogue among states with conflicting political values. Yet the CSCE was able to sustain the momentum of east–west discourse laid down in 1975, overseeing a substantive programme of contacts throughout the 1970s and 1980s. The development of the CSCE 'process', as these meetings became known, was characterised by a loose organisational structure, an eschewal of legally binding commitments and an agenda sufficiently flexible to allow both east and west and, indeed, the neutral states to emphasise issues that were deemed important. The CSCE imposed minimal obligations yet at the same time could still offer some of the benefits of multilateral diplomacy. There was then, before 1989, a sense in which the CSCE seemed functionally irresistible: it addressed a deficiency in east–west relations and embodied an inclusive ethos at a time when all other European-based organisations were premised on the exclusionary and antagonistic logic of the Cold War.[1]

In this light, the CSCE was relatively well positioned for enlargement when the Cold War came to an end and it is distinct from the other institutions covered in this book in the sense that the expansion of its membership has proven to be swift, comprehensive and, generally speaking, uncontroversial. In 1975, the CSCE could boast a membership of thirty-five participating states. Since 1991, nearly twenty new members have been added, bringing the total, as of early 1997, to fifty-four.[2] In other respects, the process of change has been somewhat more involved. The amorphous nature of the CSCE was, after 1989, no longer regarded as a virtue and consequently change has been effected in two further directions. First, the CSCE has adapted to the profound transformation that has attended the end of the Cold War by reassembling its functions and areas of responsibility. To an early preoccupation with human rights and other so-called 'Basket Three' issues has been added a role in military and security matters and, since 1992, a growing involvement in conflict prevention and crisis management. The second change has been organisational in nature – the formation and swift expansion of permanent working bodies. This process of 'institutionalisation' was symbolically crowned at the summit meeting of 1994, when a decision was reached on a change of name. Since January 1995 our subject of attention has carried the more sub-stantial sounding prefix 'Organisation' and has been known as the OSCE.[3]

Three types of enlargement, then, have affected the CSCE/OSCE: of membership, function and structure. Given that the first of these has, in principle, not been an issue of much contention, this chapter will devote more attention to the second and third. It will become apparent that this three-pronged enlargement has given rise to numerous problems. Add to this charges that the OSCE has failed to tackle many of its alleged long-standing defects and the case can be easily made that the organisation is poorly equipped to deal with the new challenges of post-Cold War Europe.[4] Such a position is not without its merits. However, it does not do justice to the OSCE. This chapter argues that what are taken as the organisation's faults are sometimes, in fact, its strengths. What is more, the OSCE has been, by virtue of its comprehensiveness, its acquisition of areas of specialisation and its organisational versatility, well positioned to play a clear role in defining and constructing post-Cold War order in the wider Europe.

Enlargement of membership

The landmark summit of the CSCE at Helsinki in 1975 was attended by thirty-five states. All signed the Final Act and were consequently designated the CSCE's original 'participating states'.[5] This group included all the states of Europe, with the sole exception of Albania, plus the United States and

Canada. The inclusion of the two North American states reflected the influence of the Cold War at this juncture. From 1975 until 1990 the CSCE was, in effect, made up of three blocs of states: those belonging to NATO, the east European members of the Soviet-led Warsaw Pact and a bloc of neutral and non-aligned states (Switzerland, Finland, Sweden and Austria).

The number of participating states remained settled up to 1990. The first significant change occurred with German unification and resulted, ironically, in a reduction in the number of participants following the withdrawal of the Democratic Republic. In mid-1991, the original number was restored with the accession of Albania, a consequence of a revised foreign policy in that state under President Ramiz Alia (itself a consequence of democratic reform launched in late 1990). Thereafter, enlargement accelerated rapidly as the CSCE accommodated new or restored states that had arisen with the break-up of the communist federations.

The most straightforward transition occurred in Czechoslovakia. An original participating state, its membership was succeeded by two separate entities, the Czech and Slovak republics, in January 1993. Somewhat more complicated were the cases of the Soviet Union and Yugoslavia. Taking the Soviet Union first, among its former constituent republics, the initial entrants into the CSCE were the Baltic states of Estonia, Latvia and Lithuania. As part of their quest for restored independence, these three requested access to the CSCE during the course of 1990. Although their cause was backed by the Nordic states and attracted a sympathetic hearing from some in the west, the Soviet Union was strongly opposed. Not until the Baltic states had been granted formal independence by a decision of the Soviet authorities in September 1991 was the way open to participation. When it came it was a smooth entrance; in a departure from the practice that had been applied to Albania, the Baltic states were not required to submit themselves to rapporteur missions to investigate adherence to CSCE commitments.

Admission for the other twelve former Soviet republics was also relatively straightforward. With the dissolution of the Soviet Union in December 1991, Russia was recognised by the CSCE as a 'continuing' state and automatically assumed the Soviet seat in January 1992. That same month the CSCE Council of Senior Officials meeting in Prague agreed to the admission of all but one of the remaining former republics. This followed letters of application which outlined acceptance of all CSCE commitments, adherence to CSCE documents on confidence and security-building measures (CSBMs) and ratification of the 1990 CFE Treaty for those within its area of application. All were also expected to welcome rapporteur missions along the lines of the Albanian precedent.[6] The January decision left just one former republic outside the CSCE. Georgia, which at the time of Soviet dissolution was in a state of civil upheaval against the rule of President Zviad Gamsakhurdia, did not submit a request for CSCE participation until February. The application was granted the following month.[7]

The extension of participation to the successor states of the former Yugoslavia was a more prolonged process. The first to acquire the status of participating states were Slovenia and Croatia, in March 1992. Bosnia-Herzegovina followed in April. Macedonia, meanwhile, had to wait until October 1995 (it had, however, been an Observer since April 1993), a delay that stemmed from Greek objections to the successor state's use of the name 'Macedonia' (Greece interpreted the name as an implied claim upon its own Macedonian territories). As for Serbia and Montenegro, these constitute the 'rump' Yugoslavia. Yugoslav participation in the CSCE has been suspended since July 1992 owing to its violation of CSCE commitments.

In addition to enlarging the number of full participants, the CSCE/OSCE has strengthened and, in some cases, forged new links with what until recently were termed 'non-participating states'. From the very beginning of the CSCE process in the mid-1970s, a wider Mediterranean dimension has been apparent, based on what the Helsinki Final Act referred to as the close geographical, cultural, economic and political links between the states of the region and Europe. Specially convened meetings were held in 1978, 1984 and 1990 involving Algeria, Egypt, Israel, Morocco and Tunisia. The key documents drawn up at the CSCE summits of July 1992 (Helsinki II) and December 1994 (Budapest) envisaged extending this cooperation and invited these states to attend CSCE/OSCE meetings of interest to them. Since December 1995, they have been known as 'Mediterranean Partners for Cooperation'. Two other states also deserve mention. The first of these, Japan, has, since 1992, forged a special relationship with the CSCE/OSCE. The Helsinki II summit invited Japan to attend CSCE meetings in a non-decision-making capacity, in the light of its extensive financial and trading links with European countries.[8] In 1994, a similar status was granted to the Republic of Korea. Both have, since December 1995, been referred to as 'Partners for Cooperation'.

Enlargement of functions

Again, the OSCE is somewhat different from the other institutions of European enlargement in the scale of the new activities it has recently taken on. Since 1990, the CSCE/OSCE has undertaken not just a redefinition and expansion of tasks already laid down during the pre-enlargement phase (1975–90) but has, in addition, assumed wholly new areas of responsibility, in the fields of conflict prevention and crisis management.

As conceived in 1975, the CSCE was a body directed at achieving a balanced dialogue between the opposing sides of the east–west divide. The original conference, which took place between 1973 and 1975, occurred against the backdrop of détente and can be understood as part of a process of recognising the reality of a divided Europe and 'routinising' the relationship between the two estranged halves of the continent. In this light, the Helsinki Final Act amounted to a grand compromise. For the states of the west, the key provisions were contained in Basket Three, in a section entitled 'Cooperation in Humanitarian and Other Fields'. This was ostensibly informed by abstract principles of human rights, but at the same time laid down very practical guidelines in four broad areas: human contacts, information, culture and education. Such standards, it was hoped, would be a corrosive influence upon the communist states. Why, then, was the Soviet Union and its allies prepared to accept such provisions? Although much of Basket Three was an anathema to them, in that it contradicted the authoritarian design of communist political systems, this section, it was calculated, could be tolerated if it meant the inclusion of other, more palatable, items in the Final Act. Of particular importance was Basket Two (on economic cooperation) and the 'Declaration of Principles' (inviolability of frontiers, territorial integrity, non-intervention in internal affairs) that formed part of Basket One, which were read as legitimising the political and territorial order laid down in the aftermath of World War Two. The essentially east–west character of the Act, finally, was also evident in a section in Basket One on CSBMs and disarmament and security, a set of provisions clearly directed at reducing tension between the opposing military–political blocs.

Following Helsinki, the concerns of the CSCE process developed along two tracks, which corresponded roughly to Baskets One and Three of the Final Act (Basket Two did not figure very highly after 1975). Of these, the principal achievements of the 1970s and 1980s lay in the latter, in what was to become known as the 'human dimension' of the CSCE. The special role of the CSCE in this field stemmed from two important features: first, the fact that no other inter-state body had made the upholding of human rights a defining aspect of friendly and cooperative relations between states; and second, the innovative use of follow-up conferences, as mandated in Basket Four of the Final Act, to review the implementation of CSCE commitments among participating states. The follow-up conferences were held on three occasions before 1990: at Belgrade (1977–8), Madrid (1980–3) and Vienna (1986–9). Often the scene of bitter east–west clashes, these were important in that they permitted the western delegations to highlight repeatedly the human rights deficiencies of the communist regimes and, by the device of adopting Concluding Documents, committed those regimes to standards of human rights that proved an inspiration to domestic opposition movements.[9] The impact of this process was indeed profound; in the words of one observer, 'it was the CSCE human dimension that was the special contribution of the Helsinki process to the dramatic changes in eastern Europe and to the passing of the Cold War.'[10]

The second area of CSCE concerns after 1975, that relating to military and security issues, became increasingly apparent during the 1980s, although it should be pointed out that the specific responsibility of the CSCE was a rather loose one. The clearest connection lay in the area of CSBMs. As noted above, attention to these formed part of Basket One of the Final Act, in which a range of commitments was listed that aimed at facilitating transparency and predictability of military activities. At Madrid, a mandate was given for negotiations on CSBMs, which subsequently gave rise to the 1986 Stockholm Document. At the Vienna follow-up meeting, further CSBMs negotiations opened in 1989, on this occasion resulting in the 1990 Vienna Document.

Less clear cut was the role of the CSCE in the framing of the 1990 CFE Treaty. Often described as falling within the CSCE framework, this was so only in a symbolic sense. The Vienna Document had provided a mandate for the CFE talks and the 1990 Paris summit of the CSCE was the setting for the signing of the treaty. However, that mandate had been granted only to the twenty-three states of NATO and the Warsaw Pact, which signed a separate agreement to that effect. This was done deliberately to exclude the European neutral states and to ensure that the final document would have legal force. The CFE Treaty was, in other words, distinct from CSCE documents, which were traditionally characterised by comprehensiveness and a non-legal, political status.[11]

The post-Helsinki development of the CSCE reached a watershed in 1990. The end of the Cold War transformed the security and political order in Europe and with it the operational basis of the CSCE. The inter-bloc character of the organisation that had persisted since 1975 was rendered obsolete by two parallel developments: the end of communist rule in Europe (a process begun with the coming to power of Solidarity in Poland in 1989) and the disbanding of the Warsaw Pact. This alone required a fundamental functional reorientation of the CSCE. Add to this subsequent developments such as the eruption of civil wars in Yugoslavia and parts of the former Soviet Union and the need was even more apparent.

The manner in which the CSCE has altered in response has depended on the outcome of debates that reflected the interests of specific states. This will be considered in some detail under the heading 'Perceptions of the OSCE', below. But first we shall examine the enlargement of CSCE functions from a somewhat more detached position, considering how these have been defined in official documentation since 1990, and looking briefly also at the development of CSCE/OSCE activities in this same period.

The most authoritative documents have been those adopted at CSCE/OSCE summits. The Paris summit of November 1990 was convened at the height of euphoria in Europe at the prospects for continent-wide co-operation. At this juncture several assumptions fed a general optimism concerning the emerging post-Cold War order. In the first place, there was a belief among all the CSCE participating states that the Soviet Union, while it might transform itself (Mikhail Gorbachev's project of economic and political reform was, by 1990, in full flow), would continue to exist and that an attenuated Soviet power was material to the unfolding new order in Europe. To this was added an assumption that threats to security would continue to be defined in inter-state terms. There was no real perception even as late as 1990 of the dangers of dissolution that were soon to be visited upon both the Soviet Union and Yugoslavia, or of the problems that minorities might face in these fragmenting states. Even though the CSCE was half-prepared for intra-state issues as a consequence of its prolonged attention to human rights, the notion of it undertaking intrusive protection was at this point absent. A third assumption was even more sweeping, to wit, that with the Cold War and the ideological competition between states over, a natural harmony of state interests, or at any rate great power interests, would emerge. Such thinking was apparent not just in President George Bush's much-maligned notion of a new world order, but also in Gorbachev's espousal of pan-human values and the notion of a 'Common European House'.

This sense of optimism imbues the key document adopted at the Paris summit, 'The Charter of Paris for a New Europe'. It speaks of the end of confrontation and division in Europe – of a continent 'whole and free', in which states are bound by a new spirit of respect and cooperation. Furthermore, the Charter, while redolent in parts of the Final Act (it makes constant reference to the Declaration of Principles and its thematic sections – on the human dimension, security and economic cooperation – closely mirror the baskets outlined in 1975), also broke new grounds in its unabashed commitment to democracy, the rule of law and economic liberalism. With the demise of communism well advanced in eastern Europe and the Soviet Union, no state was able to mount a defence of political or economic alternatives and the Charter marks the first time in which the values associated with western democratic capitalism are posited as the preferred political and economic norms for all the states of Europe.[12] This marked an important step in the standard-setting function of the CSCE.

By the time of the Helsinki follow-up and summit meeting of 1992, most of the assumptions underlying the Paris summit had evaporated. The formal winding up of the Warsaw Pact during 1991, coupled with the collapse of Yugoslavia and the Soviet Union, ended what had, during the period of the Cold War, been a moratorium on inter-state and inter-ethnic conflicts in eastern Europe imposed by centralised communist federalism and Soviet regional hegemony. The consequent outbreak of Serbian–Croatian hostilities (followed in 1992 by the expansion of war into Bosnia-Herzegovina) and the escalation of localised conflagrations throughout the former Soviet Union (FSU) were testament to the reappearance of armed warfare in Europe. These hot disputes were complemented by a proliferation of ostensibly non-violent, yet potentially escalatory, disagreements over borders and the status of minorities. The resurgence of nationalism and ethnic exclusivism that largely underpinned this catalogue of ills was made that much more lethal, moreover, by the presence in both eastern Europe and parts of the FSU (notably, Russia, Ukraine and Belarus) of bloated militaries, awash with weaponry yet uncertain of their new role in the security vacuum left by collapse of the Warsaw Pact and, in the case of the FSU, the largely unsuccessful efforts to construct a collective security arrangement under the umbrella of the CIS.

The documents issued at Helsinki consequently reflect a rather sombre mood. The summit declaration refers in paragraph 12 to 'Gross violations of CSCE commitments' and the threats of economic decline and political instability in the former communist states. Paragraph 13 is even more forthright and is worth quoting in full. In it, fifty-one heads of state or government (Yugoslavia was excluded from the meeting) state:

> For the first time in decades we are facing warfare in the CSCE region. New armed conflicts and massive use of force to achieve hegemony and territorial expansion continue to occur. The loss of life, human misery, involving huge numbers of refugees have been the worst since the Second World War. Damage to our cultural heritage and the destruction of property have been appalling.

The weight attached to the particularities of Europe's deteriorating security situation was also apparent in the 'Helsinki Decisions'. This document dedicated an entire chapter to early warning, conflict prevention and crisis management and, in the process, endorsed the concept of CSCE peace-keeping. While other, more traditional, CSCE concerns are also evident in the 'Decisions', notably a renewed commitment to negotiations on dis-armament and CSBMs and a further elaboration of human dimension commitments, for the first time at a follow-up meeting such matters were overshadowed by the immediate problems of destabilisation throughout parts of Europe.[13]

The rather jaded feel of the Helsinki summit was also apparent at Budapest two years later. Its concluding compilation document, 'Towards a Genuine Partnership in a New Era', is informed by a desire for a consolidation of the CSCE in what by now was viewed as an enduring environment of instability. With an eye to the challenges of post-communist transition and the continuation of conflicts in some of the Soviet successor states and the former Yugoslavia, the summit declaration observed the need for 'resolute action', to allow the organisation 'a cardinal role in meeting the challenges of the twenty-first century'. While there are few innovations in this document, it is nonetheless significant for its systematic itemisation of ongoing CSCE concerns. Thus, in addition to the familiar sections dedicated to the human and economic dimensions and security issues, there is a further adumbration of CSCE 'capabilities' in the areas of conflict prevention and crisis management. There is also, for the first time in such documentation, an enumeration of 'the future role and functions' of the body.[14] This attends to both old concerns (the setting of standards and norms, work on the human dimension and the enhancement of security through disarmament and CSBMs) and new areas of attention (preventive diplomacy, conflict resolution, crisis management, peacekeeping and 'post-conflict rehabilitation'). A 'Code of Conduct on Politico-Military Aspects of Security' was also adopted at Budapest. This is a similar compendium document; it reaffirms the 1975 Declaration of Principles and builds on a provision mooted at human dimension discussions in 1991 on the civilian control and proper use of armed forces in internal security missions.[15]

Pragmatism and consolidation were also characteristic of the Lisbon summit, held in December 1996. The concluding summit declaration on this occasion was brief and precise, reaffirming as it did tasks outlined at Budapest, or highlighting areas of special concern (Chechnya, Nagorno-Karabakh and Bosnia-Herzegovina).[16] Those lengthier documents adopted at the summit, relating to security issues, similarly confirmed ongoing business (see below).

Moving on to the practical activities of the CSCE/OSCE in the period since 1990, it might be useful to adopt a classification employed in the OSCE's own recent literature. This considers the 'operational profile' of the organisation as embracing, *inter alia*, the following areas:

1 early warning, conflict prevention and crisis management;
2 the human dimension;
3 military aspects of security;
4 the economic dimension.[17]

The first of these has been the main area of expansion in CSCE/OSCE activities. It has developed since 1991 largely in response to the proliferation of local conflicts and seats of tension in the eastern half of the CSCE/OSCE area. Work in the field has taken place in several ways.[18] The long-term mission is the most commonplace – ten such operations had been mandated as of July 1998. Their work has been rather diverse, being aimed at either promoting political solutions in areas of recent or ongoing conflict (Georgia, Moldova, Tajikistan, and in Sarajevo and Bosnia-Herzegovina more broadly) or staving off conflicts in areas of major dispute (Kosovo, Sanjak and Vojvodina in Serbia, Skopje in Macedonia, and in Estonia, Latvia, Ukraine and Croatia).[19] At times, missions working in these fields have complemented the efforts of the OSCE High Commissioner for National Minorities, a post created at Helsinki in July 1992 with the express purpose of providing 'early warning' and 'early action' aimed at diffusing situations of tension. Working to similar ends, the OSCE has also provided representatives to sit on commissions tasked with the implementation of bilateral inter-state agreements. Thus far, this has applied to two agreements, one signed by Russia and Latvia (on the rights of Russian military pensioners and the operation of the Skrunda radar station) and one between Russia and Estonia (again, concerning military pensioners).

It is also worth noting three rather *ad hoc* CSCE/OSCE undertakings in this field. That in Nagorno-Karabakh (Azerbaijan) has been the subject of two OSCE innovations. Here, the OSCE has, since March 1992, through the so-called Minsk Group, prepared for a conference to endorse a unified peace plan. The conflict is also, under decisions taken at Budapest, the potential site of the first ever OSCE peacekeeping operation. Neither of these innovations, however, has yet materialised, owing to the entrenched differences between the parties to the conflict itself (Armenia, the Karabakh Armenians and Azerbaijan).

The Assistance Group to Chechnya (part of the Russian Federation), established in April 1995, also has some operationally distinctive features. Unlike formal long-term missions – which it resembles in some respects – the engagement in this case has, uniquely, been tasked with assisting the return of refugees and the delivery of humanitarian aid. It also helped organise elections in the territory in January 1997. In all these areas, the Group may be regarded as path-breaking, representing as it does a rare example of international involvement in Russian domestic affairs.

In Albania, in the face of a near collapse into civil war in March 1997, the OSCE Chair-in-Office appointed a special representative, who was able to mediate a political settlement that both contained the crisis (preventing any spill-over into the Kosovo region of the Federal Republic of Yugoslavia) and paved the way for the holding of parliamentary elections in June. An OSCE 'presence' (as distinct from a formally mandated long-term mission) was subsequently established in the country to undertake on-going efforts at political mediation.

The second area of post-1990 OSCE activites has been work related to the human dimension. The importance of this topic during the 1970s and 1980s was noted above and it would be fair to say that the standards associated with the human dimension continue to inform all aspects of the

OSCE's work. During the 1990s, activity in this field has, in OSCE parlance, moved 'from standard setting to implementation', a shift based on a recognition that work related to the former had reached a satisfactory level (in addition to Basket Three of the Final Act, important documents were elaborated between 1989 and 1991 at three meetings in Paris, Vienna and Moscow dedicated specifically to the human dimension). Since 1991, attention to the new task of implementation has been based on two principles of action: first, that human dimension undertakings apply equally throughout the OSCE area – they are as relevant in the participating states of the former communist east as they are in the western democracies; and second, human rights issues are a matter of common concern. In the language of the document of the 1991 Moscow meeting of the human dimension, violations of human rights cannot be hidden behind the right of the offending state to exclude outside interference in its internal affairs.[20]

As for work on the ground, the OSCE has, during the 1990s, concentrated its human dimension efforts on the former communist states. Through its Office for Democratic Institutions and Human Rights (ODIHR), the OSCE has, since 1992, monitored elections and referenda in Russia, Hungary and most of the new participating states of the former Yugoslavia and the FSU.[21] The ODIHR has also organised a series of seminars on issues ranging from local democracy and legal reform to national minorities and migrant workers. It has offered advice on the framing of new constitutions (in Tajikistan and Georgia) and has overseen wide-ranging Implementation Meetings that have reviewed the practicalities of human dimension monitoring.[22] In the important case of Bosnia-Herzegovina, the 1995 Dayton agreement mandated the OSCE to appoint a human rights ombudsman, to oversee negotiations between the warring parties on local CSBMs and disarmament, and to organise and monitor elections. The latter have been especially significant. In September 1996, the OSCE helped organise and oversaw voting for six separate categories of office in elections described by its monitors as being among the most complicated in history.[23] Twelve months later, the OSCE also undertook an equally sensitive supervisory role of parliamentary elections in Republika Srpska, the Serb-run part of Bosnia-Herzegovina, and in September 1998 it organised a further series of ballots, on this occasion monitoring seven separate elections.

Turning to military issues, here the work of the OSCE may be characterised as being directed towards 'cooperative security' among its participating states.[24] Its activities have entailed neither the provision of security guarantees nor formal defence commitments, but have been aimed rather at the construction of a security regime that commits its members to peaceful change, compliance with certain norms of behaviour and the furtherance of practical measures that enhance confidence and trust.[25]

Reflecting these principles, several documents were approved at the Budapest summit. The 1994 Vienna Document on CSBMs (itself an enlargement of similarly named documents agreed in 1990 and 1992) and the Code of Conduct mentioned above were perhaps the most noteworthy. Others related to non-proliferation, arms transfers, the exchange of military information and military contacts. A decision was also taken to develop within the OSCE a 'Common and Comprehensive Security Model for the Twenty-First Century'. This has subsequently given rise to discussions on two documents: a 'Platform for Cooperative Security', intended to outline the scope and technicalities of cooperation between the OSCE and other security bodies, and the 'Charter on European Security', a politically binding text that is meant to reflect in 'a comprehensive way the changes that have occurred in Europe [while] outlining the foundations for identifying the responses [of the OSCE] to them'.[26] In addition to these initiatives, the OSCE has, following the precedent of the CFE Treaty, also assumed the status of 'political guardian' of a number of military-related agreements. These include the 1992 CFE-1A agreement on military personnel limits, the 1992 Treaty on Open Skies and the 1995 EU-initiated Pact on Stability in Europe.[27] At the 1996 Lisbon summit a decision was reached on a 'Framework for Arms Control', which foresaw linking these and other more obviously OSCE arrangements (specifically, CSBMs) into a 'web of interlocking and mutually reinforcing arms control obligations and commitments' that would 'serve as a guide for future arms control negotiations ... and as a basis for the establishment of a flexible agenda for future work on arms control'.[28] Negotiations on a revision of the CFE Treaty, the cornerstone of the envisaged arrangement, began in January 1997. While the treaty is, strictly speaking, not an OSCE measure, the mandate for the negotiations did nonetheless reaffirm the organisation's political connection to CFE issues.[29] Under the mandate, the treaty's adaptation was seen as a part of ongoing OSCE discussions within the framework of the Common and Comprehensive Security Model. It was also envisaged that the negotiations would be reported to the OSCE's Ministerial Council and Forum for Security Cooperation.

Finally, the fourth aspect of the CSCE/OSCE's operational profile, the economic dimension, has always been a rather marginal area of its activities. Despite the aim of pan-European economic cooperation expressed in Basket Two of the Final Act, political considerations during the 1970s and 1980s precluded the development of substantive economic ties across the east–west divide. The fall of communism removed these political obstacles and opened the way to a modest role for the OSCE. This has been limited largely to encouraging dialogue among the participating states on the problems associated with the transition from planned to market economies. For these purposes, an OSCE Economic Forum has convened annually since 1992 and occasional seminars have been held on matters such as tourism, infrastructure and the promotion of small and medium-sized business.

Enlargement of structure

In the first fifteen years or so of its existence, the CSCE was organised in a rather unique manner for an international body, in that it lacked permanent political or administrative structures. This was, in fact, deliberate and reflected the vested interests of the states of both east and west during the Cold War. The communist states, led by the Soviet Union, wished to prevent giving permanency to any body that might constrain their freedom of action or, indeed, question the political basis of their regimes. By contrast, many western states felt that an organisational enhancement of the CSCE would have the effect of legitimising the status quo in Europe and, equally pernicious, of allowing the Soviet Union a say over developments in western Europe.[30] These calculations had the effect of creating a CSCE that was less an organisation than a 'roving conversation', moving from one capital city to another without any long-term schedule or body of administration. Yet these activities were more than simply a gravy train for the diplomats of CSCE participating states. The length of follow-up meetings reflected both the importance and the arduous nature of the work of the CSCE. Taking account also of the practice of convening expert seminars and inter-sessional meetings on selected topics (the Mediterranean, peaceful settlement of disputes, the human dimension, etc.), this meant that the CSCE was vested with an air of dynamism and a sense of organisational identity. Moreover, the absence of an institutional base was in one sense an asset, allowing the CSCE a flexibility absent in more formal organisations. Untrammelled by a large bureaucracy and unnecessary procedure, its meetings could be held without time limit and were free to engage in 'linkage' politics. This often encouraged showmanship and deadlock, but on occasion proved fruitful in arriving at package deals that contained mutual concessions and agreed compromise across the east–west divide.[31]

Under-organisation, then, was closely tied to the CSCE's position as a bridge across the bloc system of the Cold War. With the winding down of the Cold War, and with it the emergence of putative new areas of CSCE responsibility, this state of affairs began to be viewed as both anachronistic and inappropriate. In the run-up to the Paris summit, proposals for the development of the CSCE were offered from various quarters that reflected differing expectations of and assumptions about its role in post-Cold War Europe. All these suggestions shared a common appreciation of the need for organisational development of some kind. This ensured that the inclusion of a chapter on 'New Structures and Institutions' in the Paris Charter was achieved without any real controversy, despite the fact that it bore a close resemblance to proposals contained in NATO's 'London Declaration' of the previous July (see chapter 2).

The 'institutionalisation' initiated at Paris has continued. Functions have been redefined, certain bodies renamed and new structures created. By the close of 1996, the OSCE comprised the following organs:[32]

- *Summit meetings* of heads of state and government have, as noted above, been held at Paris, Helsinki, Budapest and Lisbon. Their purpose is to 'set priorities and provide orientation at the highest political level'.[33] The summits are preceded by a review conference (before Budapest, known as a 'follow-up' meeting).
- The *Ministerial Council* (formerly known as the CSCE Council). This meets at least once a year, is designated under the Helsinki Decisions as the OSCE's 'central decision-making and governing body' and is made up of the foreign ministers of participating states.
- The *Senior Council* (known until December 1994 as the Committee of Senior Officials). This body is subordinate to the Ministerial Council and is responsible for preparing and carrying out its decisions, as well as setting budgetary guidelines for the OSCE as a whole. It meets at least every three months and is based in Prague. Once a year it convenes as the *Economic Forum*.
- The *Permanent Council*. Set up in December 1993 (when it was known as the Permanent Committee), this meets weekly in Vienna, is made up of permanent representatives and is responsible for 'the day-to-day operational tasks' of the OSCE. When the Senior Council is not in session it takes important decisions on all areas of OSCE concern.
- The position of *Chair-in-Office* (CIO) was established in December 1992. It is taken by the foreign minister of the state that last hosted a meeting of the Ministerial Council. The Chair-in-Office presides over meetings of the three separate councils listed above and is responsible for co-ordinating OSCE business. The holder of the office has the power to appoint personal representatives, create *ad hoc* steering groups and is assisted by the previous and succeeding Chairs-in-Office (thereby forming a group known as the 'troika') and a *Secretary-General*.
- The OSCE *Secretariat* was originally established in 1991 and was located in Prague. This office is responsible for servicing the Senior Council. As OSCE activities have increased in recent years, so too has the work of the Secretariat. Since 1993 it has acquired an additional site in Vienna, concerned with supporting the Chair-in-Office and housing the Conflict Prevention Centre, the Department for Conference Services and the Department for Administration and Budget.
- In line with a call in the Paris Charter for greater parliamentary involvement in the CSCE, a *Parliamentary Assembly* was established in

April 1991 from parliamentarians of the participating states. It has a permanent secretariat based in Copenhagen and meets annually to discuss OSCE affairs. Its decisions are relayed to the Ministerial Council, although these carry the force only of recommendations.

- The OSCE also embraces a number of specialised bodies. These include the *ODIHR*, the *High Commissioner for National Minorities* and the *Forum for Security Cooperation*, which have already been noted, and the Geneva-based *Court of Conciliation and Arbitration*.

The OSCE's threefold enlargement – of membership, functions and structure – has so far been presented in largely neutral terms. Yet one should not lose sight of the fact that this outcome conceals a wide variety of opinions among the participating states on the mechanics of enlargement itself and, more generally, on the purposes of the organisation in the new European order. It is to these debates that we now turn.

Perceptions of the OSCE

Opinion of the OSCE among its participating states has never been uniform. Yet, crucially in the context of this book, there has been little disagreement over the desirability of enlarging the organisation's membership. The two waves of enlargement that have occurred since 1990, involving first the Soviet successor states and latterly the former Yugoslav republics, occurred with little controversy. In late 1991, the United States did table some reservations to the effect that the admission of a large number of new entrants would upset the 'chemistry' and the approach of the then CSCE, and the Committee of Senior Officials at its meeting in March 1992 was reportedly divided over the Yugoslav cases. However, in both instances differences of opinion did not prove a lasting obstacle. American concerns, for instance, were short lived. By the time of the Soviet Union's dissolution, a consensus was apparent among the western states. The inclusion of the Soviet successor states within the CSCE was seen as necessary, both for promoting the standards associated with the human dimension and for linking these new states with European structures, in the process reducing the possibility of their gravitating towards other regional groupings. This was a calculation born of fears of Iranian influence in central Asia,[34] but, equally, of Russian-led structures in the area of the FSU. As for the former Yugoslavia, at issue here was not the principle of enlargement itself, but rather its timing and the method by which it was to be achieved. Greek concerns over Macedonia have been noted above and to this one might add calls from Russia and the EU 'twelve' that preference be accorded to Slovenia and Croatia.[35] Yet here, too, agreement was soon reached. Indeed, somewhat ironically, the major dispute over membership in this case was occasioned not by enlargement, but rather by the suspension of an existing participating state – Russia taking particular exception during 1992 to moves to eject the rump Yugoslavia.

Rather than the size of its membership, what has divided the OSCE's participating states to a far greater degree is the question of the organisation's purpose in the post-Cold War era. Here the debate has fallen into two distinct periods – the first centres around the time of the Paris summit and was related to the place of the CSCE in various proposed schemes of European security. This debate had tapered off by the time of the Helsinki summit in 1992. It was revived in 1994 as a consequence of NATO's mooted enlargement, although in this second period it has been somewhat less existential; with the important exception of Russia, a good deal of agreement has been evident in this period on avoiding the grandiose and confining the OSCE to delimited, specialised fields.

Returning then to 1990, at this juncture views of the CSCE were conditioned by the seismic changes then unfolding on the European continent, notably the process of east–west rapprochement, the removal of communist rule in parts of eastern Europe and the emergence of a unified Germany. The importance accorded to the CSCE was evident in a variety of proposals put forward in the run-up to the Paris summit. The then West German Foreign Minister, Hans-Dietrich Genscher, for instance, saw the CSCE as a body whose development as a pan-European security organisation might eventually supplant both NATO and the Warsaw Pact.[36] This was seen explicitly as a means of assuaging concerns in the Soviet Union over German unification, in that a greatly empowered CSCE would, in Genscher's phrase, provide Moscow with 'a guarantee ... that it can play a full role in Europe'.[37]

The Soviet attitude toward the CSCE, however, was not so straightforward and cannot be seen as primarily linked to the German question. Soviet leader Mikhail Gorbachev, having called in December 1989 for a CSCE summit as a means of reaffirming the permanence of the two Germanys,[38] soon after reversed this policy and gradually shifted towards acceptance of German unification. He was, however, reluctant to agree to the enlarged country's inclusion in NATO, proposing at one point a pan-European security body based on the CSCE as an alternative. Yet endorsement of NATO membership did eventually follow. And when it came, at a Soviet–German summit in July 1990, it was not the result of any assumption that the Alliance would be replaced by the CSCE. It was rather the product of a complex of reasons relating to German pledges on military policy and the shift in NATO strategy (signalled in the 'London Declaration') away from forward defence and flexible response.[39] Yet while Gorbachev was seemingly prepared to accept the reality of NATO's survival, it was hoped that the Alliance could still be marginalised in some way by an invigorated CSCE. Here, his motives were linked to fears of a possible security vacuum in eastern Europe in the event of the Warsaw Pact's dissolution and any consequent Soviet military withdrawal. The CSCE, in this context, was seen as providing a means of averting the prospect of NATO encroachment into this sensitive area.[40]

The wisdom of Gorbachev's approach appeared to be borne out by the fact that post-communist regimes, notably in Poland and Czechoslovakia, were, during 1990, among the strongest proponents of a strengthening of the CSCE. Indeed, these states argued that the CSCE could become the cornerstone of a new collective security system on the continent, replacing both NATO and the Warsaw Pact – two organisations whose rationale, it was claimed, had vanished with the winding down of the Cold War.[41]

Affection for the CSCE, however, was less pronounced in Washington and London, where the assumption was shared that NATO would remain the linchpin of European security. Secretary of State James Baker's speech on the 'architecture' for a 'New Europe', delivered in December 1989 in the wake of the fall of the Berlin Wall, significantly conceived the role of the CSCE as limited in the security sphere to enhancing CSBMs; its primary responsibilities were, in fact, seen as facilitating economic and political transformation in eastern Europe.[42] In an address on the CSCE the following June, Baker stuck largely to these themes, although by this point the organisation was conceded a further security role, in the form of dispute management.[43] This view of a clearly delimited CSCE was one shared by British Prime Minister Margaret Thatcher;[44] and the communiqué of NATO's London summit largely reflected the Anglo-American position. This document did accord the CSCE a prominent place in Europe's future, but not as a security organisation. Security aspects were admittedly foreseen, but these again were limited to CSBMs and the establishment of a conciliation mechanism. Moreover, with the partial exception of giving an imprimatur to a CFE Treaty, the purpose of the CSCE's Paris summit scheduled for later that year was seen as preparing to adapt, in the service of expressly political and economic objectives.[45] The institutionalisation endorsed at Paris largely reflected this assumption, hence Thatcher's boast on her return from the summit that the CSCE 'is not a defence organisation and we should not try to make it one'.[46]

The outcome of the Paris summit led to a rapid disillusionment with the idea of transforming the CSCE into some form of pan-European security body. Although the organisation continued to be lauded on various grounds (it was seen, for instance, as the best device for addressing, politically, the emergent spate of inter-ethnic conflicts in eastern Europe and the Balkans), attention, even of advocates of the CSCE, such as Poland and Czechoslovakia, now turned elsewhere. The security predicaments that faced the east European countries following key events in 1990–1 – the termination of the Warsaw Pact, the dissolution of the Soviet Union and the eruption of war in Yugoslavia – were now viewed as being best addressed through the cultivation of ties with NATO. In economic matters, similarly, integration with western institutions (in this case with the EU) was held to be most beneficial.[47]

The allure of established western organisations was also apparent among the successor states of the FSU, including the new Russia. Reflecting an early Atlanticist tendency in its foreign policy, Boris Yeltsin, in a remarkable admission shortly after the Soviet Union's demise, suggested that Russia might, in the long term, seek NATO membership. Although soon moderated to calls for 'partnership', this was an outlook that nonetheless accorded a far lower priority to the CSCE than had Gorbachev.[48] Ukraine, similarly, vested its initial hopes in some form of NATO-based arrangement. During 1992 Kiev entered into negotiations with the three nuclear powers of the Alliance (France, the UK and the United States), seeking security guarantees as a precondition for relinquishing its nuclear arsenal.

Among the western countries themselves, policy in the wake of the Paris summit evolved largely along familiar lines. The Anglo-American position that the CSCE should not develop to the detriment of NATO was implicitly endorsed by the Alliance in November 1991 with the adoption of the new strategic concept.[49] Secretary of State Baker at this juncture also repeated the now standard line that the CSCE should be accorded a role in European security but one fixed to specific responsibilities in the areas of conflict prevention and resolution.[50] Moreover, where some movement in thinking was apparent, it was, significantly, towards the American position. In the case of Germany, Genscher's arguments in favour of a CSCE-based security system had been effectively rendered redundant with the dissolution of the Soviet Union. In May 1991, a form of words was agreed between Genscher and Baker that preserved the idea of an elevated CSCE, but which at the same time accepted NATO's continuing primacy in the security sphere.[51] This relationship was confirmed some twelve months later, at the June 1992 Oslo ministerial meeting of NATO. Here, a decision was taken to allow, in principle, the seconding of Alliance resources for mooted CSCE peacekeeping, but this was less a means of empowering the CSCE than a method by which NATO could retain for itself a sanction on the deployment of military force in Europe.[52]

The CSCE was downgraded also, albeit in a rather different manner, with the framing of the TEU in December 1991. Its provisions on a CFSP, by specifying the WEU as the medium for EU defence cooperation, effectively put paid to any residual European advocacy of the CSCE (on the part of France as well as Germany) as either the successor to, or even the single most important partner of, NATO.

The second Helsinki summit in mid-1992 occurred against this back-ground of rather muted expectations. On the broad matter of the place of the CSCE within European security arrangements, the clear trend in opinion at this point was towards the idea of an organisational division of labour. In the words of the Helsinki Declaration, 'a lasting and peaceful order ... [would] be built on mutually reinforcing institutions, each with its own area of action and responsibility'. At the subsequent summits in Budapest and Lisbon, a public convergence of views was also seemingly apparent on the following related themes:

1 the OSCE would continue to develop as one of a number of international organisations contributing to security in Europe and, reflecting its enlarged membership, Eurasia more broadly;
2 the main areas of practical OSCE activity should be conflict prevention, management and resolution;
3 statements of principles, such as the Code of Conduct, remained a crucial means of setting normative standards of behaviour;
4 rather than creating new bodies, more effective use should be made of existing OSCE structures.[53]

All this is not to say that disagreement has been absent since Budapest. Indeed, some very real uncertainties have continued to dog discussions of the OSCE. These debates have, however, a somewhat different flavour to those at the time of the Paris summit. By 1994, with the process of OSCE institutionalisation well advanced, and a track record of OSCE activities firmly established, most participating states have tended to devote their attentions to procedural and operational issues. Less pragmatic has been the position of Russia. However, by contrast with the early 1990s, it has been almost alone in positing the OSCE as the cornerstone of some re-fashioned European order. Differences of opinion among participating states can be categorised as falling into three approaches: minimalist, maximalist and incrementalist.[54]

The first of these has been exemplified by the United States. It has also been closely followed by a majority of NATO countries, and particularly the UK. The minimalist position has been based on the by now familiar bias in favour of NATO. In the United States, under the Clinton administration, this preference has been strengthened by a favourable appreciation of the Alliance's own operational adaptation and an assumption that enlargement and new forms of NATO association (PFP, the NACC and its successor, the Euro-Atlantic Partnership Council) provide the most important 'building blocks' of European security. This view has allowed the OSCE a role in clearly designated fields, most importantly conflict prevention, post-conflict reconstruction (as in the case of OSCE election monitoring alongside Implementation Force, or IFOR, activities in Bosnia-Herzegovina) and conventional arms control.[55] Significantly, this has complemented

NATO activities and organisationally has entailed nothing more substantial than simple readjustments of existing OSCE structures and instruments.[56] Less explicitly, US policy has also endorsed an OSCE role in monitoring political developments in the FSU, particularly in cases such as Chechnya and Nagorno-Karabakh, where this might place a check on Russian uni-lateralism.[57]

The maximalist position is diametrically opposed. It has been championed by Russia and seeks to enhance further the power of the OSCE. Russia has made three sets of proposals.[58] The first relates to norm setting, and in particular Russian efforts to widen condemnation of 'aggressive nationalism' in OSCE documentation. As Yeltsin made clear in his speech to the Budapest summit, firmness on this issue is necessary given the alleged infringement of the rights of Russian minorities in the Soviet successor states.[59] The second concerns peacekeeping and conflict mediation. Moscow has argued in favour of a strengthened OSCE role in these areas, one, for instance, designed 'to make the OSCE capable to undertake its own peacekeeping operations'. This has, however, been placed within certain limits. Moscow has been careful to point out that the OSCE should not usurp UN operations (over which Russia has an influence, given its seat in the Security Council) nor do anything that amounts to unwarranted interference in participating states' domestic affairs.[60] The apparent ambiguity of the Russian position here reflects the fact that it would rather not see the OSCE develop an intrusive capability over which it lacked a power of veto. That it has advocated an enhanced OSCE peacekeeping/mediation function at all reflects the logic of its third set of proposals. Since 1994, Russia has made a strenuous case in favour of elevating the OSCE to the position of Europe's principal security organisation. In the run-up to the Budapest summit, the then Russian Foreign Minister Andrei Kozyrev suggested that the OSCE should assume 'overriding responsibility for the maintenance of peace and the strengthening of democracy and stability in the Euro-Atlantic area'. To this end, it was necessary that the OSCE oversee the operations of regional security bodies (NATO, the WEU and the CIS), optimally through a new Executive Committee modelled on the UN Security Council (and, like that body, including Russia as a permanent member).[61] The subsequent acceleration of the NATO enlargement process has stolen the thunder from such proposals; nonetheless, Moscow has continued to pursue them, albeit in moderated form. At the OSCE Ministerial Council in December 1997, for instance, Kozyrev's successor, Yevgenni Primakov, argued that the OSCE should play 'the central coordinating role in European security'.[62]

Russia's motives in this connection appear obvious: the OSCE is attractive because it is one of the few bodies in which Moscow is still an equal of the United States and the European powers (as distinct from NATO, the WEU and the EU, from which it is excluded). Russia's juxtaposition of the OSCE and NATO has meant, however, that the western states have forcefully opposed the scheme. It was rejected at both the Budapest and Lisbon review conferences, although at the summits themselves Russia did derive some satisfaction from the inclusion of passages on the Common and Comprehensive Security Model in the concluding documents.[63] Both this and the subsequent proposal on the European Security Charter are Russian initiatives (the latter backed by France) and have allowed Moscow to continue promoting the notion of an OSCE-based security system.[64]

The incrementalist or 'middle of the road' position has been held by a majority of states within the OSCE.[65] It is somewhat more activist than the minimalist stance in seeking to refine OSCE procedures and to develop the organisation's existing operational competence. Adherents of this position have been the main initiators of recent OSCE innovations, including the 'troika' (Germany), the Court of Conciliation and Arbitration (France) and the Code of Conduct (Poland and Hungary). Importantly, all these reforms are specific in scope. The incrementalist view is premised on the assumption that the OSCE ought to eschew grand tasks and defer in such matters to more tried and tested bodies such as NATO and the EU. It, therefore, partly reflects the positive reappraisals of NATO on the parts of Germany, certain states in eastern Europe and, more recently, France. The proper role of the OSCE has been seen as carrying out limited but necessary tasks. These for Germany include oversight of the post-Cold War arms control agenda,[66] for France arbitration on minority rights and territorial issues[67] and for Poland, Hungary and the Czech Republic conflict prevention, crisis management and human dimension activities.[68]

The problems of enlargement

The threefold enlargement of the OSCE has been attended by some very real problems of both a political and a practical nature. Again, the OSCE is somewhat exceptional here. While it would be true to say that all the organisations discussed in this book have had to confront new challenges brought about by the enlargement process, the rapid and sweeping changes experienced by the OSCE mean that in its case these have been particularly urgent and plentiful. But, to repeat the obvious, enlargement has occurred. The fact that the OSCE has ridden out the process suggests that the associated problems have been addressed in some manner, not always entirely satisfactorily, but sufficient at least to prevent the organisation's paralysis. Taking this assumption as our point of departure, in this section attention will be devoted to five sets of problems that have attended enlargement.

The first concerns the OSCE's relations with other international organisations, a particularly sensitive issue in light of the proliferation of OSCE functions in recent years. OSCE participating states have addressed this issue collectively, as noted above, in the concept of an organisational division of labour and an emphasis on the functional strengths of the organisation. Certain tensions, however, have remained. A good deal of the OSCE's work in the 1990s has been indistinguishable in purpose from that of other bodies. In some cases this duplication of effort can be justified. Human dimension issues, for instance, are also tackled by, *inter alia*, the Council of Europe and the International Court of Justice, but neither of these, it has been argued, offers the comprehensiveness of approach available to the OSCE.[69] In others, however, it is less comprehensible. What need is there, for instance, for the OSCE's Economic Forum, when matters of transition and reform can be better addressed by either the EU, the European Bank for Reconstruction and Development or the UN's Economic Commission for Europe? In this case the problem has largely been resolved by virtue of the essentially marginal tasks the Forum has taken on. Somewhat more vexed has been the OSCE's relationship with the UN. Both organisations have similar mandates to carry out missions in areas of conflict. On the ground, this resulted in some early problems of coordination (as in Tajikistan) and even competition (in Georgia). Yet here, too, corrective steps have been taken. At Helsinki II, the OSCE was declared a regional arrangement under Chapter VIII of the UN Charter and a 'Framework for Cooperation' was signed shortly after by the two organisations. Since October 1993, the OSCE has had observer status at the UN and representatives of the UN Secretary-General attend high-level OSCE meetings. The notion of 'OSCE first', whereby matters of dispute between participating states will be referred to the UN only after due consideration by the OSCE, aims to codify the relationship further.[70] A number of successes have also been registered in the field. The two organisations have worked side by side in the former Yugoslavia and in the Baltic states. In the conflict zones of the FSU, meanwhile, coordination has improved since 1992, with the UN taking the lead in Tajikistan and Abkhazia (Georgia) and the OSCE undertaking such a role in Moldova, Nagorno-Karabakh (Azerbaijan) and South Ossetia (Georgia).[71]

A second set of problems that has confronted the OSCE relates to compliance, particularly in the field of the human dimension. In that the enlargement of membership has occurred largely through admittance of states with uncertain democratic credentials, the question has been posed as to whether the organisation's agreed norms of behaviour have been compromised in some fundamental sense. Flagrant violations of human dimension standards have occurred in many parts of the FSU and the Balkans, dispelling the optimistic (some might say naive) belief that membership would extend and reinforce OSCE norms.[72] This is a problem made that much worse by the procedural difficulties of activating certain mechanisms of intrusive monitoring. The 1991 Moscow Mechanism of the human dimension, for instance, is impossible to apply if the target state withholds its cooperation.[73] The inadequacy of enforcement procedures within the OSCE compounds the problem further. The organisation's guiding documents and the directives of its new institutions have, in the main, not been based on legal provisions; they are political commitments rather than international treaties. In the case of broad-brush statements such as the Final Act, the Paris Charter and the summit declarations, this might be excused by the sheer range and abstraction of the principles and guidelines laid down, and the desire to accelerate their adoption by circumventing processes of national parliamentary approval.[74] The case for non-statutory status, however, seems less clear with regard to specific OSCE provisions. While it might be argued that the political (as opposed to legal) nature of OSCE decisions does not make them any less authoritative, a problem of enforcement does arise. Whereas the violation of legally grounded decisions usually gives rise to a direct sanction of some sort, infringements of OSCE principles, by contrast, allow a fairly limited response (criticism, exhortation and, in the singular case of the Federal Republic of Yugoslavia, a suspension of participation). To date, just one exception to the OSCE's *modus operandi* has occurred[75] – the 1992 Convention on Conciliation and Arbitration, which permits the Court of Conciliation and Arbitration (through an Arbitral Tribunal) to issue binding recommendations upon participating states. It should be pointed out, however, that this is an instrument with no obvious connection to the human dimension and one that a number of participating states (including the UK, the United States, the Netherlands and Turkey) have, in any case, refused to endorse on the grounds that its legal basis is alien to the OSCE. To date, the conciliation procedure has not been used.[76]

Decision-making practices form a third set of problems. Some of the difficulties in this regard have developed as a direct consequence of enlargement. The expansion of OSCE functions and administration, for instance, has given rise to problems of both utilisation and coordination. Many OSCE mechanisms have either never been activated (e.g., the 1991 Valetta Mechanism) or have fallen into disuse (e.g., the 1990 Mechanism on Unusual Military Activities and CSBMs generally). This reflects, in part, the fact that discussions envisaged under these mechanisms can now be held through more routine OSCE channels.[77] Yet this, too, is not without its difficulties. Permanent bodies are dispersed across a number of European cities – Warsaw, Prague, Vienna and Geneva – giving rise to complaints of inefficiency and delays in decision-making.[78] Poor communications between these work sites and missions in the field have also been a subject of concern.[79] A difficulty of longer standing is the OSCE's reliance on consensus as a basis for arriving at decisions.[80] This procedure has been used since the CSCE's inception in the mid-1970s and is not without its defenders. It is seen as encouraging creativity in negotiations and as the best guarantee of durable and legitimate outcomes. It also enshrines the sovereign equality of OSCE participating states and offers a means of protection to the smaller members.[81] These perceived advantages ensured that the consensus principle went largely unchallenged in the pre-enlargement period. With enlargement, however, the case has increasingly been made that this is a cumbersome and time-consuming way of conducting business. The arrangement has consequently been modified to permit action without consensus in certain circumstances. These include activation of a number of OSCE mechanisms: measures against a state guilty of large-scale human rights violations should that state withhold its consent (the so-called 'consensus minus one' principle used to suspend the Federal Republic of Yugoslavia); and directed conciliation, agreed upon in December 1992 (but as yet unused), which permits the Ministerial and Senior Councils to direct two parties to a dispute towards arbitration even against their will (hence the notion of 'consensus minus two').[82] Yet notwithstanding these advances, consensus still prevails as the norm at the political apex of the OSCE (summits, review conferences, meetings of the Ministerial and Senior Councils). The principle has certainly not paralysed these fora, but on occasion their work has been held hostage to the self-interested strategies of particular states. Both Armenia and Azerbaijan have withheld consensus on initiatives relating to Nagorno-Karabakh. In 1992, the three Baltic states threatened to veto the entire Helsinki II package unless it contained reference to Russian troops on their territories. At Budapest, Armenia withheld the necessary consensus on the OSCE-first proposal, while Russia refused to sanction the inclusion in the final document of a passage condemning Serbian actions in Bosnia-Herzegovina. Russia repeated the tactic at Lisbon, ensuring on this occasion the removal of a passage critical of the political situations in Belarus and the rump Yugoslavia.

A lack of involvement is a fourth type of problem, one that has arisen as a consequence of the differing degrees of enthusiasm for the OSCE among the new participating states. While it would be fair to say that some have been rather active (the Baltic states, Slovenia and Croatia), others have been less forthcoming. Few, for instance, have shown much interest in the debates on the role of the OSCE in the post-Cold War order. Moreover, relatively rare in the pre-enlargement period, the OSCE has recently had to oversee meetings with less than full attendance. The central Asian and Transcaucasian states of the FSU, in particular, have shown a marked indifference even to high-profile gatherings such as the Senior Council and sessions of follow-up meetings and review conferences. This is partly a consequence of under-resourced foreign ministries, but, equally, reflects the rather parochial foreign policy concerns of these states and the distance they feel from both the principles of the OSCE and its Euro-Atlantic origins.[83] What is more, involvement, when it has occurred, has had a distinctly instrumentalist character, the OSCE being judged by some participating states seemingly only in terms of the ability of the organisation to side with it on a specific issue (Ukraine and the status of the Crimea, Moldova and the status of the Trans-Dniester, Armenia and Azerbaijan and the future of the disputed enclave of Nagorno-Karabakh). Of course, such instrumentalism has at times not been beyond the larger and more established participating states also. However, for most, satisfaction on this score has not been a *sine qua non* of action. While they may disagree with actual or potential OSCE activities, the organisation is not judged by reference to a single issue, thus allowing a more generous and committed attitude to its broad purposes.

A final issue concerns resourcing. The OSCE has suffered a simple lack of financial and material assets. Experience of the alleged profligacy of the UN and the EU has fuelled a desire among the OSCE's wealthier members to limit the organisation's scope for expenditure. Despite institutionalisation and the ballooning of operations, the permanent staff of the OSCE remains small (just 160 persons at the beginning of 1996) and its budget paltry by comparison with other international bodies. When the political will exists among participating states, extra monies can be found. The projected 1996 budget of $35 million was, for instance, increased by some $24.5 million in order to fund OSCE operations in Bosnia-Herzegovina. This was, however, an exceptional case and a lack of funding in general has been seen as a constraint on certain OSCE activities, notably in the important field of preventive diplomacy.[84]

Conclusion

The OSCE has arguably reached the tolerable limits of enlargement. The expansion of membership has been swift and all-encompassing and it is difficult to see where any new participating states might come from. Important states such as China, India and Iran on the periphery of OSCE concerns might make a case for inclusion but could not be admitted without stretching both the rationale and credibility of the organisation to breaking point. The confinement of the Mediterranean and other Partners for Cooperation to the status of Observer suggests, in fact, a coyness among the existing membership to extend participation beyond the CSCE/OSCE's traditional geographic zone of application. Tellingly, this zone is the same now as it was in 1975; enlargement of membership has occurred only because the number of independent states within it has increased.

It is also unlikely that the OSCE will expand much further in terms of either function or structure. The parameters of the organisation's purpose are now clearly established in principle and have been confirmed in practice.

A fairly elaborate institutional apparatus also exists to give it operational expression. If anything, there is now a strong case for refinement. This might take the form of elaborating more clearly the relationship between the OSCE and other international organisations, consolidating existing OSCE commitments and streamlining certain procedures.[85]

That such issues have been posed is, in one sense, a problem of the OSCE's very success in forging ahead with enlargement. Yet, having said this, the true measure of the OSCE lies not just in its ability to develop in such a manner but in the practical impact and effectiveness of the enlarged organisation itself. How, though, one judges the performance of the organisation depends largely on the expectations one holds of it. If considered from the lofty heights of collective security, then the OSCE has been a clear failure. The hopes expressed by some in the early part of the 1990s that the then CSCE might subsume the military organisations of the Cold War and erect an inclusive regime capable of deterring and, if necessary, responding to outbreaks of war have been dashed, both by the proliferation of conflicts themselves and by the transformation of NATO into the principal organ of security on the Eurasian continent.[86]

Applying somewhat less ambitious criteria, one can see that the OSCE has developed some real strengths in recent years. It has scored numerous quiet successes in the fields of early warning, conflict prevention and crisis management. It has also played an indispensable role in post-conflict Bosnia-Herzegovina and has been the only international organisation with any meaningful presence in Chechnya.[87] The OSCE also remains a valuable custodian of standards of behaviour, both between and within states. It may lack any means of enforcement, but monitoring systems have been devised that amount to an 'accountability regime', ensuring wide and authoritative condemnation of breaches of these principles.[88] There is also much that the OSCE can realistically work towards, be this post-CFE arms control, Russian–NATO understanding through the medium of the Common and Comprehensive Security Model, or peacekeeping operations along the lines envisaged at Budapest. Some optimism, then, is not out of place when considering the OSCE. Despite the fact that it was created under entirely different circumstances to those that prevail today, the organisation's threefold enlargement has transformed it into an irreplaceable component of the post-Cold War order.[89]

Notes

1 V-Y. Ghebali and B. Sauerwein, *European Security in the 1990s: Challenges and Perspectives*, New York: UN, 1995, p. 143.
2 Information used in this chapter on the number of members and dates of accession is taken from *OSCE Handbook 1996*, Vienna: Secretariat of the OSCE, 2nd edn, 1996, annex I.

3 Throughout the text we shall refer to the CSCE in the period up to the end of 1994 and OSCE in the period from January 1995.

4 I. Peters, 'CSCE', in C. Bluth, E. Kirchner and J. Sperling (eds), *The Future of European Security*, Aldershot: Dartmouth, 1995, pp. 67–84.

5 This term has been preferred within the CSCE/OSCE to that of 'member'. The *sui generis* status of the CSCE/OSCE – it is not an international organisation under international law – means it does not have a formal legal membership as such.

6 'Prague meeting of the CSCE Council, 30–31 January 1992, summary of conclusions. Annex', *International Legal Materials*, Vol. 31, No. 4, 1992, pp. 985–6.

7 Membership for the former Soviet republics is covered in detail in A. V. Zagorski, 'The new republics of the CIS in the CSCE', in M. R. Lucas (ed.), *The CSCE in the 1990s: Constructing European Security and Cooperation*, Baden-Baden: Nomos Verlagsgesellschaft, 1993, pp. 279–92.

8 See T. Ueta, 'Japan and the CSCE: toward the extended Euro-Atlantic community from Tokyo to Vladivostok via San Francisco', in Lucas (ed.), *The CSCE in the 1990s*, pp. 207–22.

9 CSCE commitments provided an impetus to the formation of groups such as Helsinki Watch in the Soviet Union and Charter 77 in Czechoslovakia. These proved tireless publicists of infringements of CSCE principles.

10 A. Heraclides, *Helsinki-II and Its Aftermath. The Making of the CSCE into an International Organisation*, London: Pinter, 1993, p. 7.

11 *Ibid.*, p. 128; see also A. Bloed, 'Two decades of the CSCE process: from confrontation to cooperation', in A. Bloed (ed.), *The Conference on Security and Cooperation in Europe. Analyses and Basic Documents*, Dodrecht: Martinus Nijhoff, 1993, p. 58.

12 S. Lehne, *The CSCE in the 1990s. Common European House or Potemknin Village?*, Wien: Braumüller, 1991, pp. 23–4, 30. The Charter is reprinted in full in *NATO Review*, Vol. 38, No. 6, 1990, pp. 27–31.

13 Bloed, 'Two decades of the CSCE process', pp. 62–6. The texts of the Helsinki Declaration and Decisions are reproduced in *International Legal Materials*, Vol. 31, No. 6, 1992, pp. 1385–419.

14 On the significance of the Budapest summit, see V-Y. Ghebali, 'After the Budapest conference: the Organisation for Security and Cooperation in Europe', *NATO Review*, Vol. 43, No. 2, 1995, p. 26.

15 J. Borawski, 'The Budapest summit meeting', *Helsinki Monitor*, Vol. 6, No. 1, 1995, pp. 13–14. The Code of Conduct is reproduced in *SIPRI Yearbook 1995: Armaments, Disarmament and International Security*, Oxford: Oxford University Press, 1995, pp. 238–41.

16 'Lisbon Document 1996', Lisbon: OSCE, 1996.

17 *OSCE Handbook 1996, passim.*

18 *Survey of Long-Term Missions and other OSCE Field Activities*, Vienna: Secretariat of the OSCE, 1996 (http://www.fsk.ethz.ch/osce/longterm.html).

19 A. D. Rotfeld, 'Europe: the multilateral security process', in *SIPRI Yearbook 1995*, p. 290.

20 A. Glover (Director of the OSCE's ODIHR), 'The human dimension of the OSCE: from standard setting to implementation', *Helsinki Monitor*, Vol. 6, No. 3, 1995.

21 As of November 1996, the ODIHR had been involved in a total of fifty-six monitoring missions. See D. Prins and H. Würzner, 'Transition or tradition? The United Nations, the OSCE and electoral assistance', *Helsinki Monitor*, Vol. 7, No. 4, 1996.

22 *OSCE Handbook 1996*, pp. 51–62.

23 See 'Chronology of the Balkan peace effort', *Transition*, Vol. 2, No. 20, 1996, p. 50.

24 *OSCE Handbook 1996*, p. 62.

25 K. Möttölä, 'Prospects for cooperative security in Europe: the role of the CSCE', in Lucas (ed.), *The CSCE in the 1990s*, pp. 28–9.

26 Niels Helveg Petersen (Foreign Minister of Denmark and OSCE Chair-in-Office), 'Towards a European security model for the 21st century', *NATO Review*, Vol. 45, No. 6, 1997, p. 6.

27 For details see Bloed, 'Two decades of the CSCE process', pp. 74–9; *OSCE Handbook 1996*, pp. 62–9; and Rotfeld, 'Europe: the multilateral security process', p. 285.

28 'Lisbon Document 1996', pp. 13–18.

29 The 'Document Adopted by the State Parties to the Treaty on Conventional Armed Forces in Europe on the Scope and Parameters of the Process Commissioned in Paragraph 19 of the Final Document of the First CFE Treaty Review Conference' was 'welcomed' at Lisbon and issued as an appendix to the formal summit document. 'Lisbon Document 1996', pp. 23–7.

30 W. Kemp, *The OSCE in a New Context. European Security Towards the Twenty-First Century*, London: Royal Institute of International Affairs, 1996, p. 11.

31 Lehne, *The CSCE in the 1990s*, pp. 14–15.

32 See *OSCE Handbook 1996*, pp. 10–15, and Kemp, *The OSCE in a New Context*, pp. 16–21.

33 *OSCE Handbook 1996*, p. 10.

34 Zagorski, 'The new republics of the CIS in the CSCE', p. 290.

35 Heraclides, *Helsinki-II and Its Aftermath*, pp. 42–3.

36 A. Hyde-Price, *European Security Beyond the Cold War: Four Scenarios for the Year 2010*, London: Royal Institute of International Affairs/Sage, 1991, p. 217. This position, however, was not shared by the West German Defence Minister, Gerhard Stoltenberg, who warned in July 1990 against 'voluntary integration in favour of a pan-European collective security system' at the expense of NATO. See R. Asmus, 'A unified Germany', in R. A. Levine (ed.), *Transition and Turmoil in the Atlantic Alliance*, New York: Crane Russak, 1992, pp. 64–5.

37 Quoted in B. Buzan, O. Waever, M. Kelstrup, E. Tromer and P. Lemaitre, *The European Security Order Recast: Scenarios for the Post-Cold War Era*, London: Pinter, 1990, p. 241.

38 Speech of Mikhail Gorbachev to the Central Committee of the Communist Party of the Soviet Union, reprinted in V. Mastny, *The Helsinki Process and the Reintegration of Europe, 1986–1991: Analysis and Documentation*, New York: New York University Press, 1992, pp. 194–6.

39 F. S. Larrabee, 'Moscow and German unification', *Harriman Institute Forum*, Vol. 5, No. 9, 1992, pp. 4–6.

40 S. Kull, *Burying Lenin: The Revolution in Soviet Ideology and Foreign Policy*, Boulder, CO: Westview Press, 1992, pp. 151–3.

41 Hyde-Price, *European Security Beyond the Cold War*, pp. 215–16.

42 Speech reprinted in Mastny, *The Helsinki Process*, pp. 196–7.

43 Speech reprinted *ibid.*, pp. 229–32.

44 *Keesing's Record of World Events*, Vol. 36, No. 4, 1990, p. 37386.

45 'London Declaration on a Transformed North Atlantic Alliance', reprinted in M. Eyskens, *From Détente to Entente. An Alliance in Transformation: A Greater Europe in Creation*, London: Brassey's, 1990, pp. 73–4.

46 *Parliamentary Debates (Hansard)*, sixth series, Vol. 181, session 1990–91, London: HMSO, 1991, p. 293.

47 A. D. Rotfeld, 'European security structures in transition', in *SIPRI Yearbook 1992: World Armaments and Disarmament*, Oxford: Oxford University Press, 1993, p. 566, and A. Hyde-Price, *The International Politics of East Central Europe*, Manchester: Manchester University Press, 1996, p. 242.

48 See Andrei Kozyrev (Russian Foreign Minister), 'The new Russia and the Atlantic Alliance', *NATO Review*, Vol. 41, No. 1, 1993, pp. 3–6.

49 This document did refer to the role of the CSCE as complementary to some of NATO's 'fundamental security tasks'. However, it was also made clear that the Alliance would

continue to be the west's principal organisation of collective defence. See 'The Alliance's strategic concept', Appendix IX, in *NATO Handbook* (online version, 1995: http://www.nato.int/docu/handbook/home.htm).

50 Rotfeld, 'European security structures in transition', pp. 565–7.

51 Baker–Genscher joint statement, cited in M. R. Lucas, 'The challenges of Helsinki II', in I. M. Cuthbertson (ed.), *Redefining the CSCE. Challenges and Opportunities in the New Europe*, New York: Institute for East West Studies, 1992, p. 281.

52 D. N. Nelson, 'Snatching defeat from the jaws of victory', *Bulletin of the Atomic Scientists*, Vol. 48, No. 8, 1992, p. 27.

53 Rotfeld, 'Europe: the multilateral security process', p. 299.

54 L. Bouvard and B. George (rapporteurs), 'The Conference on Security and Cooperation in Europe: a case of identity', draft interim report of the Working Group on the New European Security Order, International Secretariat, Brussels: North Atlantic Assembly, November 1994, paragraph 15.

55 R. Holbrooke (US Assistant Secretary of State for European and Canadian Affairs), 'America, a European power', *Foreign Affairs*, Vol. 72, No. 2, 1995, pp. 42–6; *United States Security Strategy for Europe and NATO*, Washington, DC: United States Department of Defense, Office of International Security Affairs, 1995 (http://www.dtic.mil/defenselink/pubs/europe/index.html#pre).

56 Ghebali, 'After the Budapest conference', p. 24.

57 W. Christopher (US Secretary of State), 'US policy toward the NIS: a pragmatic strategy grounded in America's fundamental interests', *Department of State Dispatch*, Vol. 6, No. 14, 1995.

58 H. Hurlburt, 'Russia, the OSCE and European security architecture', *Helsinki Monitor*, Vol. 6, No. 2, 1995, pp. 9–10.

59 See Boris Yeltsin's speech at the Budapest summit, reported in BBC, *Summary of World Broadcasts*, SU/2171 B/8, 6 December 1994.

60 Permanent Mission of the Russian Federation to the OSCE, 'An outline of the Charter on European Security', reprinted as an annex to B. George (rapporteur), 'Complementary pillars of European security: the OSCE Security Model and the Euro-Atlantic Partnership Council', draft interim report of the Sub-Committee on Transatlantic and European Relations, International Secretariat, Brussels: North Atlantic Assembly, 26 August 1997, pp. 17–18.

61 *Ibid.*, p. 19.

62 Radio Free Europe/Radio Liberty, *Newsline* (electronic edition), 19 December 1997. What distinguishes the Russian position of 1997 from that of 1994 is the shift away from any suggestion that the OSCE has executive or 'command' functions. See N. Afanas'evskii, 'The OSCE summit in Lisbon', *International Affairs (Moscow)*, Vol. 43, No. 1, 1997, p. 35.

63 The Common and Comprehensive Security Model for the Twenty-First Century introduced at the Budapest summit was based on a Russian proposal.

64 The western powers have been prepared to endorse these discussions, initially as a trade-off for Russian acceptance of the OSCE mission in Chechnya, and latterly because they have served as one venue for talks with Moscow on NATO enlargement. See M. de Kwaasteniet, 'The security model discussion and its importance for the evolution of the European security architecture', *Helsinki Monitor*, Vol. 7, No. 3, 1996.

65 Ghebali, 'After the Budapest conference', p. 24.

66 C. Bluth, 'Germany: defining the national interest', *World Today*, Vol. 51, No. 3, 1995, p. 54.

67 E. Niemtzow, 'The OSCE's security model: conceptual confusion and competing visions', *Helsinki Monitor*, Vol. 7, No. 3, 1996.

68 P. Switalski, 'An ally for the central and eastern European states', *Transition*, Vol. 1, No. 11, 1995, pp. 28–9.

69 Kemp, *The OSCE in a New Context*, p. 26; Glover, 'The human dimension of the OSCE'.
70 A version of 'OSCE first' was adopted at the Lisbon summit. Paragraph 10 of the Lisbon Declaration on a Common and Comprehensive Security Model for the Twenty-First Century suggests that OSCE participating states refer matters to the UN Security Council only in 'exceptional circumstances', the implication being that the OSCE should be the instrument of first resort. 'Lisbon Document 1996', p. 8.
71 On OSCE–UN interaction see W. Kemp 'The OSCE and the UN: a closer relationship', *Helsinki Monitor*, Vol. 6, No. 1, 1995, and F. D. Gaer, 'The United Nations and the CSCE: cooperation, competition, or confusion?', in Lucas (ed.), *The CSCE in the 1990s*, pp. 161–206.
72 Zagorsky, 'The new republics of the CIS in the CSCE', pp. 288–9.
73 U. de Vito, *Vade Mecum: An Introduction to the Organisation for Security and Cooperation in Europe*, Berne: Swiss Federal Department of Foreign Affairs, 1996 (http://www.fsk.ethz.ch/OSCE/OSCE_vae.html).
74 N. Ronzetti, 'The Conference on Security and Cooperation and its institutions', *International Spectator*, Vol. 27, No. 1, 1993, p. 44.
75 The CFE Treaty (but not CFE-1A) and the Treaty on Open Skies are legally binding, but the caveat needs to be added that these are not formal CSCE documents, but rather the product of negotiations held within the CSCE 'framework'. The Vienna Documents on CSBMs are OSCE instruments and are politically, rather than legally, binding.
76 *OSCE Handbook 1996*, pp. 49–51; *OSCE Newsletter*, Vol. 3, No. 7, 1996; George, 'Complementary pillars of European security', p. 4.
77 Vito, *Vade Mecum*.
78 Lucas, 'The challenges of Helsinki II', p. 273.
79 Bouvard and George, 'The Conference on Security and Cooperation in Europe', paragraph 21.
80 As understood in the OSCE context, consensus is taken to mean 'the absence of any objection expressed by a participating state to the taking of ... [a] decision'. See *OSCE Handbook 1996*, p. 15.
81 N. Möller-Gulland, 'The Forum for Security Cooperation and related security issues', in Lucas (ed.), *The CSCE in the 1990s*, pp. 33–4; Heraclides, *Helsinki-II and Its Aftermath*, pp. 20–1.
82 Rotfeld, 'Europe: the multilateral security process', p. 295; Bloed, 'Two decades of the CSCE process', pp. 20–1, 34.
83 M. Mihalka, 'Restructuring European security', *Transition*, Vol. 1, No. 11, 1996, p. 9.
84 Kemp, *The OSCE in a New Context*, p. 38; Bouvard and George, 'The Conference on Security and Cooperation in Europe', paragraph 22.
85 George, 'Complementary pillars of European security', p. 8.
86 Möttölä, 'Prospects for cooperative security in Europe', pp. 14–20; T. Taylor, 'Security for Europe', in H. Miall (ed.), *Redefining Europe. New Patterns of Conflict and Cooperation*, London: Pinter for the Royal Institute for International Affairs, 1994, pp. 176–80.
87 For a positive appraisal of its work in these two conflict zones, see B. George (rapporteur), 'In quest of "mutually-reinforcing institutions": OSCE, NATO and NACC', draft interim report of the Sub-Committee on Transatlantic and European Relations, International Secretariat, Brussels: North Atlantic Assembly, September 1996, paragraphs 2–11, 25–35, and F. Cotti (OSCE Chair-in-Office), 'The OSCE's increasing responsibilities in European security', *NATO Review*, Vol. 44, No. 6, 1996, pp. 9–12.
88 *Ibid.*, p. 8; Möttölä, 'Prospects for cooperative security in Europe', pp. 28–9.
89 Here we paraphrase the Czech President Václav Havel's address to the 1994 Budapest summit, reprinted as 'A new European order?', *New York Review of Books*, 5 March 1995.

6

The enlargement of the
Council of Europe

Introduction

Building security in post-Cold War Europe, it is now commonly accepted, rests on more than simply reconfiguring the military requirements of national defence. While a narrow focus on the traditional, military aspects of security could be justified by national governments during the period of east–west stand-off, the challenges to European order that have arisen since the fall of communism have led these same governments to invest consider-able energies in defining a new, more comprehensive notion of security. This still embraces military elements (arms control and defence) but equally has identified economic cooperation, conflict prevention and democratic governance as its essential components.[1] Promoting the last of these has, since 1989, been the express task of the COE.

The purpose of the present chapter is to consider the manner in which the COE has enlarged in order to face up to this task. First, progress in enlargement itself will be outlined, in terms of both the rapid growth in the number of member states (from twenty-three in 1989 to forty by July 1998) and the parallel expansion of COE activities. The next section will consider some of the debates that have arisen out of this process, focusing less on the general issue of enlargement itself (something which has provoked very little disagreement) and more on those individual cases where consideration of membership has proven controversial. A section concerned with perceptions will then consider differing views of the organisation's place in post-Cold War Europe and this will be followed by a look at some of the problems of enlargement, concentrating, first, on issues that have arisen from the COE's embrace of democratic underachievers and, second, on its relationships with other international organisations. Following on from this discussion, the chapter will conclude by noting the more exposed position the COE has found itself in as a consequence of enlargement, preoccupied as it has become with the defence of democracy, the rule of law and human rights in countries where these values have a shaky foundation.

Progress in enlargement

Enlargement of membership

The COE has since its foundation experienced an almost continuous expansion of membership. Ten founding states signed the COE's Statute in May 1949: Belgium, Denmark, France, Ireland, Italy, Luxembourg, the Netherlands, Norway, Sweden and the UK. By the time of the organisation's fortieth anniversary, in 1989, membership had grown to twenty-three states. These later entrants included the exceptional case of West Germany (which joined in 1951), some long-established parliamentary democracies (Iceland, Switzerland and Finland) and countries in the early stages of democratisation after the removal of authoritarian rule (Portugal and Spain, which joined in 1976 and 1977, respectively). Little controversy was generated by these accessions. The COE's main problem before 1989 was in dealing with occasional democratic relapses among established members. Military rule meant Greece was expelled in 1969 and was readmitted only with the restoration of civilian rule in 1974. For similar reasons, Turkish delegates were barred from the Parliamentary Assembly of the Council of Europe (PACE) from 1981 to 1984.

Despite the steady progress in enlargement throughout the first forty years of its existence, the COE remained firmly outside Europe's eastern half. The organisation's stress on human rights, democratic governance and the rule of law as admission criteria ruled out any serious relationship with the then communist countries grouped around the Soviet Union. This state of affairs did begin to change in the late 1980s, a product both of political liberalisation in the region and the foreign policy reformulation of Mikhail Gorbachev (outlined fittingly in a speech to the PACE in July 1989) that stressed the place of Moscow and the east European states in a 'Common European House'.[2] In response, the COE's Committee of Ministers in May 1989 issued a political declaration that welcomed an 'open and concrete dialogue with eastern Europe'.[3] The following month a new category of participation in the COE was introduced. Special guest status, as it was known, was extended to four countries initially: Poland, Hungary, Yugoslavia and the Soviet Union. Czechoslovakia and Bulgaria were granted a similar position some twelve months later, and Romania and Albania were to follow in 1991. As for full membership, this was formally dependent on an applicant state satisfying conditions laid down in Article 3 of the Statute, namely acceptance of 'the principles of the rule of law and of the enjoyment by all persons ... of human rights and fundamental freedoms'.[4] In practice, these criteria were interpreted rather flexibly, membership in some instances being granted once free elections had been held. Thus, Hungary joined in 1990, Poland and Czechoslovakia in 1991 and Bulgaria in 1992.

This seemingly rather tidy process of accession was to be upset, however, from the end of 1991 by new considerations arising from the break-up of the communist federations. Only the Czechoslovak case proved largely problem free – its membership in the COE was succeeded by the Czech Republic and Slovakia in 1993. Yugoslavia was to prove far more trying. Its guest status was suspended in November 1991, in view of Serbian violations of the human rights of the Albanian population in Kosovo and the role of the federal army in the then Yugoslav republics of Croatia and Slovenia. With the subsequent disintegration of Yugoslavia, special guest status was extended in 1992 to Slovenia and Croatia, to Macedonia in 1993 and to Bosnia in 1994. With the exception of the last, all these Yugoslav successor states also subsequently obtained full membership, although, as we shall see below, not without some controversy. As for the 'rump' Yugoslavia (Serbia and Montenegro), at the time of writing formal relations with the COE remain severed.

Turning to the Soviet Union, its collapse at the end of 1991 gave rise to fifteen successor states, only six of which have since acquired full membership: Estonia and Lithuania (1993), Latvia, Moldova and Ukraine (1995), and Russia (1996). Considerations of accession here have meant not just the normal process of judging the democratic credentials of successor states (see below), but also some consideration of issues of geography. Article 4 of the Statute suggests that only states within Europe may be considered for membership. A PACE report of June 1992 divided the fifteen successor states into four categories, two of which (the Baltic states plus Russia, Belarus, Ukraine and Moldova) were considered to be obviously European and one obviously not (that of the central Asian states). That category containing the Caucasian states of Armenia, Azerbaijan and Georgia did, however, occasion some problems, and discussions regarding its status were 'not entirely conclusive'.[5] A further report, in December 1993, did rule out accession on account of the fact that the 'Caucasus is part of Asia',[6] although this position was itself subsequently reversed in a recommendation adopted in October 1994. This accepted the possibility of membership for those states 'whose national territory lies wholly or partly in Europe and whose culture is closely linked with the European culture'.[7] The Caucasian states were held to satisfy this requirement and all three were granted special guest status in 1996.

The issue of a European definition has also arisen with regard to relations with the North American democracies. While full membership has been expressly ruled out on geographic grounds, US and Canadian participation of some form has long been favoured by certain established member states. Cementing such ties has not, however, been straightforward. Canada has been a willing interlocutor, but COE relations with the United States have historically been far less cordial, characterised before the early 1990s by a series of rebuffs on the part of Washington to COE overtures. The reasons for this are not hard to find. Even though the COE embodies many of the democratic values claimed by the United States, establishment political opinion within that country has nonetheless been sceptical of the organisation, fearful that cooperation would impose unwanted obligations. US constitutional and legal tradition is hostile to any notion of extra-territorial jurisdiction in domestic matters, something that clearly rules out subordination to the Conventions of the COE and the rulings of the Court of Human Rights (see below).[8] However, while unwilling to tolerate COE involvement in its own affairs, the events of 1989 did lead the United States to recognise the potential of the COE elsewhere, and in particular as part of what US Secretary of State James Baker referred to in 1991 as the 'network of political and economic support' required to buttress the new democracies of eastern Europe.[9] Presidents George Bush and Bill Clinton have consequently shown a greater degree of enthusiasm towards the organisation, culminating in January 1996 in accession to observer status – a category of involvement that avoids the obligations of full or guest membership while allowing participation in certain COE activities (attendance at expert and specialised meetings, involvement in the COE's work in the fields of health, education, cultural and social matters etc.).[10]

Enlargement of functions

The COE was set up in 1949 with a primarily political purpose – in the words of the Council's Statute, to promote a closer unity of those countries in Europe dedicated to the 'spiritual and moral values which are the common heritage of their peoples and the true source of individual freedom, political liberty and the rule of law'. This, in effect, was a mission geared to preserving democratic life on the western half of the continent and to this end a broad spread of collaborative activities was foreseen, in areas such as economics, culture, science, the law and social and administrative matters.[11] To buttress its work, the COE subsequently developed a broad organisational structure, embracing an executive decision-making body (the Committee of Ministers), a Parliamentary Assembly, institutions set up to supervise human rights, specialised directorates (youth, the environment, legal affairs, etc.) and various *ad hoc* consultative and coordinating bodies (the European Pharmacopoeia, the Congress of Local and Regional Authorities of Europe). It also undertook the task of coordinating agreements among members in these areas, encapsulated in the 140 or so conventions signed by 1990.

In many of its spheres of activity, however, the COE came to be sidelined by other international organisations, notably the EU. Yet this was not entirely to the COE's detriment, as it was consequently encouraged to develop its own specialised field, that of human rights protection.[12] Here, the COE has generally been regarded as innovative, owing to its facility for individual petition (as opposed to simply inter-state applications) and the legally binding character of its instruments and conventions. It is also, in historical terms, something of a success story. Before 1989, all COE member states had ratified the 1950 European Convention for the Protection of Human Rights and Fundamental Freedoms (more simply the European Convention on Human Rights, or ECHR) and had accepted the compulsory jurisdiction of the European Court of Human Rights – the organ set up in 1959 to supervise and enforce the rights laid down in the Convention. Several members had incorporated ECHR provisions into their domestic constitutions. In all, this machinery was held to constitute, in the opinion of one observer, 'the most advanced international legal framework for human rights in the world'.[13]

Faced with a substantially enlarged membership, since 1989 this core area of COE activity has grown considerably. The fragile nature of human rights in the new member states, coupled with the readiness of individual applicants to appeal retrospectively against the perceived injustices of communist rule, has meant a dramatic rise in appeals to the COE.[14] The number of applications to the COE's European Commission of Human Rights increased from 596 in 1985 to 3,480 in 1995, and final decisions by the Court grew from just eleven to eighty-seven in the same period. Indeed, to accommodate this, the COE undertook its major institutional reform of the post-1989 period – the phased transition under a 1994 protocol to the ECHR to a newly organised Court of Human Rights better able to deal with the increased workload.[15] Simultaneously, the COE has continued its work of elaborating human rights standards. This includes the framing of the 1989 Convention for the Prevention of Torture (backed by its own committee charged with investigative visits to signatory states) and two initiatives relating to minority issues – the 1992 European Charter for Regional or Minority Languages and the 1995 Framework Convention for the Protection of National Minorities.[16] Work in this latter area is of particular note. It has, in large part, been a quite deliberate response to the destabilising resurgence of nationalism in former communist states and, furthermore, has involved the COE in confidence-building measures. Aimed at defusing tensions between minority and majority populations, such projects have been launched in Ukraine, Romania and Estonia, among others.[17] The COE has also played a limited role with regard to institutionalising human rights protection in post-conflict Bosnia, having been mandated under the Dayton agreement to oversee a share of the appointments to a new Human Rights Chamber, Constitutional Court and Commission for Property Claims.[18]

As well as upgrading its core functions in safeguarding human rights, the COE has also taken on a more facilitative role in the new post-communist member states through the launch of a number of assistance programmes. The first, known as 'Demosthenes', was launched in 1990, with the twofold objective of strengthening democratic reforms and integrating new members into COE institutions and activities. Supplemented subsequently by 'Demosthenes-bis', targeted at states with guest status, this programme has embraced virtually all new and aspiring members.[19] Although much of its work passes unnoticed (such as seminars and workshops), Demosthenes has made a mark in some countries. Of particular note is the 'Demi-Droit' scheme. This has, under the umbrella of Demosthenes, been geared towards providing assistance in the framing of new constitutions and in reforming criminal justice systems. To promote its work, in 1990 a new COE body was formed – the European Commission for Democracy through Law (the Venice Commission). Demosthenes has also been complemented by two further COE programmes: 'Themis', devoted to legal cooperation and specifically the training of judges, lawyers as well as prison administrators and civil servants; and 'Lode', an initiative aimed at fostering local democracy through advice on finance, administration, training and trans-border cooperation.[20]

Controversies over enlargement

As the preceding section shows, in principle the notion of an enlargement of membership has never been at issue within the COE. Set against the general principle, however, certain individual cases have been a cause of some controversy. For instance, the accession of Estonia and Latvia was condemned by Russia as 'premature', on the grounds that neither state had done enough to protect the civil rights and social status of resident Russian minorities.[21] Similarly, Hungary, out of a concern for its own diaspora population, abstained from the votes that saw Romania and Slovakia join the COE in 1993.[22] Other instances have included Liechtenstein's abstention on the vote that approved membership for the Czech Republic (owing to property seized from the city-state by the Prague government in 1918) and Greek objections to Macedonian entry (overcome following a 1995 inter-state accord under which Athens formally recognised Macedonian statehood).[23]

These cases proved controversial because they provided an occasion for the ventilation of issues of a bilateral nature. Significantly, in each case, the objecting party proved unwilling to elevate what was a localised dispute into a reason for impeding the accession process. Of a far more serious nature have been instances where several member states, as opposed to a single one, have expressed concern at a possible accession. With regard to the applications of Russia, Croatia and Belarus, such objections have proven sufficient either to delay or to reverse the admission process.

Taking Russia first, it had inherited the Soviet Union's special guest status and submitted a formal application for full membership in May 1992. Admission was, however, delayed until February 1996, following an arduous and controversial accession process. Concern focused initially on the political situation inside Russia. The Committee of Ministers, meeting in June 1992, agreed unanimously that Russian membership was desirable once Moscow had demonstrated sufficient progress in the fields of pluralist democracy, human rights and the rule of law.[24] And at a special meeting of the Committee convened the following September to discuss relations with member states of the CIS, it was agreed that cooperation should be heightened with Russia, with a view to its future accession. Yet, if Russian hopes were raised by these gestures, then they were soon to be dashed. Despite the adoption of a new constitution and the holding of elections to a newly formed legislature in December 1993, membership continued to be withheld. A *Report on the Conformity of the Legal Order of the Russian Federation with Council of Europe Standards*, written under the aegis of the PACE, concluded the following September that, despite notable achievements in the post-Soviet period, the political and legal order in the country failed to meet COE standards.[25] Several member states (in particular, some of those newly admitted from eastern Europe) were also critical of the deployment of Russian troops abroad without the consent of host governments (Russia had completed a withdrawal from the Baltic states, but troops remained in Moldova). If this were not enough, the launch by the Russian central authorities in December 1994 of military operations against the Chechen republic proved decisive. Although technically an internal matter, Russia's handling of the Chechen issue was considered to be in violation of COE and other international standards. In February 1995, the PACE decided by a large majority (one abstention and one vote against) to defer consideration of Russia's application, citing the indiscriminate use of force in Chechnya and the imbalance of political power in Russia in favour of the executive (itself amply illustrated by the Yeltsin administration's Chechen policy).[26]

Despite these deep reservations, examination of Russia's application was resumed in September, according to a PACE resolution on the grounds that Russia had shown a willingness to find a political solution to the Chechen imbroglio and was ready to investigate alleged human rights violations.[27] The subsequent six months witnessed a charged debate on the merits of Russian entry. The majority opinion, voiced by the EU states and Switzerland, was that Russia should accede on the grounds that it had registered considerable progress towards COE principles and had made several undertakings to correct deficient areas of political and legal practice.[28] The positive signal sent by membership, it was also argued, would help counteract undemocratic forces; and even if such forces should prevail in Russia, the provision for a suspension of membership remained available to the COE.[29] While these views were to win out eventually, an articulate minority argued strongly against Russian entry. Amid an escalation of the Chechen war, Baltic and Czech delegates to the PACE argued that admission was tantamount to condoning Russian aggression and casting a veil over continuing human rights abuses in the conflict zone.[30]

Croatian admission proved similarly vexed. Having been formally accepted by a vote of the PACE in April 1996, the Committee of Ministers, in an unprecedented move the following month, placed Croatian entry on hold. This followed charges from EU foreign ministers that the Zagreb government had failed to live up to undertakings made to the COE on human rights, tolerance of political opposition and non-interference in the media.[31] Reflecting these concerns, the Committee of Ministers stipulated that entry would follow only after Croatia could demonstrate further progress towards political liberalisation and respect for related aspects of the Dayton peace process. The Committee of Ministers finally agreed to admit Croatia in October, citing on this occasion recent cooperation with the UN International Criminal Tribunal, improvements in Croatia's human rights record and the successful conclusion of the elections in Bosnia.[32]

While both Russia and Croatia did eventually join the COE, in the case of Belarus objections have been serious enough seemingly to preclude membership. Having been granted special guest status in 1992, Belarus forwarded an application for full membership in March of the following year. Little progress, however, was registered thereafter, owing to both the snail's pace of political liberalisation in that country and the lack of interest in the COE on the part of Belarus President Aleksandr Lukashenko. In fact, Belarus has acquired the unenviable position of being the only country since Yugoslavia in 1991 to experience a formal freezing of its relations with the COE. In January 1997, the Political Bureau of the PACE voted to suspend indefinitely the Belarus delegation from the Assembly. This followed charges of irregularities in the conduct of a referendum held the previous November on a new constitution that granted Lukashenko what amounted to authoritarian powers. In voting to exclude Belarus, the PACE made any further cooperation dependent on a greater regard for democratic norms and human rights, thereby signifying that eventual membership remained at best a long-term prospect.[33] Yet, despite Belarus's clear deviation from COE norms, suspension was not greeted with unanimity. One interesting aspect of the episode was the attitude of Moscow. In the interests of its close bilateral relationship with Belarus (an agreement on the creation of a

Russia–Belarus Community of Sovereign States had been signed the previous April), Russia was led to denounce the PACE action as 'hasty' and counterproductive and to argue instead for the application of 'constructive dialogue and real assistance' to foster democracy in Belarus.[34]

Perceptions of the COE

For all the concerns and, at times, controversy generated by the intro-duction of new members, the debates surrounding admission have had a somewhat artificial quality. The rump Yugoslavia and Belarus not-withstanding, worries and, at times, disagreement among existing members concerning the merits of potential new entrants have not prevented an influx of states into the COE. This contrasts markedly with NATO, the EU and the WEU, where divisions of opinion and the application of rigorous admission criteria have impeded a significant increase in membership. In explaining this difference, attention should be drawn to the perceived role of the organisation in post-Cold War Europe. From its rather exclusivist function as the guardian of western democratic norms among the established European democracies, the organisation has moved to take on the related, but nonetheless innovative, role of champion of these principles in the uncertain post-communist environment. And, by definition, this is a mission the COE cannot undertake unless it is prepared to embrace formerly excluded states.

Such a view of the COE has been most obviously apparent among its permanent officials. Speaking in 1990, COE Secretary-General Catherine Lalumière suggested that the COE was 'the organisation around which ... [a] future European confederation ... [could] be constructed'.[35] While this level of euphoria did not last long after 1989, Lalumière nonetheless continued to argue that the COE had a valuable role to play, particularly in eastern Europe. By promoting its core concerns – pluralistic democracy, human rights and the rule of law – and by encouraging tolerance among different ethnic and religious groups, the COE could make a unique contribution to stability in the region, engineering a 'democratic security' that would complement the potential military and economic benefits of partnership with other international organisations.[36] Lalumière's successor, Daniel Tarschys, has argued in similar vein. Writing in 1995, he contended that 'democracy and democratic security must be extended eastwards'. While this should not entail any lowering of the COE's ambitions 'for the defence of democracy and human rights', Tarschys suggested that it was better to accept new members on the basis of their *commitment* to meeting COE standards. A less than perfect record was to be expected in fledgling democracies and once an 'acceptable level of democratic development' had been attained, membership should follow, for inclusion was 'far preferable to exclusion' if democratic construction was to be encouraged in the post-communist states.[37]

To a point, these views have been supported by the COE's long-standing member states. The Vienna Declaration issued by the first ever summit meeting of COE heads of state and government in October 1993 referred, in glowing terms, to the COE as 'the pre-eminent European political organisation capable of welcoming ... the democracies of Europe freed from communist oppression'. Accession of these countries was consequently viewed as 'a central factor in the process of European construction'.[38] Individual states have voiced similar opinions. In the initial wake of the collapse of communism and the Cold War, France and Germany, in particular, were keen to emphasise the COE. François Mitterrand in December 1989 suggested that the COE could 'offer a valuable framework for dialogue and cooperation of a sort that can anchor ... [the east European] states definitively among the democratic nations'.[39] On a similar note, in January 1990, the West German Foreign Minister Hans-Dietrich Genscher proposed the establishment of a 'pan-European institution for the protection of human rights' and 'the application of the COE's human rights convention to the whole of Europe'.[40] As the accession process has accelerated, such views have continued to be voiced. Even the UK Conservative government, not known for its enthusiasm for the COE, joined the chorus; the then Foreign Secretary, Malcolm Rifkind, in a speech made in Ukraine in September 1995, for instance, referred to the COE as 'a vehicle for consolidating stability among democratising states'.[41]

At face value, these statements seemingly suggest a considerable faith in the COE among west European governments. However, underlying this support for the COE's political mission are a number of motives other than simply a desire to influence post-communist political development. There has been, in the first place, a good deal of *realpolitik* involved in the admission process. The case could be made that the ease of entry to the COE was a way of compensating states, such as Romania and the Baltic republics, that were keen to join NATO and the EU but were not at the front of the queue for admission. Considerations of an equally practical nature have also applied in the cases of Croatia and Russia. The former's admission to the COE was, as already noted, expressly tied to progress on the Dayton peace process. Western support for Russian entry meanwhile can be seen in terms of the policy of attempting to engage first the Soviet Union and then Russia in pan-European cooperation. That this has its limitations can be seen from the obvious fact that NATO enlargement threatens to undo much of the improvement in east–west relations since the late 1980s, hence the Alliance strategy of attempting to ameliorate Russian concerns through political concessions (see chapter 2), of which granting COE membership is only one of several strands.[42]

A mix of idealism and instrumentalism has also been apparent in the attitudes of the COE's new and aspiring members. In the first place, COE membership can be seen as motivated by a desire to 'return to Europe', to reforge links forcibly severed during the communist period and to signify the break with the political and economic experience of communist rule. This is a goal that applies especially to Poland, the Czech Republic and Hungary, where cultural traditions, historical experience and geographic proximity have created a 'new nationalist myth ... of return to real or imaginary European roots'.[43] Further afield, it also has an influence. For the Baltic states, membership of the COE is seen as confirmation of their true position in the European mainstream, thereby distancing themselves from the experience of incorporation within a Soviet/Russian sphere of interest.[44] In Transcaucasia, too, where European identity is even more ambiguous, membership of the COE is viewed as symbolic acceptance of 'European-ness' and with it a refutation of the region's post-communist reputation for political instability.[45]

Beyond these general expressions of political orientation, some very real practical considerations have also been at work among the new members. For a large number of post-communist states, recent interest in international organisations has been based on a sense of exposure and vulnerability. And while the COE itself is not disposed to tackle either the security predicaments or the economic challenges of these states, it has been viewed as facilitating the journey towards those organisations that can. Membership of the COE, by confirming a country's democratic status, satisfies an essential precondition of membership laid down by both the EU and NATO.[46] This is a crucial consideration for states such as Poland, Hungary and the Czech Republic. For those equally intent on membership but further back in the queue, similar considerations have also applied. One Latvian analyst, for instance, has suggested that the Baltic states have, since 1991, engaged in a strategy of 'gradual, functional integration', welcoming entry into any and all structures of multilateral European cooperation in the hope that this process will eventually extend to admission to the more prized organisations of the EU and NATO.[47] Comparable strategies have also been pursued in Romania and Slovenia.[48]

Such long-term views have also been buttressed by an appreciation of the short-term benefits to be had from joining the COE. By conferring 'a clean bill of democratic health',[49] accession to the COE has been used by sitting governments in new member states to claim an added legitimacy for themselves. This is particularly valuable when the governments in question have struggled to demonstrate their democratic credentials, as in the cases of Croatia or Russia, or have faced criticism over specific policies. Both Latvia and Estonia, for instance, have pointed to COE membership as a means of rebutting charges from Moscow of discrimination against their sizeable Russian-speaking populations.[50]

This, however, has not been the end of the matter, as the Russian leadership has been equally keen to harness the COE to its own ends. Following Moscow's admission, both President Boris Yeltsin and his erstwhile Foreign Minister Yevgenni Primakov have utilised the COE as a forum for defending the rights of ethnic Russians in the Baltic states.[51]

Problems of enlargement

The enlargement of the COE has been both swift and comprehensive and this has given rise to a multiplicity of new challenges for the organisation. In order to accommodate new members, it has had to rethink organisational practice, take upon itself new missions (see above) and grapple with the consequences of embracing states in the early stages of post-communist political development.

This last point has been especially significant given the COE's principal concern with upholding standards of human rights and democratic practice. In this regard, it has been able to claim important successes. Some countries have implemented domestic political changes, influenced in part by the accession process. Latvian membership, for instance, was granted only after it had amended drafts of citizenship laws that had been criticised by the COE (and the OSCE) as falling short of European standards.[52] The admission of Moldova, meanwhile, was facilitated by the promulgation of a new democratic constitution and the granting of an autonomous region for the Gagauz minority population.[53] The COE has also been influential in assisting the consolidation of democratic governance and the rule of law subsequent to accession. This has been, in part, a consequence of the projects described above, but due also to the individual commitment of certain states – notably Hungary and, to a lesser degree, Poland – to bring domestic legislation and legal practice into line with the ECHR.[54]

Yet, for all these good works, the criticism has been made that the principles of the COE have been diluted by the influx of new members.[55] Indeed, the enlargement process has proven in some cases so controversial as to lead to resignations from the organisation's Secretariat.[56] While Secretary-General Tarschys has defended the COE against such charges, it is beyond dispute that the implicit lowering of admission criteria noted above has allowed in countries with dubious political, legal and human rights practices. This is a state of affairs made that much worse by an unwillingness on the part of certain countries to live up to commitments made at the point of admission. Albania provides a case in point. Its admission in June 1995 followed a declared commitment to respect human rights and democracy and to introduce reforms that would promote the freedom of the judiciary and the media.[57] The following eighteen months, however, witnessed continued state interference in these areas, combined with more allegations of police brutality, undue restrictions on the right of assembly and parliamentary elections in May 1996 that the PACE itself described as 'damaging the credibility of the democratic process' in Albania.[58] During 1997, the civil situation broke down and a state of emergency was imposed between March and July, a period in which an estimated 2,000 people were killed as a consequence of a collapse of governmental authority. The situation stabilised after parliamentary elections in June 1997 and while the human rights record of the new government does constitute an improvement upon that of its predecessor, it has remained far from exemplary.[59]

Russian behaviour has also been a challenge to the COE. The PACE, when considering Moscow's case, attached a number of conditions to admission. These included ratification of the ECHR within one year, eventual abolition of the death penalty (to be preceded by a three-year moratorium), an improvement in prison conditions and the enactment of a law on alternative military service for conscripts.[60] Progress, however, has been far from obvious. Over the issue of capital punishment, Moscow has been in open conflict with the COE. The rate of executions actually increased in the first few months following admission.[61] The death penalty was also retained in the new Russian Criminal Code, which went into force in January 1997,[62] and Russian judges have continued to hand down the sentence. The Russian parliament, in March 1997, refused to support a draft law imposing a legal moratorium by a wide margin of 177 to 75. Officials at the Justice Ministry, the Supreme Court and the office of the General Prosecutor are also reportedly strongly in favour of retaining capital punishment.[63] What movement has occurred in Russia has been largely due to executive intervention. A presidential moratorium on the death sentence was introduced in August 1996 and the following April Russia signed up to Protocol 6 of the ECHR, which prohibits capital punishment in peacetime (this, however, awaits ratification by the Russian parliament). In January 1998, Yeltsin signed a law on amendments to the Criminal Procedure Code that allows the President to review all death sentences, in effect institutionalising the common practice of presidential pardons for those on death row.[64]

On other human rights issues, the Russian record has been mixed. Russia has taken note of some accession conditions; for instance, it has begun the transfer of prison administration from the Ministry of the Interior to the Ministry of Justice and in June 1997 repealed Presidential Decree 1226, which had permitted detention without charge for up to thirty days. In February 1998, the Russian parliament also ratified the ECHR, something that opens up the possibility of Russian citizens making direct appeals to the European Court of Human Rights and of the Russian government being legally required to implement any adverse findings. Should this occur (at the time of ratification some 800 complaints had already been lodged with the European Commission on Human Rights[65]) it will amount to a profound challenge, both to Russian legal doctrine and to a political culture that has generally been hostile to external influence in areas of domestic jurisdiction. This move, however, remains, at present, as much symbolic as it is substantive and in other regards Russia's record has departed markedly from COE norms. Since accession to membership in 1996, the human rights situation in Russia has attracted considerable criticism relating to prison conditions, the abuse of military conscripts, arbitrary arrest and detention, lengthy pre-trial detention, torture of detainees, curtailments on the freedom of worship (linked to the passage of a controversial Law on Religion in October 1997) and infringements of citizens' rights to privacy.[66]

As for Chechnya, PACE hearings on the situation in the region scheduled for September 1996 elicited charges from Yeltsin's office that the COE was guilty of an 'unceremonious interference in the internal affairs of [Russia]'.[67] The hearings were subsequently cancelled, in part because Aleksandr Lebed, then Russian Security Council Secretary, refused to attend.[68]

As well as having to grapple with the accommodation of new members, the COE has in parallel had to refashion its relations with other European-based international organisations. Regarding the OSCE, this body at first sight seems particularly well suited to cooperation with the COE. The values embodied in OSCE documentation (see chapter 5), particularly in the fields of the human dimension and minority rights, suggest a close complementarity of aims with the COE.[69] This, it has been argued, has presented the possibility of a mutually beneficial division of labour. The political commitments of states entered into within the OSCE could be given a legal weight by the COE, thereby promoting the shared goals of strengthening democratic norms and extending the human rights regime to the former communist states.[70] At the declaratory level, both organisations have registered a common commitment to foster cooperation.[71] Institutional links have also been forged. The COE has enjoyed an observer status in OSCE political bodies (summits and meetings of the Senior Council) and has cooperated in the work of two OSCE specialised agencies (the High Commissioner for National Minorities and the ODIHR). On the ground, the two organisations have been involved in joint projects regarding national minority and human dimension issues as far afield as Moldova, Macedonia, the Slovak Republic and the Baltic states. Finally, in the special case of Bosnia, they have cooperated in the work of the Dayton-mandated Human Rights Chamber and ombudsman.[72]

Turning to EU–COE relations, a framework for cooperation was first formalised in 1987. Since then, regular quadripartite meetings have been held between the Presidents of the European Commission and the European Council, on the one hand, and the COE Secretary-General and President of the Committee of Ministers, on the other. Channels also exist between the Commission and the COE Secretariat.[73] As for practical measures, joint programmes for legal reform, local government and human rights protection have been pursued in Russia, Ukraine, Albania and the Baltic states, partly funded by the EU's Phare and Tacis programmes.[74]

These inter-organisational links have not, however, been problem free. The similarity of some of the COE's activities with those of the OSCE has created, in the words of two observers, 'potentially unnecessary inter-institutional overlaps and duplication'.[75] This state of affairs has given rise to complaints among small, new members, concerned at the cost of repeated attendance at similar meetings in different fora.[76] It has also given grist to the mill of those longer established members, such as the UK, concerned at the need for financial restraint in international organis-ations.[77] For those with more of a vested interest in the COE, duplication has also led to some anxiety, in this case born of fears that the COE's traditional areas of concern are being encroached upon. PACE delegates have argued that election monitoring should be a task primarily for the COE and not the OSCE and also that member states of the COE should make greater use of its own conventions and institutions before investing their energies in new OSCE procedures.[78] Yet the COE itself has not been blameless, as demonstrated by its recent forays into confidence building – normally regarded as an area of OSCE expertise. So far, little has been done at the institutional level to iron out these overlapping areas of responsibility. Indeed, only in 1996 were preliminary consultations begun with the OSCE aimed at establishing a consultation procedure to coordinate activities.[79]

Relations with the EU have also given rise to difficulties. An issue of long standing has been the respective roles of the COE's Court of Human Rights and the EU's Court of Justice. While the jurisdiction of the latter has been confined to matters that fall within EU law, it has made occasional judgements with human rights implications.[80] This has led to complaints from within the PACE that legal confusion might arise, as different sets of cases could result in the laying down of different legal precedents.[81] Criticisms have also been levelled at the EU for what is seen as its increasingly political role. These refer to specific activities of the EU, in areas of culture, education and non-racism, that the COE has thought of as its preserve and also, more widely, to the process of enlargement itself.[82] Brussels' insistence on certain political conditions of membership correspond closely to COE requirements and membership of the latter, as noted earlier, is also seen as an essential prerequisite for joining the EU. Despite this implicit link, and to the clear disappointment of the PACE, no formal arrangement has materialised for the latter's involvement in the EU accession process.[83]

Turning finally to some organisational issues in-house, the COE has had to respond to what one PACE report has termed the 'serious impacts' of enlargement on its internal functioning.[84] One major change, the re-organisation of the Court of Human Rights, has already been noted. In addition, alterations have also been made in decision-making procedures. The unanimity required within the Committee of Ministers for the adoption of recommendations to governments has been altered in favour of a two-thirds majority threshold.[85] Resourcing issues have also had to be faced. In addition to financing assistance programmes, new demands have been placed upon expenditure from the bureaucratic consequences of enlargement: increased staff recruitment, expanded office space and the translation of numerous additional languages. In order to cover these costs, the COE's operational budget was increased by an average of approximately 7.75 per cent per annum between 1990 and 1994.[86] This sum, however, has not fully satisfied some within the COE. The increase was described as 'modest' by erstwhile Secretary-General Lalumière in 1992 and, in a PACE report some two years later, as insufficient to meet the new tasks of enlargement.[87] A further report, in January 1996, coming on the back of a freezing of the COE's budget in 1995, described resources as 'extremely stretched', something that placed a severe limit on the COE's 'capacity for action'.[88] A communication of the Committee of Ministers issued in April 1997 suggested that expansion had severely complicated COE budgetary provisions and expressed the hope that the organisation's 'entry into a stable period', while not removing spending pressures, would nonetheless permit more rational financial planning.[89]

Conclusion

With the fall of communism and the end of the Cold War, the COE was seemingly well suited for enlargement. The nascent transitions to democracy that began first in eastern Europe and which subsequently spread to the Soviet Union and its successor states marked what one observer has dubbed 'the beginning of the COE's second life'.[90] Having long played the role of custodian of democratic standards in the more established democracies of western Europe, the COE was now afforded the opportunity to extend these principles to the formerly excluded countries in the eastern half of the continent. This has required an institutional reorientation of sorts, as the COE has taken on the practical tasks of assisting democratic consolidation, but, in essence, enlargement has not meant any fundamental rethink of the organisation's original rationale: to promote cooperation between democratic states.

This clear sense of purpose has ensured a swift and full process of enlargement. However, in so readily embracing new members, the COE has run the risk that its core function has been demeaned and its credibility undermined. The loosening of admission criteria, coupled with subsequent lapses among newly admitted members, has exposed to criticism the organisation's claim to be a defender of democracy, the rule of law and human rights. In response, the COE can point to its continued willingness to suspend recalcitrant states, as in the cases of the rump Yugoslavia and Belarus. Whether such a defence can be sustained in the face of democratic backsliding elsewhere, however, has yet to be seen. The real test will be how the COE deals with states such as Croatia, Albania and particularly Russia – full members with a less than perfect record in meeting COE norms. With regard to these states, the COE could face a very real dilemma. To expel them on the grounds of a persistent violation would certainly boost the COE's claim to be a beacon of democratic values and human rights, but would at the same time undo much of the facilitative work it has already invested in these states in promoting democratic consolidation. Yet to retain them as members, while allowing such cooperative assistance to continue, will imply that the COE has somehow lowered its standards of membership, and in the process devalued the very principles it claims to hold dear. This dilemma could have been avoided had the COE's admission requirements been applied more rigorously at the outset of the current round of enlargement. Certainly, in the cases of Croatia and Russia entry to the organisation occurred in the midst of clear shortcomings of political and legal practice and while it is too early to judge whether their inclusion has proven a better way of encouraging beneficial change than exclusion, the record in both cases has so far been less than encouraging.

These issues suggest that the COE has been challenged in some new fundamental way by the most recent process of enlargement. Encouraging and enforcing the norms of democratic society had been relatively straight-forward before 1989. Either members were already thoroughly imbued with these values or, if they were not (as in the cases of West Germany, Greece, Spain and Turkey), entrance into the COE was accompanied by near simultaneous incorporation into the EU or NATO (or both), organisations that were able to reinforce the process of democratic consolidation. This contrasts markedly with the situation after 1989. With one or two exceptions (the Baltic states and the Czech Republic), democratic traditions are uniformly lacking in the post-communist states and, moreover, only a handful have a realistic chance in the foreseeable future of adding NATO and EU membership to that of the COE. Even so, democratic construction is not impossible. The COE has itself become much more proactive in facilitating democratic development and while NATO and the EU have so far not admitted any of the new post-communist democracies, they do have the potential to influence political developments at a distance, through their own insistence on democratic government as one important pre-condition of membership. Given that many of the post-communist states attach greater importance to NATO and the EU than they do to the COE, this may mean, ironically, that, in the long run, the COE will simply act as the junior partner to organisations for which the promotion of democracy is only an auxiliary aim.

Notes

1   See WEU, 'European security: a common concept of the 27 WEU countries', and OSCE, 'Decision on a Common and Comprehensive Security Model for Europe for the twenty-first century: a new concept for a new century', both reprinted in *SIPRI Yearbook 1996. Armaments, Disarmament and International Security*, Oxford: Oxford University Press, 1996, pp. 309–12, 320–1.
2   R. Garthoff, *The Great Transition. American–Soviet Relations and the End of the Cold War*, Washington, DC: Brookings Institution, 1994, p. 587.
3   *Keesing's Record of World Events*, Vol. 35, No. 5, 1989, p. 36668.
4   'The Statute of the Council of Europe', in *Manual of the Council of Europe. Structure, Functions and Achievements*, London: Stevens, 1970, p. 300.
5   Parliamentary Assembly of the Council of Europe (PACE), Document No. 6629, 16 June 1992, p. 10.
6   PACE, Document No. 6975, 13 December 1993, p. 2.
7   PACE, Recommendation No. 1247, 1994, as cited in COE, *The Challenges of a Greater Europe. The Council of Europe and Democratic Stability*, Strasbourg: Council of Europe Publishing, 1996, p. 27.
8   M. R. Lucas and A. Kreikmeyer, 'Pan-European integration and European institutions: the new role of the Council of Europe', *Journal of European Integration*, Vol. 16, No. 1, 1992, p. 105.
9   'The Euro-Atlantic architecture: from east to west', speech to the CSCE Council, Berlin, 19 June 1991, reprinted in V. Mastny, *The Helsinki Process and the Reintegration of Europe, 1986–1991. Analysis and Documentation*, New York: New York University Press, 1992, p. 309.
10 Observer status was also granted to Canada (May 1996) and to Japan (November 1996).
11 C. Archer, *Organising Europe. The Institutions of Integration*, London: Edward Arnold, 2nd edn, 1994, p. 59.
12 V-Y. Ghebali and B. Saurwein, *European Security in the 1990s: Challenges and Perspectives*, New York: UN, 1995, p. 170.
13 J. E. Manas, 'The Council of Europe's democracy ideal and the challenge of ethno-national strife', in A. Chayes and A. H. Chayes (eds), *Preventing Conflict in the Post-Communist World*, Washington, DC: Brookings Institution, 1996, p. 107.
14 A. M. Gross, 'Reinforcing new democracies: the European Convention on Human Rights and the former communist countries – a study of the case law', *European Journal of International Law*, Vol. 7, No. 1, 1996, p. 102.
15 This reorganised court began to function in November 1998.
16 As of January 1998, the 1995 Framework Convention for the Protection of National Minorities had been signed by thirty-six COE members and ratified by fifteen. It entered into force in February 1998.
17 These focus on areas such as educational and media access and language instruction.

See 'Confidence-building measures', in COE, *The Challenges of a Greater Europe*, pp. 153–4, and K. Schumann, 'The role of the Council of Europe', in H. Miall (ed.), *Minority Rights in Europe. The Scope for a Transnational Regime*, London: Pinter for the Royal Institute for International Affairs, 1994, pp. 94–6.

18 D. Tarschys, 'The Council of Europe: strengthening European security by civilian means', *NATO Review*, Vol. 45, No. 1, 1997, p. 6.

19 A. Drzemczewski, 'The Council of Europe's cooperation and assistance programmes with central and eastern European countries in the human rights field', *Human Rights Law Journal*, Vol. 14, Nos 7–8, 1993, pp. 229–48.

20 D. Pinto, 'Assisting central and eastern Europe's transformation', in COE, *The Challenges of a Greater Europe*, pp. 52–5.

21 See, for instance, Russian Foreign Minister Andrei Kozyrev cited in Radio Free Europe/Radio Liberty (RFE/RL), *News Briefs*, Vol. 2, No. 21, 1993, p. 13. (Russia itself was not a member at the time these charges were made.)

22 RFE/RL, *News Briefs*, Vol. 2, No. 28, 1993, p. 16; *Keesing's Record of World Events*, Vol. 39, No. 10, 1993, p. 39707.

23 RFE/RL, *News Briefs*, Vol. 2, No. 8, 1993, p. 16; Open Media Research Institute (OMRI), *Daily Digest* (electronic edition), 28 September 1995.

24 Council of Ministers, Resolution No. (92) 27, 25 June 1992.

25 The report is reprinted in full in *Human Rights Law Journal*, Vol. 15, No. 7, 1994.

26 PACE, Document No. 7372, 11 September 1995, addendum.

27 PACE, Resolution No. 1055, 1995, reprinted in *Human Rights Law Journal*, Vol. 17, Nos 3–6, 1996, p. 196.

28 PACE, Opinion No. 193, 1996, paragraphs 1–7, reprinted in *Human Rights Law Journal*, Vol. 17, Nos 3–6, 1996, p. 185. (This opinion was strengthened by the holding of elections to the State Duma, the lower chamber of the Russian parliament, in December 1995.)

29 *Keesing's Record of World Events*, Vol. 42, No. 1, 1996, p. 40925.

30 *Ibid.*; J. Blocker, 'Vote on Russia marks Council's most historic day', *RFE/RL*, 26 January 1996.

31 *The Guardian*, 14 May 1996, p. 10.

32 OMRI, *Daily Digest* (electronic edition), 16 October 1996, 6 November 1996.

33 OMRI, *Daily Digest* (electronic edition), 17 January 1997.

34 Foreign Ministry spokesman V. Andreev, cited in OMRI, *Daily Digest* (electronic edition), 17 January 1997. (Russia, along with Ukraine and Finland, voted against Belarus's suspension.)

35 Cited in PACE, Document No. 6216, 26 April 1990, p. 12.

36 From a lecture given by Catherine Lalumière to St Anthony's College, Oxford, cited in A. Hyde-Price, *The International Politics of East Central Europe*, Manchester: Manchester University Press, 1996, p. 194.

37 D. Tarschys, 'The Council of Europe: the challenge of enlargement', *World Today*, Vol. 51, No. 4, 1995, pp. 62–4.

38 'Vienna Declaration of the Heads of State and Government of the Member States of the Council of Europe on the Reform of the Council Mechanism of the ECHR, on National Minorities, and on a Plan of Action against Racism', reprinted in *Human Rights Law Journal*, Vol. 14, Nos 9–10, 1993, pp. 373–6.

39 Cited in PACE, Document No. 6168, appendix II, p. 13.

40 Cited in A. D. Rotfeld, 'New security structures in Europe: concepts, proposals and decisions', *SIPRI Yearbook 1991: World Armaments and Disarmament*, Oxford: Oxford University Press, 1991, p. 596.

41 http://www.fco.gov.uk/current/1995/sept/04/rifkind_speech_ukraine-fulltext.txt.

42 Other concessions could be seen to include negotiations on a Russian–NATO charter during 1996–7 and redefined CFE Treaty flank area quotas for Russian arms agreed in June 1996.

43 V. Zaslavsky, 'Nationalism and democratic transition in postcommunist societies', *Daedalus*, Vol. 121, No. 2, 1992, p. 110, cited in Hyde-Price, *The International Politics of East Central Europe*, p. 60.

44 See the speech of Toomas Savi (speaker of the Estonian parliament) to the PACE, 22 January 1996 (http://www.vm.ee/speeches/1996/96jan22.html).

45 M. Woollacott, 'Stuck in a great cultural divide', *The Guardian*, 20 July 1996, p. 26.

46 The Copenhagen European Council meeting (June 1993) laid down criteria to be met by states applying for EU membership; these included stable democratic institutions, adherence to the rule of law and respect for human rights. As for NATO, paragraph 70 of the 'Study on NATO Enlargement' released by the Alliance in September 1995 outlines several conditions prospective new members are expected to fulfil: the first is to conform to the principles of 'democracy, individual liberty and the rule of law' (http://www.nato.int/docu/basictxt/enl-9501.htm).

47 A. Ozolins, 'Limits and opportunities at the eastern edge', in I. Gambles (ed.), *A Lasting Peace in Central Europe?*, Chaillot Papers No. 20, Paris: Institute for Security Studies Western European Union, 1995, pp. 70–1.

48 V. G. Baleanu, *Romania 1996: From Autocracy to Democracy*, Sandhurst: Conflict Studies Research Centre; T. Melescanu (then Minister of Foreign Affairs of Romania), 'Security in central Europe: a positive-sum game', *NATO Review*, Vo. 41, No. 5, 1993, pp. 12–18; S. Markotich, 'Slovenia inches ahead', *Transition*, Vol. 3, No. 2, 1997, p. 34.

49 Tarschys, 'The Council of Europe: the challenge of enlargement', p. 62.

50 V. Kand, 'Estonia: a year of challenges', *RFE/RL Research Report*, Vol. 3, No. 1, 1994, p 92; S. Girnuis, 'Latvia. Political squabbles, financial crisis take their toll at home', in *Building Democracy. The OMRI Annual Survey of Eastern Europe and the Former Soviet Union, 1995*, Armonk: M. E. Sharpe, 1996, p. 65.

51 See Primakov's speech to the COE's Committee of Ministers (2 May 1996), reprinted in *Diplomaticheskii vestnik*, No. 6, 1996, p. 5; and Yeltsin's comments during a meeting with the COE's Secretary-General Daniel Tarschys and the president of the PACE, reported in BBC, *Summary of World Broadcasts*, SU/3047 B/11, 11 October 1997.

52 M. A. Jubulis, 'The external dimension of democratisation in Latvia: the impact of European institutions', *International Relations*, Vol. 13, No. 3, 1996, p. 71.

53 C. Lee, 'Council of Europe', in A. J. Day (ed.), *The Annual Register. A Record of Events, 1995*, London: Cartermill International, 1995, p. 400.

54 A. Drzemczewski, 'Ensuring compatibility of domestic law with the European Convention on Human Rights prior to ratification: the Hungarian model', *Human Rights Law Journal*, Vol. 16, Nos 7–9, 1995, pp. 258–60; P. Hofmanski, 'Poland after ratification of the European Convention on Human Rights and Fundamental Freedoms', *Helsinki Monitor*, Vol. 6, No. 1, 1995.

55 M. Janis, 'Russia and the "legality" of Strasbourg law', *European Journal of International Law*, Vol. 8, No. 1, 1997.

56 Deputy Secretary-General Peter Leuprecht resigned in July 1997 in protest at what he saw as a watering down of the COE's values owing to its overly fast expansion. At the time, Leuprecht referred to the admission of Croatia, Romania and Russia as being mistaken. See J. Blocker, 'Council of Europe's "soft" standards for east European members', *RFE/RL Newsline* (electronic edition), end note, 8 July 1997.

57 OMRI, *Daily Digest* (electronic edition), 30 June 1995.

58 PACE, Document No. 7633, addendum III, 9 September 1996, p. 1, and Resolution No. 1095, 26 June 1996.

59   US Department of State, *Albania. Country Report on Human Rights Practices for 1997* (http://www.state.gov/www/global/human_rights/1997_hrp_report/albania.html).

60   PACE, Opinion No. 193, 1996, reprinted in *Human Rights Law Journal*, Vol. 17, Nos 3–6, 1996, pp. 185–7.

61   *The Guardian*, 2 May 1996, p. 12.

62   The number of offences carrying the death sentence was reduced from twenty-eight to five; however, as a PACE report noted, none of the prisoners condemned to death in recent years were sentenced on the basis of the twenty-three offences for which punishment had been revised. See PACE, Document No. 7746, 28 January 1997, p. 5.

63   *Moscow News*, 16–22 October 1997, p. 5.

64   *RIA Novosti*, 13 January 1998, as carried in Johnson's Russia List (electronic edition), 14 January 1998 (available at: davidjohnson@erols.com).

65   *RFE/RL Newsline* (electronic edition), 20 February 1998.

66   International Helsinki Federation for Human Rights, *Annual Report 1997* (http://pgsc.polar.on.ca/pages/ihfr97ru.htm). See also PACE, Document No. 8127, 2 June 1998, 'Honouring of obligations and commitments by the Russian Federation', which contains a more balanced but, at times, still critical assessment.

67   BBC, *Summary of World Broadcasts*, SU/2716 B/11, 13 September 1996.

68   OMRI, *Daily Digest* (electronic edition), 18 September 1996, 24 September 1996.

69   PACE, Document No. 6607, 5 May 1992, pp. 8–9.

70   F. Benoît-Rohmer, *The Minority Question in Europe. Texts and Commentary*, Strasbourg: Council of Europe Publishing, 1996, p. 56.

71   See the COE's Vienna Declaration, and 'Charter of Paris for a New Europe', *NATO Review*, Vol. 38, No. 6, 1990, p. 29.

72   Tarschys, 'The Council of Europe: strengthening European security', p. 7; D. Tarschys, 'The Council of Europe: towards a vast area of democratic security', *NATO Review*, Vol. 42, No. 6, 1994–5, p. 11; Benoît-Rohmer, *The Minority Question in Europe*, pp. 56–8; COE, *Human Rights. A Continuing Challenge for the Council of Europe*, Strasbourg: Council of Europe Press, 1995, pp. 88–90.

73   H. van den Broek, 'The Council of Europe and the European Union: complementing each other', in COE, *The Challenges of a Greater Europe*, p. 174.

74   Pinto, 'Assisting central and eastern Europe's transformation', pp. 56–7; PACE, Document No. 7637, 10 September 1996, p. 7.

75   Lucas and Kreikmeyer, 'Pan-European integration and European institutions', p. 96; see also PACE, Document No. 7637, 10 September 1996, p. 6.

76   See the remarks of Jüri Luik (Minister of Foreign Affairs of Estonia) at the Committee of Ministers of the COE, Strasbourg, 10 November 1994 (http://www.vm.ee/speeches/1994/94nov10.html).

77   R. Lambert, 'Council of Europe', in A. J. Day (ed.), *The Annual Register: A Record of World Events, 1993*, Harlow: Longman, 1993, p. 421.

78   PACE, Document No. 6607, 5 May 1992, p. 11, Document No. 7280, 12 April 1995, p. 11, Document No. 7637, 10 September 1996, p. 11.

79   These discussions were partly begun to address concerns in both the COE and the OSCE that in the sphere of election monitoring the two organisations were able to arrive at different assessments. This had been the case with the 1995 parliamentary elections in Belarus and the 1996 local elections in Albania. In the latter case, the OSCE's ODIHR had withdrawn its mission in protest at Albanian tardiness in granting accreditation to its monitors. The COE observation mission remained and was to subsequently register its satisfaction at the conduct of the elections. See OMRI, *Daily Digest* (electronic edition), 21 October 1996, 23 October 1996.

80   A. H. Robertson and J. G. Merrills, *Human Rights in Europe. A Study of the European*

   Convention on Human Rights, Manchester: Manchester University Press, 3rd edn, 1993, pp. 363–6.
81 J. Blocker, 'Council of Europe: are the Council and EU partners or rivals?', *RFE/RL*, 29 January 1997.
82 C. H. Church and D. Phinnemore, *A Handbook and Commentary on the Post-Maastrich Treaties*, New York: Harvester Wheatsheaf, 1994, p. 489.
83 Blocker, 'Council of Europe'.
84 PACE, Document No. 6629, 10 June 1994, p. 17.
85 PACE, Document No. 7443, addendum D, 2 January 1996, p. 64.
86 Figure calculated from annual budgetary increases detailed in PACE, Document No. 6168, 23 January 1990, p. ii; PACE, Opinion No. 171, 1993, p. 2, and Opinion No. 179, 1994, p. 2.
87 PACE, Document No. 6685, 1 October 1992, p. 6, Document No. 7180, revised, 17 October 1994, p. 2.
88 PACE, Document No. 7443, addendum D, 2 January 1996, p. 64.
89 PACE, Document No. 7788, 3 April 1997, p. 2.
90 Pinto, 'Assisting central and eastern Europe's transformation', p. 49.

7

Conclusion

The enlargement processes involving the various organisations in Europe have been played out against a complex backcloth of events. The first and most important one, the end of the Cold War, transformed the political and security situation of the continent and shattered the east European bloc. In so doing, it created a group of CEECs that perceived themselves as languishing in a political, economic and security vacuum. Communism had left behind a legacy of economic mismanagement, underdeveloped civil societies and a host of deep-seated nationalist tensions. In order to escape from this situation, the CEECs were eager to join with other states, from southern Europe, that were seeking admission into west European organisations. These organisations had survived the Cold War and, because they embodied western values, they appeared to offer stability and economic prosperity to the aspirant states.

A second factor that has served as part of the background for the enlargement processes has been the manner of European integration. The ending of the Cold War raised the complex question in the west of whether to pursue the goal of the enlargement of the EU or to seek its deeper integration. The desire to anchor the newly united Germany into the existing range of institutions in Europe resulted in the speeding up of the integration process. In addition to the plan for monetary union, France and Germany pressed for the creation of a political union, which led to the TEU. These developments acted as a warning beacon to the CEECs, because they signalled that states in the western half of the continent were determined to draw closer together and raised the spectre of the exclusion of the eastern countries from the focus of prosperity.

Nevertheless, the period after the signing of the TEU witnessed a faltering in the momentum of the integration process. This resulted from a number of causes, including the absence of sufficient popular support for further integration in many EU countries, the difficulty of securing ratification of the TEU and the paralysis demonstrated by the EU during the Balkan conflict. It was no longer clear in which direction the EU was heading and this raised doubts over the issue of enlargement. There was growing hesitation, even among robust supporters of enlargement such as Germany, about the impact that a diverse group of new members could have upon the homogeneity of the organisation. Additionally, there was a broader appreciation of the potential costs that could be incurred by admitting states whose economies had not converged significantly with those of existing members.

The uncertainty regarding the future role of the United States also increased the complexity of enlargement issues. Because of its traditional position as a highly influential state in continental affairs, it was inevitable that the United States would be a leading voice in the debates on enlargement. Yet, in the early part of the 1990s, there was an absence of clarity within the United States, as well as among its allies, over the role that it was willing to play in Europe. In the light of the reductions in US forces based on the continent and the competing calls on its resources from other theatres, there were doubts as to the willingness of the United States to provide future leadership.

Lastly, the Europe in which organisational enlargements were being determined was one in which disorder and conflict were increasingly endemic. This was particularly evident in the eastern half of the continent, as the old system of communist rule crumbled away. Conflicts in some of the former Soviet republics and the territories of the former Yugoslavia proved that the new European environment would be far from peaceful and harmonious. This state of affairs helped to focus attention on those pre-existing organisations that were able to draw on military force to offer hard security guarantees, particularly as many of the CEECs still regarded Russia as a potential threat to their welfare. The growing evidence of disorder also had the effect of deepening the sense of caution among some organisations regarding the speed of their enlargement. It was feared that the latent instability in parts of the continent could all too easily be imported into western institutions.

The chapters of this book have argued that past experiences of organisational enlargements have not been appropriate to the transformed situation of the continent. The uniqueness of the post-Cold War environment has militated against drawing upon the past as a guide. The admission of new members into the Atlantic Alliance and the WEU during the Cold War was undertaken in order to bolster the strength of these organisations against the perception of threat from the Warsaw Pact. Such a rationale has no counterpart in the current circumstances, when there is no overarching security threat. History has also proved to be an unsatisfactory guide in the case of the OSCE, as it had no experience of admitting new members before 1990.

However, although no models can be discerned from the past, it would be erroneous to deny that earlier enlargements can provide lessons and insights for the future. First, it is salutary to remember the EU's experience of earlier enlargements and the length of time it took in the past to agree upon the terms of entry. It is likely to take as long, if not longer, to bring the CEECs into the EU, particularly in light of their differing historical developments. Second, past experience points to the irreversibility of enlargement processes: once a state has been granted access to an organisation, then the decision cannot be reversed subsequently (although the OSCE has taken the step of suspending states). This places pressure on those organisations pondering enlargement to weigh the decision carefully before granting admission to new countries. Finally, attention must be paid to the need to secure ratification of enlargement decisions by appropriate member states in organisations such as NATO and the EU. Each government must be convinced of the wisdom of accepting new entrants, so that they may be committed to securing ratification in their own domestic legislatures.

The end of the Cold War has forced many of the organisations analysed in this book to adapt their functions, as well as to consider enlarging their memberships. The transformed situation on the continent has demanded that existing organisations reach out to assist states in the east to resolve a broad array of problems. These have included issues of domestic governance, economic weaknesses, refugee movements and environmental degradation. The new prominence of such issues has meant that organisations that fulfilled particular roles during the Cold War were required to adapt, often in fundamental ways. This has led to considerable soul-searching among the various organisations and has contributed to a period of confusion. It has even resulted in overlap and institutional competition for roles. This, in turn, has undermined the optimistic rhetoric of the early post-Cold War period, which declared that institutions would be mutually supportive and interlocking.

Some organisations have continued to emphasise the carrying out of their traditional core functions. The COE, for instance, has remained focused upon democracy and human rights issues. Others have expanded the scope of their activities but remained within the same broad area of responsibility. Thus NATO has remained concerned principally with military security, but it has expanded its remit from just territorial defence to include crisis management and peace enforcement. This has been demonstrated by its involvement in Bosnia in Operation Deliberate Force and the Implementation Force (IFOR) and Stabilisation Force (SFOR) missions. Other organisations, such as the EU, have always enjoyed a broad area of responsibility, while the WEU has retained its focus on defence and also expanded into quasi-police tasks.

In relation to function, one question that dominated the agenda was over which organisation was going to enjoy primary responsibility in the field of security and defence. The early post-Cold War period led to a sense of disorientation, partly because awareness of the security and defence tasks to be performed was only gradually materialising. There was a good deal of optimism surrounding the future role of the then CSCE, because it was a pan-European body that represented the broadest possible cross-section of states. Indeed, there was hope, particularly among some CEECs, that the CSCE would become a collective security body that would transcend the old east–west divide. However, it became apparent that the CSCE lacked sufficient support among the key western countries. The competencies of the organisation were developed instead in the areas of preventive security, assistance to refugees and election monitoring. Only Russia has continued to argue that the OSCE should be Europe's principal military security body, in the hope that it would guarantee Moscow a leading voice in continental affairs.

Each organisation has attempted to chart its own course in the enlargement process. It was widely acknowledged that expanding the membership of an organisation would influence its position in the continent's institutional architecture. There was uncertainty, however, over which institutions were going to enjoy the widest support. Some organisations that sought to represent the broadest cross-section of states chose to enlarge quickly. The COE and the OSCE, for example, have admitted most of the independent states in Europe. Others, such as NATO and the EU, while recognising the importance of enlargement to their own futures, exhibit greater caution about accepting new entrants.

Over a period of time, inter-organisational tensions and 'turf wars' have been increasingly managed through a process of specialisation. This has been an *ad hoc* process, but one in which each organisation has been able to refine its own area of responsibility. The EU has emerged as the organisation with primary responsibility for trade, economic assistance and environmental issues. NATO has retained its position as the foremost security and defence framework and the organisation that could be relied upon to mobilise collective military capabilities in Europe. The WEU has played an important role as a bridge between NATO and the EU. The COE has continued to be wedded to human rights issues, while the OSCE has been unusual in assuming a range of new and important tasks, such as preventive diplomacy.

Yet it would be wrong to imply that these specialisations have led to harmony between the organisations, for rivalry and competition still exist.

NATO, for example, has been developing an interest in environmental matters, in competition with the EU; it has overlapped in some of its activities with both the OSCE and the COE; while debate continues to rage over whether the WEU should concentrate on its status as the European pillar of the Alliance or whether it should advance a more muscular European role. Although more clearly defined mechanisms for managing the relations between the institutions have been developed, these have not succeeded in eliminating all forms of competition.

Rivalry has not been the only characteristic of enlargement processes. States enjoying membership of several organisations have used this position to send different messages to aspirant countries. It has been possible to discern a pattern of trade-offs between organisations so that states refused entry into one forum have been compensated by access to another. For instance, allowing states with poor reputations on human rights to enter the COE has been interpreted as a form of compensation for entry into the EU being barred. Thus it has been possible to offer encouragement to states undergoing a process of reform, while holding back from offering them membership of the core organisations. In this way, entry into the COE has served as a sort of pre-accession strategy for the EU and a hierarchy between the organisations has emerged. Similarly, a form of linkage has been traceable between the EU, the WEU and NATO. The EU and the WEU reached out to the Baltic states in their Association Agreements as a way of offsetting the fact that NATO was unable to consider these countries as being in the front rank of potential new members. Such tactics are unsurprising, in that the same west European states are members of the major institutions.

It has been notable that the criteria laid down for the entry of aspirant states into the various organisations have been vague and ill-defined. Common ideas have been evident in all the organisations, based upon the 1975 Helsinki Final Act and the 1990 Charter of Paris. Adherence to democratic structures of government, such as multi-party political systems and the rule of law, evidence of transitional arrangements to market economies, observance of human rights provisions and the principle of parliamentary control over the armed forces have all been important elements. Yet no objective standard for assessing these criteria has existed across all the organisations. In part, this reflects the difficulty of assessing compliance over a host of countries each with its own idiosyncrasies. But it reflects also the differing priorities of organisations in relation to their enlargement processes. To have agreed a common set of guidelines for admitting new states would have narrowed the room for manoeuvre between institutions.

The criteria chosen for accession provided an insight into the institutional definitions of 'Europe', as well as the vision for the future of the continent. It was evident that liberal capitalist values had triumphed at the end of the Cold War, with CEECs seeking to model themselves upon the example of their western neighbours. Allowing post-communist states into key international organisations required them to subscribe to these goals. Unless they did so, there was the danger that new members might come to reject the values upon which the organisation was founded. This has led to problems for those states that wish for membership but represent social systems based on different values. Turkey is one such example and has come to feel aggrieved that its own application to join the EU has been ignored while states from central Europe have moved to the front of the queue.

The rigour with which the entry criteria have been applied has varied between the organisations. Some have compromised their criteria in order to facilitate a rapid enlargement process and export stability to other parts of the continent. The COE, for example, admitted Russia and Croatia, even though there were protests that these countries fell short of its human rights standards. This was undertaken in order to signal the willingness of the west to include such states within the European family and because it was hoped that membership would encourage these states to improve their behaviour. Other organisations have either interpreted their criteria stringently or have kept them ill-defined so as to enjoy the greatest flexibility over the accession of new members. NATO, for example, kept its criteria vague despite undertaking a detailed study of the enlargement issue, thereby enabling it to dictate the speed of entry by new members.

The EU and the WEU waited until the Copenhagen Council in June 1993 to make explicit criteria for membership. The approach to enlargement of the EU and the WEU was to concentrate upon a specific group of nine states (later increased to ten). The EU signed Association Agreements with these designated states and provided forms of financial assistance, while the WEU granted them Associate Partner status. Other organisations have adopted a different approach. NATO began by allowing all states to enter into a dialogue with it through the NACC and then, after the PFP announcement, NATO allowed aspirant states to pursue a policy of self-differentiation. This enabled those countries eager for NATO membership to develop their own strategies to prove their worthiness to the Alliance.

Although the focus of this book has been upon institutions, it has remained a central tenet throughout that individual countries have played a vital role in the enlargement process. Contrary to the expectations of some that the importance of institutions would diminish after the Cold War, countries have set great store by fashioning the orientation and future membership of key organisations. Owing to their size and historical influence, some countries have enjoyed a disproportionate degree of influence. The United States, as the only remaining superpower, has been the key actor in deciding the process of NATO enlargement. It performed a pivotal role in the creation of the NACC, along with Germany, and then master-minded the PFP initiative. It subsequently took the lead in determining that three invitations for NATO membership would be extended at the Madrid summit in July 1997.

In contrast to the leading role that the United States has played within NATO, no such state champion has been evident within the EU. To a large extent this has been because no country in the EU has arisen to become substantially more powerful than the rest. The only country that comes close to such status, Germany, has largely eschewed a leadership function for fear of causing disquiet among its allies. Germany has proved to be a vigorous supporter of the enlargement of the EU, owing to its proximity to valuable markets in central Europe. Germany has also supported NATO and OSCE expansion as a means of ensuring the stability of the eastern half of the continent. Other west European countries have held different perspectives on EU enlargement: the UK has actively supported EU enlarge-ment, but for different reasons to that of Germany. It has regarded enlargement as a way to dilute the process of European integration.

Just as states have advanced their views on the enlargement process through support for certain organisations or for particular countries, so it has been possible to detect the emergence of regional perspectives on these issues. Both northern and southern viewpoints have become discernible among the European states. The northern perspective, from countries such as Germany, the UK and the Benelux states, has focused on enlargement to the CEECs. The Nordic members of the EU, such as Sweden and Finland, have been ardent advocates of the three Baltic states. On the other hand, a southern viewpoint has emerged among states such as France, Italy and Greece. This viewpoint has argued against attention being devoted exclusively to central Europe and has championed the cause of those states from the Mediterranean area. It has led to a Mediterranean dialogue being adopted by both the EU and NATO.

As well as exhibiting preferences, states have also opposed the enlarge-ment of those institutions to which they have attached less importance. Some have recognised the role that enlargement can play in preserving the relevance and renewing the mission of an organisation after the Cold War. Hence France was eager, in the early part of the 1990s, to arrest the entry of new members into NATO. This was because France was reluctant to see the Alliance take in new states that might augment NATO's – and hence the United States' – influence in the security structure of the continent. When it became evident that NATO would enlarge, France accepted the inevitable and argued strongly for the inclusion of Romania into the first round of new members. France's lobbying in this case was to be un-successful. In addition to opposing the early enlargement of NATO, France has also been against taking new states into the EU. It expressed the reservation that new entrants might undermine the integration process and weaken the sense of solidarity.

Furthermore, some states have not hesitated to place their own selfish interests above the demands of creating a Europe 'whole and free'. They have demonstrated a willingness to subordinate the enlargement process to the pursuit of their own prejudices against other states. For example, the antagonism between Greece and Turkey has spilled over into the area of organisational enlargement. Greece has made clear its opposition to Turkish membership of both the EU and the WEU, on account of their long-standing hostility. Turkey has responded by threatening to disrupt the process of enlarging NATO as a protest against the application of the Greek part of Cyprus into the EU. This dispute has reinforced the lesson that European organisations need to ensure as far as possible that aspirant members have resolved all outstanding differences with their neighbours before being granted membership.

The influence of the bureaucracies within the organisations has been of limited significance in relation to enlargement. All of the bureaucracies have demonstrated the desire to ensure their own survival, but they have played only a secondary role in comparison with the member states. The European Commission exercised its influence over the countries invited to be the first states to enter into accession negotiations with the EU through the 'Agenda 2000' document. In addition, the Secretary-General of NATO has been an important figure in structuring the Alliance's approach to the issue of taking in new members. Yet this capacity to exercise influence has taken place within a context that has been determined to a large extent by the member states.

In similar fashion, the aspirant countries seeking entry into such organisations as the EU and the WEU have been relegated to a mainly passive role. The place of the CEECs in the hierarchy of aspirant states has been decided in pre-enlargement forums outside of their control and they have found it difficult to influence the process. The CEECs have naturally engaged in extensive discussions with representatives of the organisations, but they have often been forced to respond to external demands not of their making. One such example was the French-inspired 'Stability Pact', which sought to address the problem of tensions between states in the eastern half of the continent as a precursor to EU membership. The Stability Pact was imposed on the central Europeans without them having a significant voice in its formulation. It has been apparent that keeping prospective members in anticipation of entry has granted organisations influence over their continuing development. This would be likely to disappear once states were offered the right of admission to the institution. Only in the OSCE and, to a lesser extent, in the COE have states been granted almost automatic access.

The only threat of sanction against new members has been the possibility of suspending them from the organisation for an unspecified period of time.

One state that has fallen outside this norm has been Russia. Like other states, it was able to secure immediate admission to the then CSCE and, after a period of delay, to the COE. But it has also enjoyed a unique degree of influence over the enlargement of other organisations, in spite of the fact that it was not seeking membership of these forums, and regardless of Moscow's diminished strength. Russia's influence stemmed from the fact that, in spite of its decline, it remained a pivotal actor on the continent and because the enlargement of organisations could be interpreted as impinging upon its sphere of interest. Moreover, there were fears that the enlargement processes could strengthen anti-democratic political forces in the Russian Federation. Hence, Russian views were sought over enlargement of the EU, the WEU and, in particular, NATO. Russia voiced little concern in relation to the first two of these, but warned of the dangers of a 'Cold Peace' in relation to NATO expansion. As a result, Russia was accorded extensive consultative rights, which led to the formulation of the NATO–Russia Permanent Joint Council in 1997. Although it was not considered acceptable to grant Russia a veto power over the enlargements of western organisations, many states have considered it politically prudent to grant Moscow a unique voice in the process.

Those institutions, such as the OSCE, that have enlarged have experienced profound changes. Inevitably, they have admitted states with different sorts of historical experiences and a variety of perspectives on the future development of Europe. The COE enlarged to take in a range of new states, but was subsequently faced with the question of whether to expand beyond what it has traditionally regarded as Europe. It has to decide whether to embrace the Transcaucasian countries of Georgia, Armenia and Azerbaijan, something that would stretch its earlier definition of European culture. While organisations have become more representative of the variety of opinions in Europe, undeniably they have also experienced drawbacks associated with larger membership. These have included a greater diversity of views among the participants, slower decision-making and more complex working procedures.

Such implications have induced the cautious approach of NATO and the EU towards enlargement. As the organisations that have delivered military security and economic prosperity for their members, there was an understandable reluctance about admitting additional states that might alter the existing structures. Both organisations have been fearful of losing their homogeneity. For its part, NATO has been worried about assuming additional security burdens that it could not carry out, such as defence guarantees towards states bordering Russia. The offer of such commitments would be highly contentious within the American Congress and perhaps the parliaments of other member states.

As for the EU, it has recognised that its enlargement would be the most technically difficult of all the organisations, because of the breadth of competencies, its supranational characteristics and its constant process of evolution. In practical terms, new members will have to incorporate the existing *acquis*, while former members will have to modify the CAP and the disbursement of structural funds. The EU has also been forced to acknowledge that enlargement will require it to reform its internal decision-making structures and the composition of its institutions, such as the European Commission and the European Parliament. It would be unrealistic to believe that the EU could operate in the same way with over twenty-five states as it has done with twelve and then fifteen.

Even a decade after the end of the Cold War, there remains considerable variation among the organisations in regard to their timetables for enlargement. Some have gone as far as they can in welcoming new members, while others have still to embark on their first round of new entrants. NATO will admit its first three new members in 1999, but there is a lack of clarity about enlargements after the initial wave. Leaders of the Alliance have made clear that they foresee successive waves of new members, but there has been no substantive statement as to which states will be invited to apply in the future, nor whether there will be any limit to this process. This has been a source of concern to those aspirant states excluded from the first wave of expansion, as they fear that events might undermine future prospects. Although it was once thought that NATO and the EU would enlarge in tandem, it has now become inevitable that the next wave of EU enlargement will follow after the first, much smaller enlargement of the Alliance. At the end of 1997, the EU identified which states will be invited to begin negotiations on admission.

The issue of subsequent waves of enlargements relates to a broader question: What vision is held for the future of the continent? One clear conclusion of this book is that there has not been an overarching vision driving the enlargement processes. However, it is evidently the case that the enlargement processes will lead to a new European political reality for the early part of the next millennium. Two alternatives appear to be possible.

One vision might be of an all-inclusive Europe, in which the expansion continues, albeit according to different timetables. Eventually this may result in all states becoming members of the various organisations, or enjoying levels of membership if they are regarded as unsuitable to be full members. According to such a view, all institutions would advance eastward to include the former Soviet republics, and perhaps even Russia itself. Concomitantly, western norms and standards of behaviour would, over time, become accepted across the entire continent.

The second, alternative vision would be one in which western leaders might calculate the dangers of taking organisations up to the borders of Russia as being too great, particularly if this should stimulate a nationalist reaction. Although it would sacrifice the goal of an integrated Europe, it might be judged unwise to risk compromising the values of a 'core' of western and central European states by the admission of countries with discordant outlooks. Such a vision would therefore draw back from including the Soviet successor states, at least from NATO, if not from the EU. This would heighten even further the problem of dealing with the Baltic republics. This view might also set greater store by fostering integration among smaller groups of states, rather than attempting to create broad but disparate organisations. But such a policy would risk two eventualities. One would be the potential for a sense of rejection and disillusionment among those states with no prospect of joining the most desirable institutions. The other would be to generate permanent zones of unequal security and prosperity that could become the focal points for future patterns of instability.

These are the central and most important questions in the enlargement processes. It is easy to focus on the immediate practicalities of particular enlargement decisions and on their implementation, to the exclusion of grand strategy. But any detailed analysis of the enlargement debate in Europe requires answers to four fundamental questions: What are the boundaries of Europe? How should the 'insiders' in Europe's organisations treat those that are 'outside'? Are European values strictly coterminous with western ones? And how far are the rich, secure and democratic states prepared to compromise what they have achieved in order to share what they value with their neighbours?

Appendix 1. Membership of Euro-Atlantic international organisations

	NATO	EU	WEU	COE	OSCE
Albania				•	•
Andorra				•	•
Armenia					•
Austria		•		•	•
Azerbaijan					•
Belarus					•
Belgium	•	•	•	•	•
Bosnia-Herzegovina					•
Bulgaria				•	•
Canada	•				
Croatia				•	•
Cyprus				•	•
Czech Republic				•	•
Denmark	•	•		•	?
Estonia				•	•
Federal Republic of Yugoslavia					suspended
Finland		•		•	•
France	•	•	•	•	•
Georgia					•
Germany	•	•	•	•	•
Greece	•	•	•	•	•
Holy See					•
Hungary				•	•
Iceland	•			•	•
Ireland		•		•	•
Italy	•	•	•	•	•
Kazakhstan					•
Kyrgyzstan					•
Latvia				•	•
Liechtenstein				•	•
Lithuania				•	•
Luxembourg	•	•	•	•	•
Macedonia				•	•
Malta				•	•
Moldova				•	•
Monaco					•
Netherlands	•	•	•	•	•
Norway	•			•	•
Poland				•	•
Portugal	•	•	•	•	•
Romania				•	•
Russia				•	•
San Marino					•
Slovakia				•	•
Slovenia				•	•
Spain	•	•	•	•	•
Sweden		•		•	•
Switzerland				•	•
Tajikistan					•
Turkey	•			•	•
Turkmenistan					•
Ukraine				•	•
United Kingdom	•	•	•	•	•
United States	•				•
Uzbekistan					•

Appendix 2. Forms of association with Euro-Atlantic international organisations

	NATO				EU				WEU		
	A	I	PFP	EAPC	A	AA	EA	PCA	Ass. M.	O	Ass. P.
Albania			•	•							
Andorra											
Armenia			•	•				•			
Austria			•	•						•	
Azerbaijan			•	•				•			
Belarus			•	•				•			
Belgium	•			•							
Bosnia-Herzegovina											
Bulgaria			•	•			•				•
Canada	•			•							
Croatia											
Cyprus					•	•					
Czech Republic		•	•	•	•		•				•
Denmark	•			•						•	
Estonia			•	•			•				•
Federal Republic of Yugoslavia											
Finland			•	•						•	
France	•			•							
Georgia			•	•				•			
Germany	•		•	•							
Greece	•		•	•							
Holy See											
Hungary		•	•	•	•		•				•
Iceland	•		•	•					•		
Ireland			•	•						•	

Italy			•		•	•		•	
Kazakhstan			•		•	•		•	
Kyrgyzstan			•		•	•		•	
Latvia	•		•		•	•		•	•
Liechtenstein	•		•					•	
Lithuania			•		•	•		•	•
Luxembourg								•	•
Macedonia			•						•
Malta		•							
Moldova			•		•	•		•	•
Monaco									
Netherlands								•	
Norway	•		•					•	
Poland	•		•		•	•	•	•	•
Portugal								•	
Romania	•		•		•	•		•	•
Russia	•		•					•	
San Marino									
Slovakia	• •		• •		• •	• •		• •	• •
Slovenia	•		•					•	
Spain								•	
Sweden		•						•	
Switzerland								•	
Tajikistan								•	
Turkey	•		•		•	•		•	•
Turkmenistan								•	
Ukraine	•		•					•	
United Kingdom								•	
United States								•	
Uzbekistan			•					•	

A, applicant (as of 1998); I, invited to join (as of 1998); PFP, Partnership for Peace; EAPC, Euro-Atlantic Partnership Council; AA, Association Agreement; EA, Europe Agreement; PCA, Partnership and Cooperation Agreement; Ass. M., Associate Member; O, Observer; Ass. P., Associate Partner.

Index